CY LAURIE

LUCKY OL' ME

SUNSTREAMER
ENGLAND

DEDICATION

LOVE AND BLESSINGS TO ALL

ACKNOWLEDGMENTS

Heart-felt thanks go to Ron & Chris Bussey for making it happen and musician and broadcaster Mike Pointon for his help and encouragement. My thanks also to my family and close friends who are always there for me.

Veronica Laurie

FOREWORD FOR LUCKY OL' ME

Cy Laurie was an inspirational figure for me when I first became interested in jazz. Hearing his band for the first time in the late 50s in his Great Windmill Street club just off Piccadilly Circus, with its bohemian atmosphere of sprawling sofas and enthusiastic fans, created a strong impression on a teenage fledgeling jazzman. Significantly, his policy of encouraging younger musicians by featuring sitting-in sessions run by my old colleague Bill Brunskill on Sunday afternoons was, in retrospect, more productive for would-be jazzers than many a so-called 'educational' course available today. By the time I had began to play professionally I remember seeing an ad in the Melody Maker for a trombonist in Cy's band. I rang the appropriate number and was told to show up at a certain time and place (perhaps the club itself?) but couldn't summon up the courage, so I didn't meet him in those days. Luckily, I did get to know and work with Cy in later years and if somehow I helped persuade him to write this fascinating book I am delighted. It not only captures the dedicated atmosphere of the Jazz Revival in Britain and reminds us how major Cy's input was it takes us inside the mind of a man whose apparent reticence could be misunderstood. He shares with us courageously the inner conflicts that must have beset him for many years and adds an extra dimension to make this much more than a musical memoir. For those with perception he gives much philosophical food for thought and at the same time sets to rest many of the myths and rumours that surrounded his life. We should be grateful to Ronnie, his devoted partner who has made the publishing of this autobiography possible.

Mike Pointon

When Cy finished writing his autobiography he said 'thank goodness thats done' and I replied 'I don't think so' and, of course, it wasn't. He re-arranged paragraphs, revised and added and this took many months, as did the cover design, but at last it was finished.

As fate decreed, it fell to me to bring the book to publication and although it has been emotionally draining and a somewhat lonely journey, I feel great joy and achievement, for Cy and myself, that it is now in print.

Meeting with Cy all those years ago changed my life direction. My life became en-riched. I shared in his world of jazz and travelled all over this Planet with him. I walked in his other world, meeting teachers, seekers, healers, those with advanced ideas and gifts and those practising alternative and complementary medicines.

Cy was a greatly gifted musician, a kind, wise and loving man who sought a meaning to life and beyond, which took precedence over all. He showed me an alternative path which I still tread and explore today. I have the gift of his love and strength and shared the knowledge and wisdom, highs and lows, music and laughter that was Cy and he has my love and blessings forever - the Spirit lives on!

To those who knew Cy only through his jazz I say keep an open mind on the side that you don't know, there is much to take in and if you find yourself saying no to some aspects and statements (and Cy has only touched on the rudiments in his story) try saying why not and go forward again, there is a rich seam to tap!

Veronica Laurie

My life is not my own to live
It's Theirs who gave it me to give
With motives for self-gain destroyed
For Love is Will and skill deployed
I seek but opportunity
To serve all Life efficiently

Cy Laurie ©

TABLE OF CONTENTS   Page No

"LUCKY OL' ME"

BY CY LAURIE

THE AUTOBIOGRAPHY OF A JAZZMAN'S QUEST FOR MEANING

By Way of an Introduction

It had often been suggested by various people over the years that I write an autobiography, or at least, an account of those incidents in my life which others might find interesting.

I have always been reluctant to do so for many reasons. Nor was I ever a writer, such a means of expression never came easy to me, even though I had on occasions put pen to paper when really necessary, albeit reluctantly. Also by nature I am a very private person and have always tended to keep myself to myself, besides which, I would never have considered people would be particularly interested in hearing about my life, much of which I felt was quite ordinary - with the exception, of course, of certain incidents and experiences of a more spiritual nature that I consider important. Of those, a certain type of person might find it helpful to hear about them, yet for others, they would probably find it just one big yawn.

From the persuasive requests of some jazz friends, not only those personally interested in my jazz background but also those connected with either professional jazz publications or organisations involved in the collection of jazz archives, both of sound and written material, I conceded that maybe I should, at some future date, put something down on paper.

Also, many of those with whom I have been connected in my search for a greater understanding of life's meaning and purposes have often urged me to write an account of my experiences and what, if anything, I have gained from my years of questing. This too I have intended to write about, but again at some future date.

However, as fate would have it, not so long ago I agreed to record an interview for the British Library Sound Archives as it was felt that certain incidents in my early musical career were of importance in building up a picture of the beginnings of the jazz revival movement in Britain during the mid-to-late 40s and 50s, in which I was involved.

Early on during the interview, on hearing the initial test playbacks, I felt that my raw verbal offerings were not as detailed as they should be, mainly owing to my not too spontaneous memory, and that I could not do them sufficient justice.

I therefore thought that as I had finally decided to recount aspects of my jazz career, writing would more likely be the most reliable and accurate medium. Also, in this way, I could do the work in my own time and at my own pace, as well as give more consideration to the specifics of what I had to say.

In addition, somewhere among all the dust and debris of my Farmhouse loft therein lie some early photographs, diaries, press cuttings, band notes, letters, and what-have-you, that I had collected over the years, and which could be useful to verify certain details for me, such as dates, names, places, etc.

In the past, in spite of being obliged to write various personal and business letters, essays on certain philosophical subjects, attempting spasmodic diary entries, the occasional magazine article, my own publicity leaflets, record sleeve notes, and the like, and even at one time compiling a training course on Meditation and Philosophy (which in effect amounted to a summary of my studies over the years - but that's another story), I have always found writing a bit of a chore.

However, another reason for my decision to embark upon this memoir project is that, over the years there have been quite a few articles, commentaries, etc. written about me by others which, without first checking my version, had got many details woefully wrong and had misconstrued many others. Where some of these journalists get their info has always been a mystery to me.

So to help put the record straight and for future reference, not to mention the fact that life's needle is about to clock up three-quarters of a century for me, I came around to thinking that there should at least be some general documentation of what I've been up to in my life, not only my jazz activities and contacts for the sake of my many jazz friends but also for those whose priorities in spiritual matters, being my major life pursuit, were akin to my own.

Once the decision was made to put something down on paper, the first thought that struck me was how to tackle the problem of writing about these two primary interests of mine which are not necessarily compatible in most peoples' minds and which I have always endeavoured to keep separate.

It seemed that there were three possible approaches: I could write two distinct pieces, one for each type of reader, or I could include both under one cover, each having its own separate section, or I could combine them both, presenting them in chronological sequence in which they occurred.

I reasoned that, recounting my musical activities would probably have a broader appeal, yet because in this area it is the music itself which I felt was of importance and not necessarily the incidents relating to it (I was never a great jazz historian), there was not a great deal for me to write about. Besides, certain names and places which would be significant to jazz followers would probably have little or no meaning to those who were not.

On the other hand, although the side of my life connected with meditation and philosophy would possibly have a more limited appeal, yet being my major interest - in fact the raison d'etre of my life - I would have more to say on that subject, but it might be of little interest to the majority of those whose interests are solely in the jazz aspects - in fact, it would probably bore the pants off them.

After much thought, being one who always tries to take the easy way out, I decided to settle on the third alternative and to place the incidents in chronological order as best I can remember them. Who knows, possibly some may come to share both my interests?.

Essex, England. - Summer, 2000.

APRIL 1926 - A Royal Welcome

Imagine, the early morning hour of great national excitment, the whole of the United Kingdom festooned with Union Jacks and coloured bunting, the peal of church bells echoing throughout the land, the populace rejoicing, and all anticipating the awaited country-wide street celebrations. For on that day, 21st April 1926, in the stateliest of England's homes, was born a child who was to make her mark among royalty, who was destined to become the sovereign ruler of all Great Britain and the British Empire.

Also, not so far away, in the East End of London, another was born who, now a mere 8 hours old, was also to make his mark, yet, in a much less auspicious way, upon those who had a taste for the style of jazz in the New Orleans idiom which was to become of prominent and world-wide interest.

The mother of this 8 hour old boy, of Jewish stock from London's Stepney area, was a chubby-faced, outgoing, friendly woman, oozing with love, yet very firm when needing to be. His father, a Russian Jewish immigrant, from Riga, in Latvia, was a quiet, gentle person, yet industrious and conscientious in his profession as a trained watchmaker, a real craftsman of the old tradition, who seldom got involved in the upbringing of his children.

After marrying and settling themselves in a small shop in the East End, on the minimum of income and resources, they raised a family of seven children, the youngest of whom was the one born 8 hours prior to who is now, Queen Elizabeth the Second of England.

He was named Cyril after his great grandfather and, as was the general custom of those days, the children of the families of such communities were, from an early age, tutored and encouraged to learn to play certain musical instruments, even if it strained the parents' already meagre finances. So it was in this case where all of Cyril's elder brothers and sisters were given the required training on one or other musical instruments.

Yet, ironically, when he was old enough to follow in that family custom, possibly because all previous efforts with the other children had come to naught, or money was not available and such expenditure was felt unwarrented, or both, the opportunity for musical training was not given to him.

It was a very close-knit family, due principally to the love and care that their mother showered on them all, with seldom a disruption to the household atmosphere. The father was the main workhorse of the family, immersed daily in his intricate chronometric operations from early morn till late at night, whilst his ever resourceful wife,

4

with her friendly and engaging personality, took care of the business side of things and the running of the shop. Together they built up a substantial amount of goodwill within the neighbourhood which contributed much to their eventual financial solvency during those difficult and competitive times where one had to work hard to scrape a living.

To the rear of the shop behind father's work enclosure was a living room where the family's day-to-day activity took place. Adjoining this was a kitchen which led out through a latched wooden panelled door into the small garden. Above the shop and these living quarters were three small bedrooms where the family slept - and where most of the children were born. The domestic facilities were of the standard 'outside toilet, kitchen range cooking, tin bath by the fire, etc.' type of existence, so common in those days for that level of society.

The tastes in music of the elder children as they grew up were mainly influenced by the popular music of the day, which naturally rubbed off on their kid brother.

This was reinforced during his teens when, due to the world war he was evacuated with his school to Somerset. There he teamed up with a small group of fellow pupils who had similar musical tastes and together they followed the current trends in the popular music of those days, little suspecting that one day this teenage interest of Cyril's would flower into a highly successful and internationally acclaimed professional activity.

EPISODE ONE

CHAPTER 1 - LAYING THE FOUNDATIONS

1930'S - Early Years

As an individual, I suppose I was generally of a quiet disposition, and maybe some-what a bit of a dreamer. I was also inclined to be on the naive side, even impres-sionable at times, and therefore an easy target for the critical and sarcastic, as some kids often are, something which I may have felt too keenly. Yet I believe I had a mind of my own and was not too easily led. There was also, of course, a mischievous side which often came to the fore - and could get me into trouble at times.

Education wise, I was never the top of my class, probably considered of average learning ability, although as with most, if there was a subject which caught my interest, I could more easily apply myself, and do comparatively well in it.

My childhood years were spent in the East London area where I was born and brought up with my elder brothers and sisters by parents whose livelihood centred around the watchmakers and jewellery shop which they ran. The shop was situated in a promi-nent position in Roman Road, Bow, about two hundred yards from the lively and popular Roman Road street market. The main entrance to my school was in this market road and small groups of us kids could often be found during lunch and after school hours mingling with the crowds and the assortment of stall-holders plying their wares. It was a very mixed market, and probably still is, with a wide variety of goods on display from fruit and vegetables, flowers, clothes, shoes, haberdashery, toys, books, and the like.

One particular stall which distastefully sticks in my memory was one run by the jellied eel man who would, in front of all his onlookers, grab from a large galvanised iron tray of tightly packed live slithering eels his next unlucky victim. This he would place on a well worn wooden block and then with his large cleaver-type knife, quick as a flash, decapitate the creature, slit it along its length, de-bowel it, and then would chop it up into about inch length pieces, after which he would scoop up these unholy remains and place them in small white cardboard tubs of jelly, ugh! - and people used to eat these things!

As for my home life, it very much centred around my capable and loving mother who, its seems, doted on her children. She was a thoughtful, caring person, full of life and with a keen sense of humour, in spite of the fact that she had suffered much anguish during her married life with the unfortunate loss of three of her children during their youth, and this before I had reached my ninth year. Her first born, a daughter, Rose died before I appeared and two of my elder brothers died during the early thirties. I recall little of their presence except that around 1933 they had an accident on the local boating lake in Victoria Park and their little craft had sunk, and they arrived home wringing wet. Apparently as a result of this, the elder of the two, Sonny, caught a serious bout of pneumonia, which proved to be fatal, whilst the other, Arthur, died about a year or so later. To have gone through such a series of traumatic experiences could have added to the reasons why my mother gave the rest of us kids all that extra love and care which, it seems, was her especial quality - particularly where I was concerned.

From my early childhood, I was forever being told by my brothers and sisters how, being the youngest, all the family had spoilt me. I never really understood what that meant except that I was invariably allowed much of my own way. This may well have been the case as it was not unusual in those days for me to be found behind the counter of our shop, tugging at my mother's skirts (even while she was serving a customer), asking for pennies with which I could go out and buy my little childhood delights from the market: some sweets, a small toy, a new gadget, or a comic such as the "Beano", "Dandy", "Boy's Own", "Comic Cuts", "Film Fun", etc. (copies of which I gather are worth a small fortune these days), all of which I enthusiastically collected.

Later on, when I made myself a big enough nuisance and my scrounging proved particularly successful, I could extract sufficient funds from my mother to treat one of my friends and myself to a bus ride into London's Charing Cross where we would take ourselves into Lyons Corner House to order tea and toast from the friendly, daintily clad white-aproned waitresses there. How posh we felt, two scruffy-looking East End urchins mixing with the well-to-do, funning with the young waitresses (or "nippies" as we called them), gawking at and listening to the resident string orchestra who were happily sawing away on their violins on the potted palm bedecked stage. It was a real treat for us. There were even occasions when we were served up tall ice cream sundaes after our tea and toast, courtesy of one or other of the near-by customers who found our presence there worthy of their generosity. These trips were really cheap enough for us youngsters in those days and I came back home with money to spare from the sixpence I had managed to cajole from my mother, and this included our return bus fare - and I enhanced my reputation in my friends' eyes into the bargain.

1939-46 - My Teenage Period

Immediately following the declaration of the Second World War in September, 1939. I was one of the many London youngsters who were compulsorily evacuated to one of the country areas, to be billeted out into distant and often alien homes.

I was first sent to Buckinghamshire where I was taken in by a small family who ran a kennels for hunting dogs. Attached to the kennels was a small abattoir, the smell of which I found absolutely nauseating.

On one occasion early on in my stay there, I witnessed the slaughter of a cow and a goat, which was positively horrifying to me, to the point of near collapse, especially when the goat, not being dead after the first attempt, had to have its throat cut by the farm-hand's knife - right there in front of me!

Back home in London life was pretty worrisome as air raids were a constant threat. I was only allowed home during school holidays but it seemed that these were the times when the intensity of the air raids were stepped up.

There was one occasion, when the first doodle-bug dropped. My family and I were about to rush to our local air raid shelter, which was the practice after the air raid siren sounded, when the overhead engine noise of what was thought an approaching enemy aircraft suddenly cut out (a characteristic of such instruments of war before plummeting to earth to complete their mission of indiscriminate and wholesale devastation), the significance of which was new to the whole country.

Thinking it was an aircraft that had been shot down or something, we felt safe to take our time before walking to the air raid shelter. Then all of a sudden the whole world seemed to shatter around us as it landed just down the street, demolishing whole blocks of buildings and levelling a vast area in its wake. We were lucky to be alive.

Another lucky life-saving situation took place when during one of my holiday trips home

Colchester 1939 - 13yrs

8

around that period, my mother and I took the
short bus ride to a cinema in Bethnal Green Road (3rd March 1943). During the performance, the air raid siren had sounded and we were all requested to vacate the
theatre and proceed to the nearest air raid shelter. It was
common for people to gather on the platforms of London's Underground stations
during the air raids, sometimes sleeping there for nights on end, as such places were
supposed to provide the best protection from bomb and shrapnel incidents.

This being the case, on this occasion, we decided that Bethnal Green Underground,
which was a little walk away, would be the best and safest bet for us. On our way there
we saw the bus coming and thought if we waited for it it would get us to the Under
ground Station faster than if we walked. Of course, we were not the only ones who had
this idea and by the time we arrived at the bus stop, a sizable queue of people had
gathered before us. By the time we reached the conductor's platform the bus was filled
to overflowing and we were not allowed to board. We had no alternative but to walk to
the Underground - and jolly lucky for us that we did because the morning after the
harrowing night's air raid we discovered that a great tragedy occurred there on the
previous evening. Apparently excess crowds of people seeking refuge from the air- raid
crammed themselves through the entrance and down the stairs to Bethnal Green
Underground resulting in the trampling, suffocation, and death of 173 people, 62 of
them children under sixteen years of age and with 62 detained in hospital overnight.
Apparently the lighting on the stair was extremely dim being a 25 watt bulb fixed in the
bulkhead and some reflected light from the landing below. A woman said to be leading
a child fell on the third step from the bottom and then a man fell to her left. So great was
the pressure of people behind that they too lost their balance and fell on the bodies
beneath. And we were nearly among them!

It was not all fun going home for the holidays!

Many billeted kids were not particularly well cared for and invariably returned home
after the first few weeks. It was a similar case with me when, after being shifted and
shunted from one billet to another, as was often the case with school youngsters in
such conditions, I was taken back home to London with other members of my school.
It was a little after this period when I was advised to start thinking about a future career,
which was then the expected procedure as I was 13 years old and nearing school
leaving age.

With help from my family, we tossed around a few ideas and really, there was hardly
anything that appealed to me at the time; the only likely possibilities were, in my
innocence, the more abstract professions like becoming an Astronomer (because I
had been recently reading about the Planets and the Stars, etc., which I found fascinating), or an inventor (due to my interest in a film I had seen recently, at least three
times, called "Young Tom Edison").

9

Marie, Pop, Myself, Mum, Ethel.   11th July 1943

My brother pointed out to me that to be an Astronomer one would need to be well versed in mathematics, and an inventor would need to be familiar with mechanics. So after consulting the possible Technical schools available that might cover such subjects, a compromise was made for me to apply to take the entrance examination for an East London engineering school, which covered the favoured subjects. These I successfully passed - unexpectedly, I might add.

I then once again left home, this time to Bridgwater, Somerset, where my chosen school had been evacuated. It was in the company of some fellow school chums that my musical interests were then being stimulated. Together we followed the current trends in popular music, visiting the local cinemas to see the latest musicals, hanging around record shops, etc., as is common with most teenagers of many generations.

It was during the period at this school, between 1939 and 1943, that my interest in music began to seriously make itself known. I just couldn't get enough of the bands of the period, Glenn Miller, The Dorsey Brothers, Benny Goodman, etc. and all the popular vocalists who were doing the rounds.

Many of us were often found in the record shops listening to the latest issues, which were easily obtained by just asking for them at the counter and then taking them into one of the record booths to enjoy them undisturbed - and without any obligation to buy. This was a sales facility available in those days of which we took the utmost advantage, even though we seldom made a purchase.

On leaving school at 17 I trained as a mechanical engineer draughtsman-designer and undertook a five-year indentured apprenticship with a small engineering company in North London. The company was involved in the war effort manufacturing numbering machines and rev. counters for vehicle and aircraft instruments. It was due to this essential production line that I qualified for exemption from conscription to the armed services.

Academically, I had qualified at National Certificate level and was studying to take my Higher National exams. Come my late teens-early 20's these studies were being overshadowed by my interest in music, which was becoming more important to me. I never did take those final exams as I gave up my studies two months before the exams were due. This was either due to an aversion to the intensity of work involved in swatting for them or I was diverted from them by the greater attraction of music, or both. I know that I spent most of my leisure time in the company of some of my old school chums frequenting all types of dance halls, from the London Palais to local hops, not for the dancing - I was too shy to chase after girls - but to listen to the bands.

I had been attracted to the clarinet for years and to have one of my own was just a distant dream for me as then I would have not only had to save up to buy one from the

11

surplus of my meagre apprenticship earnings but also to persuade my parents, my mother in particular as it was she who controlled the purse strings, to allow me to do so. Permission for such a major expenditure was always necessary in a family whose financial circumstances were as critical as ours.

As luck would have it, a frequent customer to my parent's shop who had a long outstanding debt for a watch repair or something, which he found difficult to pay,offered to settle the debt with a musical instument, a clarinet, he said, which he no longer had a use for. In spite of this instrument, which came in a long narrow case, being in a very dilapidated state and apparently nowhere near the value of the debt, the deal was agreed (my parents were known for their sympathetic nature in these instances, a quality which helped to build up the good reputation of their business).I was unaware of this transaction as my mother kept the instrument tucked away from me for some time. At an opportune moment, probably on the occasion when I next bent her ear on the subject of purchasing a clarinet, she told me she had acquired one for me and duly presented me with this long narrow case containing a "clarinet" - which turned out to be a straight soprano saxophone, and not in the best of health either. I knew why the previous owner no longer had a use for it!

Fate works in such mysterious ways, and it seemed I was on the lucky end of it. I did my best to repair this instrument and get some semblance of noise from it - and I DO mean "noise" - but was never quite happy about it. I persevered with it on and off (mainly 'off') for a few weeks until my parents finally relented and agreed that I should get myself a clarinet instead. I wouldn't say it was a pressurised decision on their part but it could have been due to them preferring something (anything!) that made a more acceptable noise.

So in went the sop. in part-exchange for a clarinet, which then became my pride and joy, even though that too had obviously seen better times. I spent much of my spare time tucked away in my bedroom trying to grapple with it and make it work for me - "If you are a musical instrument, why aren't you making music?"

I forget whether it was due to my own frustrated efforts or on my family's persuasive advice (insistence), but I finally agreed to take a few clarinet lessons, something I felt in my bones was not appropriate for me. However, I could at least learn the academic fingering necessary for forming the correct notes.

With Soprano Sax

With brother Bon 22nd Nov 1945 Aged 19 years   London Studios. Oxford St.

It turned out that after the first two or three lessons from the local private music teacher,a Mr. Popkin, that my self-invented fingering was the main obstacle to me not being able to produce any form of tone. He suggested that I learn to read music and learn to play in an academic way, working with the written pieces which he assured me were tried and tested and would help me develop a techique.

I felt instinctively that this was not the right way for me to go about it and, possibly due to some romantic notion I had acquired of playing in an improptu fashion, explained how I really wanted to play the music that was in my head, without being influenced by the academic approach. At first he didn't appear to be too sympathic, he couldn't understand why I wanted to play this way, or even if it was possible to do so, but after I explained that if I could whistle or hum musical lines from my own head, why couldn't I learn to do the same on a clarinet? He kindly tolerated my attitude and took the trouble to persevere with me, until he could at least help me correct my faulty fingering.

Needless to say, I was not under his tuition for long, yet what he did for me helped greatly at the time. He was also instrumental (if you'll pardon the pun) in opening up an important door into my musical life for which I remain ever grateful. It was he who suggested that I attend, just as a spectator at first, one of his local band tuition evenings which, his pupils there being "readers" might encourage me to learn to read music with the purpose of joining the band. I thought it worth a try.

However, my visit served a different purpose.The group were practising some military band-type pieces and one of the cornet players, who I got talking to during the tea break, told me how the music he was playing that evening was not his main musical interest. He said he was really a jazz player, playing mainly by ear. Of course, this fired my interest - and lady luck seemed to smile on me again.

He introduced himself as Bill Brunskill, and said he followed the bands of Bunk Johnson and the like. Of course, I admitted that I had never heard of such bands but was learning to play the clarinet myself and that I too wished to play by ear. He enthused about the music of Bunk Johnson and suggested that I should hear it for myself, etc., and why not come over to his house and listen to some records.

Of course, I jumped at the chance, and as he only lived a few minutes down the road from me, I soon became a regular visitor, not only to listen to his records but to have little jam sessions together with Bill on cornet, a young relation of his on guitar, and myself on clarinet.

I had to confess that the style of jazz which he was interested in was not exactly that which I felt I would like to play. Nevertheless, we enjoyed what we played together, with Bill playing the melody lines and me improvising around them with much gusto - and cacophonous abandon.

Occasionally, Bill invited other budding musicians to join us on our musical forays.We had regular group sessions, meeting at various members' houses (with the din we created, we had to keep moving from house to house!) and developing our raw talent. On one occasion, a clarinet player turned up to join us carrying his instrument in a brown paper bag. He and I made friends immediately and from then on we jammed together often. His name was Monty Sunshine and, although I thought he was a good clarinet player, of course I was better - I had a case for my clarinet.

Our paths still cross occasionally and he delights in ribbing me about those days and how he always considered me his musical mentor.

1947-49 - My Early Twenties

In spite of the fun that we all had at these sessions, we were improvising in our own separate ways and the results were not as musical as I would have liked, I felt that the sound we were making could have been a little more organised for my taste. I tried to get a bit more structure into what we were doing, but as we were never sure who would turn up at any of the sessions, it was difficult to get anything musically more constructive going.

I was also spending a lot of my spare time sessioning with pick-up groups in and around London with various musicians that I got to know - there weren't that many around in those days - and from these I managed to gather together a more consistent sort of group.

After a few regular sessions and a lot of hard graft, a pattern of playing eventually began to take shape with this group until I felt that we were beginning to sound more like a band.

Bill who was on cornet with the group band, being a plumber by profession, was in contact with various local social clubs with whom, suprisingly enough, he managed to arrange public performances for the band - what amount of arm-twisting was involved Bill never ventured to discuss.

After a few of these performances, the confidence of the band increased, the standard of music improved, and we even started to get a small stipend for our fun. I thought it was time therefore that we had proper rehearsal sessions and started branching out.

The line-up for these sessions was Bill Brunskill - cornet, Eric Goode - trombone, Norman Day - piano, who also played guitar, and Jimmy Devine - banjo. We went under the name of the Cy Laurie Dixie Hot Shots until the group was augmented by Denny Dyson on drums - who was really a trombone player - at which time I changed the name to the Cy Laurie Dixieland Six.

In my innocent enthusiasm I decided to run a special Jazz Band Ball. I booked a hall, one of the biggest in the area, the Bow Public Town Hall, for the Saturday night, 20th, November 1948; bought crates of soft drinks, my mother pitched in and made stacks of assorted sandwiches, I designed and had printed tickets, leaflets, posters (many of which I drew by hand), etc., with which I flooded the neighbourhood. It was really an ambitious project for an amateur such as I to promote, but I was keen, and happily it turned out to be a resounding success - with nobody more surprised than I.

Building on this success, we booked a room above the "Seven Stars" public house in Bow where we not only had regular weekly rehearsals but unexpectedly attracted an audience of keen listeners. Often among such audiences were visiting musicians who sat in with the band. It turned into a regular jazz venue where I met George Melly, Mick Mulligan, Charlie Gallbraith, and a host of new jazz friends.

It was during this period I used to attend various private record recitals which were

15

going the rounds, given by jazz notables such as Jimmy Asman, Ken Lindsey, Dave Carey, Max Jones, Charlie Gallbraith, et al. Not being a jazz record collector myself, my knowledge of jazz and its history was extremely limited, and like many others, based mainly on what the Hollywood film industry led us to believe.

I also made it my business to visit as many of the places featuring live jazz as I possibly could. There were really not that many around but I recall going to Cookes Ferry Inn a fair amount and the Leicester Square Jazz Club, which was run by jazz buff, Ken Lindsey. I also remember visiting the Jelly Roll Club on occasions (in a pub in the Kings Cross area, I think), and sitting in with the John Haim Jelly Roll Kings. I also managed to catch Graeme Bell's Australian Jazz Band at, what was then the London Jazz Club - that was one great band! I was not only getting an idea of the different styles that were around but in the process I met many a keen jazz musician.

It was also around that time when I first visited Eel Pie Island, a small island in the Thames just off Richmond and Twickenham which held the occasional jazz session. Access to the island could only be gained by taking the small ferry boat, an old wooden flat-bottomed vessel which held about three or four people at a time and was paddled by a little elderly man who charged the exhorbitant sum of one penny for the trip. Jazz on Eel Pie Island was eventually to become a main promotional venture for me.

Pete Payne was another prominent jazz enthusiast of the period who ran a record shop in Catford, South London. Behind his shop was a room that he put aside decked out with some early recording equipment. It was, I think Bill who one day received an invitation from Pete to bring me over to his shop to make an impromptu recording with some other musicians. It was there that I first met Ken Colyer and Sonny Morris, both cornet players who apparently ran a group in Middlesex. We duly made the record-ings, four tracks if I remember rightly, and I think about a half-dozen acetate copies were made which have now been swept away into the misty past - I hope.

Another jazz acquaintance of mine was Doug Whitton, an aspiring cornet player and jazz collector who was rather keen on the band and offered to take over the trumpet chair. As we already had Bill on trumpet, I declined his offer but he said that instead he would manage the band and get us some more engagements. OK, I thought, we had nothing to lose by it .....oh, how innocent I was.

I had only been playing a few months and here was I, leading my own band, playing regularly in public, had successfully promoted my own Jazz Band Ball, a 'featured' recording artist (??), running my own jazz venue, and even had my own band man-ager, and all the time widening my circle of jazz friends.

Even so, somehow the style of music that the band was playing was still not satisfying for me, yet I wasn't aware of exactly what would satisfy me - that is, not until I heard George Webb's Dixielanders. I saw a poster advertising a session of theirs and although I was not familiar with the name, felt that if they played jazz, I should hear them - and when I did I was quite bowled over!

Here was the nearest sound that I had heard to what I wanted to play. They featured a two trumpet line-up and a banjo and a tuba in the rhythm section, a completely different sound to the band I was at the time running. From then on I was a regular visitor to their weekly Monday jazz sessions at the Red Barn.

I would never have considered myself "pushy" by nature but over the weeks and months of the Red Barn days I got to know not only the members of George's band but many aspiring jazz musicians who were also regulars there, as well as some very influential jazz enthusiasts, such as Les Perrin, Jimmy and Dot Asman, Dave Carey, Doug Dobell, Jim Godbolt (who I believe helped manage the band at that time), etc. and particularly Owen and Iris Bryce, whose role in establishing jazz in England, I have often thought, has never really been given the credit it deserved.

Although, it was indeed George Webb who deservedly came to the fore as the one who laid the foundations of the British jazz revival, in my eyes, however, the one who really brought jazz into public prominence was Humphrey Lyttelton, who, once he joined the Webb band during the Red Barn Days and then reformed it under his own name, took it to a far wider audience than was ever thought possible for what was then known as a minority interest.

Jazz was also taking off in other parts of the world and I was often a visitor to Paris where I would do the rounds of the clubs, particularly the Vieux Columbier where The Claude Luter Band regularly played.

London's Soho was my main hang-out though and on one visit there I caught a club session which featured, I was told, a great American jazz trumpeter, Rex Stewart, who apparently had played with many important jazz bands and was very famous. Not being very discerning at that time,although I was struck by his energy and volume, I was not particularly impressed by his style. What impressed me more was the supporting band of Mike Daniels.

I got chatting to Mike's trombone player, Bernie Newlands, during the interval who told me that the band had only been going for a few months and he kindly introduced me to Mike and the rest of the boys, thus adding to my growing circle of jazz friends.

There were two jazz enthusiasts who I feel played a very pivotal role in my early jazz education. One being Charlie Gallbraith, an ardent record collector and a budding trombone player. After the "Seven Stars" sessions came to an end (the publican of the

17

time was not exactly an enthusiast of our musical endeavours), there was a change in the band personnel which necessitated a new trombone player. As Charlie was available, and as Bill Brunskill and I felt his style of playing would be suitable for the band, and being a jazz buff, and having good knowledge of jazz he became our first choice.

Charlie and I pal'd up together and he was always going on at me as to how much like Johnny Dodds I played. At the time I had never heard of this Dodds fellow until Charlie invited me over to his flat to hear some original records. It was a one-roomed flat as far as I remember, sparsely furnished except for the walls which were lined with stacks of orange boxes turned on their sides, each jam-packed with old jazz records (78s of course).

He was eager for me to hear his favourite American clarinet player, Johnny Dodds, and selected from his vast collection "Perdido Street Blues". This had as an opening, a clarinet passage which I felt in my own naive way, not unlike certain phrases which I had developed, the slurs and the blue notes and things, except that here they were executed with perfection and experienced professionalism.

Charlie then followed this with some of the original King Oliver's Creole Jazz Band sides. At the time I was not too impressed with these, principally I suppose because I was not accustomed to listening to music through a foreground of unpleasant surface scratching, as was characteristic of those pre electric 78 recordings. The 'microphones' consisted of a number of large horns about 10 foot in length, into which the musicians would point their instruments as they played. A very primitive set-up which I believe was very much a touch and go affair, often requiring repeat takes.

On first listening, such records sounded like the microphones were immersed in a pan of frying fish in order to drown out the band that was playing in a back room somewhere. However, with perseverance, and after many listenings (to learn how to listen to these records became an art form in itself), the beauty of the distant music slowly began to reveal itself, and it wasn't long before I took to it like a duck to water. They were eventually to become my main source of musical inspiration.

From then on my musical treats were confined to the likes of King Oliver, Louis Armstrong's Hot Fives and Sevens, Jelly Roll Morton's Red Hot Peppers, and the specialised groups who played in this Classic jazz idiom.

Here was a style that appealed to me and that I really wanted to play, and it was to have a group of musicians around me who were able and who desired to play in the same style that became my musical aim.

Another person who had an important influence on my musical education was Owen

Bryce. Owen was also a jazz enthusiast; he ran a record shop in the Southside of London and he often invited me over for record sessions and discussions on jazz. He was not only very knowledgable on jazz and its early history, but he was an acomplished trumpet player - who also understood the rudiments of music and the theory behind it.

It was he who first acquainted me with chord structures and how they formed the har monic background to melody lines, etc., explaining to me the various chord sequences and musical patterns of which certain jazz tunes were composed, etc.

I was a regular visitor to Owen and Iris's tea-time get-togethers where groups of jazzers like myself would chat and listen to records way into the early hours. It was during these sessions and my chats with Owen that another side of my life was beginning to emerge. I had come across two or three people, one in particular with whom I used to work at the engineering firm, who were practicing a system of diet reform which, after thumbing through two or three books on the subject, sparked my interest. It involved a serious questioning of one's conventional dietary habits, the possible detrimental effects they had on one's health, and the alternatives that were available.

There was apparently a small but growing school of thought on these lines which I found very rational and attractive to my way of thinking. Owen and Iris also happened to be followers of this school of thought and they introduced me to many new aspects of it. It recommended a readjustment of one's diet, the balancing of one's intake of proteins, starches, and mineral salts, etc. In particular, it advocated lots of fresh fruit and vegetables, plenty of fresh air, exercise, positive thinking, and even encouraged a meatless diet, although this was not obligatory.

Although I was enjoying very good health anyway, it seemed a sensible way of life and I felt it was certainly worth experimenting with, including a try at the meatless diet - even if it did cause astonishment and confusion, not to mention some resistance, in my family life. But that soon resolved itself as my mother and brother, through the sheer common sense of such a life-style, also became adherents.

My interests in health, both physical and mental well-being, and generally living as far as possible in accordance with nature, was emerging as a very important factor in my life.

Early in 1949 my involvement in jazz was also beginning to take new directions. Ken Colyer and Sonny Morris, who were playing regular sessions at a pub in Cranford, Middlesex, the "White Hart", I believe, invited Charlie Gallbraith and me over to play with them with a view to us joining their band.

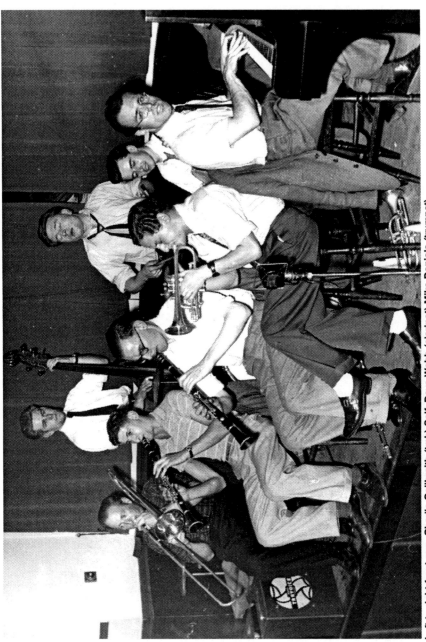

Left to right front row Charlie Gallbraith (tmb) Self. Dave Webb (clarinet) Mike Daniels (trumpet)
Back row Micky Ashman (bass) Red Townsend (drums) Freddy Legon (guitar/banjo) Allen Johnson (piano)

20

It was at a time when I was becoming more disenchanted with the style of jazz my own band was playing and welcomed the prospect of working with others who possibly might play the more classic style of jazz which Charlie and I preferred.

Although I enjoyed playing with Bill, he was always a lovely guy and we were good friends - and still are - I felt that due to a conflict of styles, it seemed on the cards that we were heading for a parting of the ways.

Charlie and I took up Ken and Sonny's invitation to go over to one of their Cranford sessions and I recall that it was a very enjoyable get together. Ken and Sonny made a good cornet team to work with, giving a very definite lead. But to my dismay, it was a lead which was based in a similar style to Bill's one which I was hoping to distance myself from. Charlie was also of the same mind and we therefore had to say no to their offer to join their band. I told Ken that I knew of a good clarinet player, Monty Sunshine, who would probably suit their style far better. I duly put them in touch with each other and, for the followers of Ken's music, the rest is history.

As for my own band, no extra jobs were ever forthcoming from our 'manager', Doug Whitton, who in February, 1949 decided to form his own group, taking with him in the process, my whole rhythm section - which was half my band!

What with this incident and my increasing unease with the style that Bill played, the band, or what was left of it, broke up, and with it the "Seven Stars" weekly venue came to an end.

It was about this time that Owen Bryce was re-forming the Dixielanders and Charlie and I were invited to audition for the band - it was a big thrill for us, especially for me who had comparatively little experience under my belt. Charlie got the job, I got the 'some-other-time-thank-you-very-much' routine. Owen later tactfully explained that the whole band thought I was very good but added that my harmonies were not always correct - which, on reflection, could well have been the case. Years later on one of my tours Owen turned-up to sit in with the band I was guesting with and after I had finished my solo and the applause had died down he stepped up to the microphone and said with a grin on his face "and this is the man I turned-down for my band" Praise indeed!

Still, all was not lost, and I was fully aware that I had much to learn. I got together with some of my jazz musician friends (among whom were the now well known Chris Barber and Lonnie Donegan), organising sessions where and when I could, mainly in the cellars and backrooms of pubs and clubs in and around London.

Apart from that I spent all my spare hours (I stIll had my full-time job at the engineering firm), listening and playing along to records, improving my fingering, developing my style, training my ear (if such a thing was possible when playing with records that were invariably way off pitch or in keys that were yet to be invented), and cultivating my ability to spontaneously improvise, which to me was the essence of that style of jazz and which seemed to be my prime asset (always something fresh seemed to be coming out - both good and not so good), that and the ability to "swing", that intangible something which cannot be defined, only experienced.

By the Spring of that year I was acquiring much more musical ability and improving my sense of improvisation. I still had a long way to go and much criticism could justifiably be laid at my door; I may not have then had a perfect ear, I may not have had a good technique, and my musical accuracy may have left much to be desired - but repetitious and unrhythmic I was not!

Throughout the summer of 1949 I made various attempts to reform a band with another jazz friend of mine, Spencer Dunmore, a trumpeter who had similar musical tastes to myself, but there were not that many musicians available in the style and so our efforts eventually came to naught.

It was around this time Mike Daniels made some changes in his band personnel and asked Charlie Gallbraith and myself to join him. Charlie was still with the original Dixielanders (as Owen Bryce had named his reformed band) at the time but he confessed that he would much prefer to play with me, and left the Dixielanders and together we joined Mike's group. Mike had retained his existing clarinet player, Dave Webb and, with two clarinets in the front line, we did our first job with Mike Daniels Delta JazzMen on the 27th August 1949.

The line-up was; in the rhythm section, Red Townsend, drums, Allen Johnson, piano, Freddy Legon, guitar and banjo, and Micky Ashman, string bass. The front line consisted of, Mike on trumpet, Charlie Gallbraith, trombone, and Dave Webb and myself, clarinets.

The band manager was a Dave Davis, who I understood was an employee of Mike's father's firm, and who was responsible for the band's fairly healthy date-book. This entailed us playing a variety of engagements, from hospital wards for charity to pubs, clubs, dancehalls, etc. It was a group of musicians of good musical standard and during my time with them I worked with many who are now jazz notables, among which were, pianist Johnny Parker, blues singer Beryl Bryden, vocalist, entertainer, and raconteur, George Melly, and many others who are now familiar names to jazzers.

CHAPTER 2 - CY LAURIE JAZZ CLUB

1950 - 53 - My Mid-Twenties

On January 1st 1950, Pete Payne booked the Mike Daniels' band to open his new club, The Delta Jazz Club, in a basement in Soho's New Compton Street. The band was becoming much more widely known and an established part of the London jazz scene. On February 5th we cut four tracks for Mike's new Delta label: "Snag It", "1919 Rag", "Gatemouth", and "Savoy Blues", all of which received good write-ups in the musical press.

But for me, all was not roses. Mike played a good lead trumpet and the general band sound was competent. However, I found the clarinet playing of Dave Webb very difficult to work with. I have always maintained that one of the essential qualities a jazz musician should have is the ability to "listen" while they are playing, to be aware of what the other musicians around them are doing (and endeavouring to do), to sympathetically play in relation to them and to musically complement their efforts. Otherwise the overall sound would be mingled with individualised elements which could often be conflicting, making it more difficult to play one's proper role, particularly during ensemble passages. It requires a certain musical sensitivity which I found wanting in some of the members of Mike's band at the time.

Dave Webb had been with the band some time and he was a good technician, but it seemed to me that he wasn't able to "listen", and musically we kept getting in each other's way. Although I had tried to tactfully explain to Dave what I thought would better our work together, things never really improved. In fact they got worse, but whether Dave understood what I was getting at, I never really knew.

It's not my intention, nor is it ever my place, to lay down how jazz should be played. Jazz to me is a free improvised musical expression and it has to be left to each individual player to interpret according to their own lights. Yet the style to which I am attracted, although conforming to the above free self-expression mode, requires a certain musical discipline, the role of each of the instrumentalists being very specific.

Briefly (in fact very briefly, for fear of tiring the reader with details), regarding the interplay of the front line instruments: the trumpet's job is to lay down the lead by playing the main melody line yet leaving appropriate spaces in which the trombone may underpin that melody with a patterned base line, which with the aid of selective key notes, helps bridge the harmonic sequence from one chord to another. What I have in mind is known as the tailgate style (so named because, it is said, the original trombonists in New Orleans bands played that way whilst sitting facing rearwards on the tailgate of their street parade wagons).

The clarinet, on the other hand, has the job of weaving in, out, and around the trumpet's melody to create a specific counterpoint line which should not only complement the melody but relate to the harmonic structure.

It all sounds so academic and clinical on paper. Nevertheless, the result should be an ensemble sound which gives each instrumentalist the freedom of creative musical improvisation yet within an organised disciplined framework - only really successful when the musicians involved are able to "listen".

This was not how I found it with the line up Mike had. It was when Mike required me to play mainly in low register, possibly thinking that would help balance the dual clarinet sound, that I found I was being too restricted. All in all, I was becoming so frustrated musically that I had to ask Mike if he would replace me. I eventually left the band in March of that year - as did Charlie Gallbraith, who was equally unhappy about the band sound. Charlie then went on to form his own band.

This might have motivated Mike to make further changes in his band as about ten days or so later Red Townsend, the drummer, and Allen Johnson, pianist, had been asked to quit.

I played a few more gigs with trumpeter Spencer Dunmore and the group I was running then, but it wasn't long before I decided to give up playing altogether to see if it would help me get out of the rut that I had got myself into.

By this time my day job as an engineer-designer, being part of a team designing intricate instrumental equipment which although a very creative, absorbing, and challenging occupation under normal circumstances, was becoming less attractive to me. This was due both to my increasing interest in playing jazz and my growing desire to learn more about and follow the principles of Diet Reform, a subject becoming more and more important to me.

I recall avoiding the food served up in the firm's canteen, and taking to work my mother's home-made vegetable soups, wholewheat salad sandwiches, fresh fruit, nuts, milk, and all sorts of health-giving foods.

Guided by the few books on the subject at the time, I came to realise how those companies and organisations that we look to who produce, prepare, and market the food that we rely on to keep us in good health seem to have less concern for our well being than they have for making excess profits. In fact, according to statements in the literature on the subject, it is often the case that, to the extreme detriment of their consumers, they specifically and knowingly adulterate and devitalise the food they supply for the purpose of such profits, irrespective of the effects upon the health of those consumers. At first I couldn't believe it. But then in many respects it was a more innocent age.

On top of that, the medical fraternity we rely upon to help us back to health when necessary seemed to place their emphasis upon the treatment of the symptoms of our ill health by their over frequent and less than discriminate use of drugs, antibiotics, operations, etc., rather than to seek out the causes of those symptoms which, in many cases, was due not only to the intake of adulterated and devitalised food which is so deceptively inflicted upon us and the prime factor in the cause of disease, but to a general, unhealthy life-style where a deficiency of fresh air, exercise, sufficient and regular sleep (plus the excessive intake of stimulants, and the lack of a positive outlook), is really a major contributory cause - and unfortunately one which is commonly accepted as being the "normal" way to live.

All these ideas revived thoughts in my mind of the situation my father was in a few days after my 21st birthday. He was ill in bed with a slight fever. I was there sitting by his side when the doctor who attended him, after confiding that he couldn't diagnose the problem, gave him a shot, I believe of morphine . . . . . my father died the day after. Whether there was any connection between the administered injection and my father's death, one will never know, but, in spite of being brought up to look upon doctors as experts in matters of ill health and to therefore have utter faith in their decisions, it struck me as odd that I should become very suspicious of this doctor's action in this instance. My bewilderment stayed with me for some long time after.

Be that as it may, the more I learned of these unorthodox views as to not only the causes of ill health and the means of avoiding such causes through natural methods, but the unexpected fallibility of medical practitioners in dealing with those who are ailing, the more I came to align myself to this somewhat then novel way of thinking.

As my conviction along these lines increased, I became more determined to do something about my situation, even if it meant changing my life style, my job, and even my profession. What with this and the frustration I felt musically, it seemed I was coming to a bit of a cross-roads in my life. It didn't take much deliberation on my part to reach a decision as to what I should do.

As I had accrued some savings and the completion of my contracted apprenticeship at work was long behind me. I was free to hand in my notice there - which I did. My playing work had dwindled down to all but nil, and I had little incentive to do anything about it so, that Spring, of 1950, with the agreement of my mother, I gave up my job, gave up my playing, upped sticks and left the country for the South of France, firm in the belief that with a complete change of living patterns, I could shake off the old and build up the new.

I had been to the South of France on holiday with Spencer Dunmore the summer before so I knew roughly what to expect. It was during that holiday I saw the legendary New Orleans reedman, Sidney Bechet, playing in a theatre as the feature artist with a French jazz band. I had so far admired this great man's music by listening to his records so it was a great thrill for me to hear him in the flesh, and I even plucked up courage to go backstage to chat to him. He was very friendly to me and asked me about myself, I explained that I was a budding clarinet player who was a great admirer of the New Orleans style of jazz. Although we had an interesting talk together, I always regretted that I could have made much more of the opportunity.

I realised that although we should consider ourselves lucky to have the benefit of their recorded work, so much of the true tone, spirit, and talent, of these great exponents of our music is inevitably lost in the recording process - there is hardly any comparison with the thrill of their live performances. This was forcibly brought home to me on hearing Sidney Bechet during this excursion of mine to the South of France.

The following year, on my trip there alone in 1950, I stayed in a room of a small villa about a couple of miles or so the other side of the railway track which ran parallel to the sea front of Juan les Pins. I got into a daily routine of going to the beach for swimming and playing volley-ball with friends I had made there, plus plenty of sun bathing sessions (I was always a lover of the Sun). I spent the rest of my time studying the books on Diet Reform which I had brought with me, such as, "Nature Cure In a Nutshell" by Alex Milne, "Your Diet in Health and Disease", by Harry Benjamin, also the various books and publications from the Edinburgh Clinic of C.J. Thompson.

I kept to a strictly balanced vegetarian diet, eating as much fresh local produce as I could and at times, according to the recommended 'cleansing' regimes, living solely on fresh orange juice for days on end - so much so, that at one point even my skin took on an orange hue!

I know such a routine may sound extreme to many and obviously not suitable for everybody, but I enjoyed it and felt that it was right for me at the time. It was an important growth period for me, I gave my body a good clean up, cleared my mind of some unwanted debris, got to know more about the laws of healthy living, and all in all, it provided a complete and constructive change for me.

South of France

Also staying at this villa (which at the time catered exclusively for vegetarians - a rare type of establishment for those days) was Charles C. Abbott. Charles, who I got to know shortly after his arrival there, was a professional therapist who, as one of the few pioneers of the period specialised in alternative methods of healing. He was a very dedicated worker in that 'unorthodox' field who was snatching a couple of weeks' break from his highly demanding occupation. He practiced a wide range of alternative therapies, all based on natural methods of healing, but I gathered his forte was developing the work of Dr. Albert Abraham's radionic techniques of diagnosing and treating the energy processes of the body which apparently determine the state of health, or disease, of a person. He wrote many books on the subject, some of which I still have in my collection, particularly one of a court trial in which he was involved during the 30s where he had had quite a lot of trouble convincing the orthodox medical fraternity, steeped in their well-entrenched prejudice, of the efficacy of his methods.

I learnt much from him how best to live in our modern world in harmony with nature and was very much encouraged by him in my efforts in that direction. In fact, I became so impressed with him and his work that I made it my business to visit him in the following years, whenever I possibly could, at his home in Lancashire. On looking back, if I had had the clarity of mind, I could have taken more advantage of his knowledge and experience by entering the healing profession myself under his tutelage. However, I didn't, and it was an opportunity missed.

After spending such a physically, and mentally, stimulating period in the south of France, I returned to England that Autumn, very tanned and disgustingly healthy, ready to pick up the threads of my clarinet playing, as I had not taken my clarinet with me to the South of France, nor did I hear any jazz during that period. Although I was intent on forming another group, I was quite determined not to work regularly with musicians who were not sympathetic to my musical aims.

I recall that there was a long wait ahead for me before finding anyone with whom I could form a satisfactory group. I spent much of my time for months on end scouring the clubs and pubs in and around London where jazz was being featured. Places such as, London Jazz Club, Cranford's White Hart, Cooks Ferry Inn, Wood Green Jazz Club, and many others, some in the basements of London's Soho, and others spread around the London suburbs, of which there was an increasing number, it seemed that jazz was really taking off.

I renewed my links with many musician friends, did a lot of sitting in with many of the bands around, of which there was a growing number. Those led by musicians whose names are now well-etched in the minds of early jazzers, such as Freddy Randall, Humphrey Lyttleton, Chris Barber, Eric Silk, Mick Mulligan, Len Beadle, Ken Colyer, Steve Lane, Christie Brothers, etc., to name but a few. Many of semi-professional standing but some now playing on a professional basis.

There was even an official body set up to promote jazz, The National Federation of Jazz Organisations, the President of which, I think, was the Marquis of Donegal, and having many jazz notables on its staff, including Harold Pendleton, a follower of my earlier band. I see I still have a copy, rather worse for wear, of their little blue book, giving details of the jazz movements that were around in those days. I seem to recall this organisation eventually disappeared only later to resurface as the National Jazz Federation.

The search for suitable and available musicians to form a group of my own went on for several months until eventually I was amply rewarded by coming across three very fine players with whom I thought I could happily work.

First there was Fred Hunt, an outstanding pianist who had a natural feel for the music even though he wasn't too familiar at the time with its origins. Then there was Les Jowett, a trumpet player who played a good, clean, firm lead, full of fresh and inventive ideas. Finally, guitarist Ron Dean, whose rhythmic ability admirably complemented Fred's piano style.

After a couple of preliminary rehearsals, in March, 1951, I launched the 'Cy Laurie Four' around the jazz venues - the group took off like a forest fire. Jobs came in thick and fast, and the favourable write-ups the group received were beyond expectations; those which I still have, faded though they are, show that our musical efforts were being well appreciated.

Cy Laurie Four   Fred Hunt (piano) Self. Les Jowett (trumpet). Ron Dean (guitar).

Within a few short weeks of our launch our date book was choc-a-bloc full, we were developing our own sound and we were booked for our first recording session on April 28th, where we cut a couple of numbers, "Gatemouth" and "Reefer Drag", for Carlo Krahmer's Esquire Label.

The following few months saw us playing stacks of out-of-town engagements, radio work, and further recordings. On Sunday, 2nd September 1951, we broadcast a session from the Cooks Ferry Inn, and another from the Aeolian Hall in London's Bond Street on the 29th September. Our recordings of "Jelly Roll Blues" and "Flat Foot" were issued by Esquire in December followed by "Baby Doll", featuring Beryl Bryden on vocal, and "I'm So Glad", with Beryl on washboard, issued in January, 1952, also on Esquire label. Beryl occasionally featured with the group on gigs, she sang songs in the idiom, her washboard playing fitted well with the style of the group, and she was a popular attraction.

It was a time when jazz bands and clubs seemed to be springing up all over the country. In and around London alone there were such clubs as the London Jazz Club,

29

Humph's Club, both at 100, Oxford St., West End Jazz Club, at 44, Gerrard Street, Delta Jazz Club, 39, Gerrard Street, Cook's Ferry Inn, Edmonton, Wood Green Jazz Club, etc., all featuring the jazz groups of the day, including those of Humphrey Lyttleton, Chris Barber, George Webb, Eric Silk, Mike Daniels, Freddie Randall, Mick Mulligan, Ken Colyer, Joe Daniels, Crane River - to name but a few. On top of that, there were hosts of record recital clubs meticulously delving into the origins and history of the music.

The "Four" was going great guns as we were being featured at most of the clubs all over the country, and we made good money for those days. We were featured in an ongoing series of multi-band concert tours, where a selection of usually three or four well known bands were booked to perform throughout a two hour concert. I recall one particular session which featured, among others, Mick Mulligan's Magnolia Jazz Band, with George Melly. Emblazoned in bright lights across the outside fascia of the theatre, as was the method in those days to publicise their programme, were our names together with "Mick Mulligan's MONGOLIAN Jazz Band"- it took some time before George Melly let Mick forget this.

Despite our busy schedule, I was still arranging minor sessions around London in between times, bringing various musicians together, more or less on a casual basis. I was missing the fullness of a larger band, with its wider scope of sounds and variety of musical voicing.

There was a fair size basement room that I used to hire for rehearsals on a Friday evening behind a jewelery-cum-antique shop in St. Martins Lane, just around from Leicester Square. It had a high ceiling, brick walls painted in a wishy-washy light blue and a concrete floor, in the corner of which was a small stage supporting a very out-of-tune upright piano, (to encounter an in tune piano in any of these places was quite a rarity). It was appropriately called the 'Blue Room'.

The echoing acoustics were not that favourable for a jazz band to play in but it was in a fairly central position in town and many student friends of mine, mainly from St. Martins School of Art where I had played a number of times, used to visit us during our rehearsal sessions there. They liked listening and dancing to the music and mixing with the musicians and we built up a large circle of friends in the bargain.

It gave me the chance to try to develop a band sound that embodied what I thought were the essential elements of the type of jazz I was trying to recreate, a group sound that was organised and harmonious structurally yet, through the freedom of improvisation, was able to swing with a rhythmic "heat" that was so characteristic of the early New Orleans jazz pioneers.

Another essential element of the style is a quality called the "blues", derived very much from the unorthodox musical intervals, like the flattening and bending of notes as practisced by many of the Southern American Negro musicians and singers, particularly during the period of their slavery. As this unique quality was very attractive to me and one that I felt very sympathetic towards, it was natural that I should take to the recordings of the black blues singers of the '20's such as Ma Rainey, Sippie Wallace, the Smiths, Bessie, Mamie, Clara, and Trixie Smith (I don't think they were related), and more.

I also became a great admirer of gospel artists like Marie Knight and Sister Rosetta Tharpe, and in particular, Mahalia Jackson. When Mahalia came over in November '52 for her European tour, to my great delight I got the chance to meet her and to get to know her.

I was travelling up to Leicester, De Montfort Hall, I think it was, to catch one of her first UK concerts, and with good ol' lady luck once again on my side, I was not only on the same train as her but she was accompanied by her road manager that her British agency had assigned to her, Harold Pendleton. He was the same person I had been associated with on some of my own band jobs, a member of the then National Jazz Federation and a professed admirer of my playing. He invited me into their carriage to be introduced to her - and that did it! From then on I was by her side throughout most of her stay here.

There was one occasion when a small group of us, including her piano accompanist, Mildred Falls, and her American manager, returned to her London Hotel just before 11pm after a local performance. She went straight to bed as she was coming down with what seemed to be a severe bout of flu', but none of us had eaten since lunchtime and the ensuing disturbance her manager provoked among the Hotel night staff when he tried to order some food for us at that hour was really something to behold. There was nobody on duty in the kitchen, all the food was refrigerated and locked up for the night, all the equipment there had been turned off, etc., not even a slice of toast was possible. This, for the Americans who were used to a wide variety of hot dishes being available on a 24 hour basis, was too much to tolerate from one of London's foremost hotels. After much ado and irate complaining, we ended up with a few measly cheese and tomato sandwiches, thanks to the condescending offices of the night porter. I doubt if it was anything to do with this incident but I seem to recall Mahalia was laid up with this flu' bug for some days after.

She had a few friends over here in England who belonged to the same Chicago Baptist Church as herself and who I got to know fairly well, keeping in contact with them long after she returned to the States. One was a Rev. Bradley, a leader of a gospel group, whose voice, both speaking and singing, was of a deep rich quality and an extreme delight for me to listen to.

As to my interests in diet reform, I was becoming really sold on the idea of living a healthy life, as near to nature as possible. I had a few life habits which prevented me from doing so: I was never a drinker as such, maybe the occasional dinner or festive glass of wine, and if I smoked at all, it was just a pipeful, and only at times of relaxation. Both habits gave me up with little resistance after a while.

My family ate an average amount of meat, chicken, and fish, which I had been brought up to accept as being required for the maintenance of one's physical wellbeing. It was only when I came across the persuasive arguments in favour of vegetarianism that I began looking deeper into the subject to see how valid and appropriate such a radical regime would be for me. I take the liberty of here setting out some of the factors which influenced me to adopt this unusual (as it was then) vegetarian life-style, as it had a significant bearing upon much of my future approach to living.

I first learnt that the structure of the human body indicated that it was naturally designed for a non-carnivorous diet, not being endowed with such equipment as meat tearing fangs in the mouth, a short intestinal tract as opposed to a non-carnivore's extended one, the chemical ability to easily deal with the highly acid-forming constituents of a flesh diet, etc.

Secondly, I understood that when an animal is slaughtered for human consumption all the waste products produced by its normal metabolic functions are there retained within its tissues, especially those of the organs of elimination such as the liver, kidneys, intestines, etc. In addition, the conditions in which the creature is transported, and subsequently treated in the house of its slaughter, and the blood-soaked atmosphere in which it instinctively knows it will follow its companions to their untimely extinction, fills it with such an intensity of fear that the state of toxicity of its bodily tissues is enormously increased. It is this highly poisonous flesh which I had been brought up to continually and habitually consume, which, I was forced to concede, was much to my detriment.

Another factor which I was obliged to consider was that of putrefaction: flesh foods are particularly prone to decay in heat and when held in the body for any length of time (as is the case with the extended intestinal tract of a human), this decaying substance, if not eliminated rapidly (as is done in carnivores with short intestines), adds an even further burden of toxic waste for the body to eliminate. This being particularly so when such food comes to our plate sometimes after many weeks, or even months, after the slaughter, and it is further devitalised by being necessarily subjected to a wide variety of chemical and physical processing to keep it looking edible - and saleable.

In the wild, when one creature kills another for food, all the constituent elements of the victim's body are there to be consumed in their fresh, raw uncooked condition, supplying the much needed protein and mineral salts which such elements contain. The fact that most people nowadays would find such a method of obtaining their food totally revolting was for me another indication that man was, by nature, meant to be a vegetarian, even though such an idea was contrary to his traditional habits and cherished opinions.

So in the face of such rational and, to me, incontestable arguments, I easily lost the taste for such carnal dietary items.

However, what really clinched it for me was that at some special family occasion on visiting our relatives, the whole tongue of a cow was cooked and placed on the table in front of me. Such a dish at that time was considered quite an expensive delicacy, but to my naive mind, with all the tongue's roots and taste buds on full display, it was a virtual horror show! After that, I was easy meat - if the phrase be pardoned - to be converted to vegetarianism.

At this period, in my efforts to live a healthier life, I took a job in the local park during the day, doing various kinds of unskilled menial tasks, like weeding flower beds, clearing paths, sweeping leaves and debris from roads and gutters, etc., mainly to be out in the fresh air and to keep trim, and to help counteract the stuffy, smoky atmospheres of the halls, club, and cellars, in which a jazz musician was obliged to play.

It was not unusual for me to spend my day cleaning paths and sweeping the roads and gutters, then shooting off to play a concert or a broadcast in the evening. Of course, it was not long before such a contrast in life styles attracted the attention of newspaper reporters, resulting in more than dramatic articles on the topic, and the inevitable frequent visits to the park of jazz followers to see how true it was - or maybe to inspect my work.

As flattering as it was, it became rather embarrassing after a while and eventually led to my departure from such a healthy and publicly exposed daytime venture.

As to the progress of my four piece group; Les Jowett, the trumpeter, decided to leave the 'Four' and form his own group in the Brighton area where he lived. I seem to think that he had trouble with his health as he died at an early age. For a while Allan Littlejohn took over his place in the 'Four', yet the sound of the group, although still very competent, was never the same, and when Fred Hunt left to join another band (he finally joined Alex Welsh who came down from Scotland), over a period, after a series of replacements, the "Four" eventually folded.

However, the sessions down in the Blue Room were swinging along nicely and it wasn't long before we had a regular Friday club with a thriving audience of friends who were bringing along their friends. The band at this time consisted of, Jerry French, trumpet, Jim Thomas, trombone, Dick Hughes, piano, Jim Perry, double bass, Nobby

33

Willett, banjo, and Arthur Fryatt, or Ron McKay on drums.

No entrance charge was made for these sessions as we all knew everybody and most were students, anyway. But there came a time when I had to limit the number of people to those we could verify were connected to our regular friends.

This was becoming more and more difficult as our following increased almost beyond the capacity of the room. The owners of the premises from whom I rented the place were, understandably, less than happy with the situation, especially as we all had to file through their shop premises to get to the narrow stairway that led to the basement room. When I look back on it, the security laxness was quite unthinkable. Fortunately there were no incidents of any theft or breakages, but inevitably, after a time they decided to ask me to leave.

I tried many other premises around Soho but it was not easy to find anything suitable and available. After spending much time and energy traipsing around the area, talking to pub landlords, restaurant and club owners, etc., and pulling a blank at each, I finally managed to arrange two or three consecutive Friday evenings in the basement room at Mac's in Great Windmill Street, just opposite the famous Windmill Theatre. The basement itself consisted of two largish rooms, both were normally used during the day for rehearsals and they had various activities going on in the evenings, in fact I had used the rooms for rehearsals myself on previous occasions.

The main room was a bit too large for what I had in mind, it had austere white-washed brick walls around which were three or four long, large unattractive maroon sofas, but it did have a wooden floor (much more suitable for dancing), also a stage and a grand piano. The smaller room was decked out in a sort of papier-mache material, moulded and designed to resemble the inside of a cave, streaming with imitation water droplets and false stalagmites and stalactites all over the place - very effective it was too. It was actually called The Cave. This room housed a small upright piano but due to the 'decor' material and its size, the deadened acoustics were not as suitable as the larger room.

Mac, the owner of the premises, seemed a very accommodating person, though a very shrewed businessman, who himself ran a night club on the ground floor called the Panama Club, which had an adjoining room fitted up as a bar, yet independent from the club so that non-Panama Club members could use it - it was often frequented by the stars and performers of the Windmill Theatre opposite. The three other upper storeys of Mac's building housed a famous boxing gymnasium and their offices.

I spread the word around that a temporary home had been found where we could continue with our Friday evening jazz sessions, at least for two or three weeks, until a more permanent venue could be found. Mac himself became taken with the band and,

34

after clearing his Friday evening booking commitments for the room, which I believe were only a further two or three, he said I could have the use of the room on a week-to-week basis - which in effect meant that he could remove us whenever he wanted at short notice. This was quite acceptable to me as I had no long term thoughts about it at the time as not only was the size of the room too large but so too was the rent he charged.

The rent for the Blue Room had come out of my own pocket, after all, it was my project and my band that I was rehearsing, and I naturally considered it was my responsibility to foot the expenses, even though I split any gig money evenly - because I was in it for the sheer enjoyment of the music.

But that situation soon had to be rethought as after the first few weeks at Mac's our audience began to build up far more than I had anticipated; friends, and friends-of-friends, and friends-of-friends-of-friends, etc., all became regular visitors to these Friday evening sessions. Of course, when Mac twigged all this, he just kept raising the rent, with the advice that I should consider asking our audience to help out with these expenses as payment for their evening's entertainment. I was being backed into a corner, so it wasn't long therefore before I was obliged to make a nominal charge for entrance to these sessions. But this brought its own complications which involved tickets being printed, hiring someone at the door to take payment, and someone else at the door to check that only those with tickets were admitted, etc.

Also, having to become an official "members club", by law, only members and their guests were permitted entry. That meant membership cards, keeping records of members, and adhering to the strict ritual of members and their guests signing a special book on entering, etc. It was obvious that the whole thing had to be more organised, which was something I didn't really want the bother of - I just wanted to enjoy playing. Fortunately, my brother, Bon, agreed to take some of the responsibility from my shoulders in that department.

The personnel of the band underwent some changes and I was to experience a situation which was to be a repeated occurrence throughout my band-leading career; Jerry French left me to form his own band, taking with him my trombone, banjo, bass player and drummer. My line-up was now changed to, Vince Sheriden, trumpet, Charles Sonnenstein, trombone (who was over here temporarily from the States), Dick Hughes, piano, Dave Wood on double bass, John Potter, banjo, and Ron McKay, drums. We were building up a good stock of numbers with some very interesting head arrangements too, which seemed to be my forte.

Many of the original American small groups of the 20s featured a washboard in the rhythm section and when I came across Alf Payne, (real name Awotwi Paynin who ran his own West African High Life band) a washboard player who wanted to join the band,

Cy Laurie Club 1955/56   Charles Hewitt. Picture Post

I could not turn him down, thinking that it would give the band sound a more authentic flavour.

The success of the club was quite overwhelming. The large room, and the large rent, became amply justified. The word was getting around and these friends of friends of friends were beginning to pack the place, listening to the band, making up all sorts of new dance styles, and generally using the club as a weekly meeting place - and all of us making stacks of new friends in the bargain.

In fact, it became so successful, that the room which I thought was too big became too small. Also I discovered that people were beginning to come in who were not connected to any of the members, and being strictly a members club, it was illegal in those days to allow anyone in who was not a registered member or a guest of a registered member - and beside that, I was beginning to lose the personal contact that I had with the audience.

After some weeks of this increasing popularity, Mac, with his sharp eye for further business, not only put the rent up again but suggested we have an additional night during the week to accommodate our expanding audience. I, of course, was agree able to this as it would not only bring in further members but I could keep the Friday evening numbers down to the originally intended idea of catering only for invited friends, and use the extra evening (I choose a Sunday, being one of the evenings Mac had available), for I hoped, a wider audience. So henceforth, I booked the Sunday evenings too - more money in Mac's pocket.

With the help of a couple of band followers, I smothered the appropriate walls of Soho with fly posters and handed out reams of leaflets to all who would likely be interested, to announce the new Sunday evening venue.

As a result, the Sunday evenings immediately took off and it wasn't long before that too became a popular rendezvous for jazzers. There was a small kiosk-like room in the corner of the hall that Mac used for selling refreshments, sandwiches, soft drinks, sweets, chocolates, crisps, etc. - nothing alcoholic whatsoever - for the members, and he did a roaring trade there, especially during the short interval period that we had, as it invariably got steaming hot down there.

I had a limited quantity of separate membership cards printed for the Friday's specially invited friends plus those they chose to invite. This helped to keep the original atmosphere going where we all knew each other, the dancers had more freedom on the floor to experiment and 'strut their stuff', and I was able to try out new numbers and new arrangements with the band. This was becoming more necessary as, apart from the sessions at the club, work was coming in from all quarters for the band and an extended repertoire was becoming essential.

The admission charges for the Sunday sessions were; Members, four shillings (20p), and guests, five shillings (25p), and I had a strict policy where all known musicians were allowed in free of charge and all students were given free membership - on production of a certified student's card.

As the Friday evening annual membership was also free, yet strictly selective, and the admission charges were less than the Sundays, it became a 'privileged' evening and membership was very much sought after.

There was a small restaurant that we used to frequent called the A and A Club, located at 6, Flitchcroft Street, a cul de sac, just behind Charing Cross Rd, a large multi-storey building with various activities going on. On the very top floor there was this smallish restaurant which held about 50 or 60 people and which conveniently stayed open all night, being often the haunt of London's taxi driving fraternity. It wasn't uncommon for some of us musicians, after an evening gig, to pop in there for something to eat then to follow it up with a little impromptu jam session on the small stage they had fitted up for us. This led to occasional bookings there for me for which I used a variety of line-ups, according to those I could round up at the time.

I was eventually asked to play a regular spot there on a Friday and Saturday night between midnight and 2 am, starting with a full seven day week during Coronation week, 2nd June '53. It attracted a largish audience for the size of the place and we had some enjoyable sessions there. There was always food available throughout the night and the only condition for admission was a five shilling (25p) annual membership card.

There were during this time various small groups springing up, especially washboard groups which tried to emulate the New Orleans sounds of the 20s. Some of these groups, those who were promising players, I offered the interval spots for the evening sessions at my Windmill Street club. Many of these groups were of the standard three front, four rhythm instrumentation, others were a bit more unorthodox in their line up, which included, apart from washboard, such devices as, kazoos, jew's harps, horns, guitars, jugs, tea-chest-and-broom basses, etc., playing more in the American folk idiom. They made a good contrast in sound to the standard line up of my band and went down very well.

It was the time when Ken Colyer and Lonnie Donegan were also experimenting with the skiffle sound, which they featured at the club when I booked them, and that too was getting a good following with lots of little groups latching on to the style - Ken and Lonnie had their skiffle groups and I had my washboard bands. However, I used both, either a washboard band or a skiffle group for club sessions. And why not? Both types of groups were derived from the same folk sources, as was jazz itself. In fact I might say that the club played a very prominent part in establishing and promoting skiffle and small group music in those days.

That Autumn, once again there was the necessity for me to make further changes in the personnel of my band. When trombonist, Charles Sonnestein, returned to America, I was fortunate enough to recruit John R. T. Davis to replace him. John R.T. is one of those rare musicians, a multi-instrumentalist who knew the music inside out, being an ardent and long-standing jazz record collector. John has done so much for the cause of jazz, being a prominent contributor in the reissuing of rare and collectable jazz recordings, being himself a fully trained and competent sound engineer, as well as playing a full and gutsy trombone.

Also Vince Sheriden, the trumpeter, returned to his home town of Carlisle to form his own band. John R.T. suggested we use Dennis Field, an up and coming cornet player that he had heard recently at the Wood Green Jazz Club. Fresh from his spell of military service, Dennis took over the trumpet chair in the band - and once again with thanks to Lady Luck's generosity, I was saved in time to fulfill my forthcoming musical com- mitments.

It wasn't until much later in our association that I discovered that Dennis and I had both been evacuated to the same Somerset town of Bridgwater during the war, and we even attended the same school premises. It was required at the time for those pupils from various London schools who were evacuated to the lesser populated areas to utilise the appropriate school premises of these country schools. In this case, Dennis' school and my school were both assigned to Dr. Morgan's Bridgewater campus, and although I was there a year or so ahead of him and our presence there must have overlapped, I don't think we ever actually met.

So now, the club was featuring two sessions a week, both exceedingly well attended and musically a big success. The membership numbers were increasing rapidly as was the band's following.

This also might have had something to do with the fact that I had started running the occasional All-night session after the regular Friday evening one. These I repeated every few months, particularly at holiday times, booking additional bands to fill in the long hours so that a continuous night of non-stop jazz was on offer. It was quite a daring venture in those days for youngsters to stay out after a respectable hour, especially if it was spent in a Soho 'jazz cellar', and was not exactly conducive to harmonious family relationships for them.

I recall one of the first I held at Christmas, 1953, when I also booked the smaller room, The Caves, adjoining the main room of the club so that there would be jazz groups playing all the time in both rooms. This became an added feature of all subsequent all-nighters.

Apart from my own band, among others that I booked on that occasion, the Christmas of 1953, were the bands of Ken Colyer, with his Skiffle group, Graham Stewart, and a selection of guest musicians who sat in with both the main bands and also the change-over bands. These latter groups were mainly of the smaller washboard and skiffle type combinatiions which I was keen to encourage. Their function was to fill in the gaps and keep the music going while the main bands took a breather before setting up for their next stint.

We opened on the Friday evening of Christmas Day and went right through, non-stop till 7 am Boxing day morning, some dancers going all that time practically non-stop themselves. It was a prolonged night of hot, hectic, entertaining, innocent, fun, for a lovely crowd of steaming, energetic, perspiring, young enthusiasts.

THE **Cy Laurie**
MAC'S, A1 GT. WINDMILL ST.
PICCADILLY CIRCUS, LONDON, W.1
(OPPOSITE WINDMILL THEATRE) *Jazz Club*

GRAND XMAS SESSION

JAZZ ALL NIGHT PARTY

FRIDAY DECEMBER 25th 1953

XMAS NIGHT 9.00 p.m. to 7.00 a.m. BOXING MORNING

DANCING

TO

NEW ORLEANS JAZZ

WITH THE

CY LAURIE BAND
KEN COLYER'S JAZZMEN
INCORPORATING THE SKIFFLE GROUP
GRAHAM STEWART'S JAZZMEN
Many GUEST ARTISTS, MUSICIANS, etc.

SNACK BAR   LOUNGE

Admission 10/6
Member's Tickets — 8/6 (available at desk of CY LAURIE JAZZ CLUB)

LONDON TRANSPORT CONTINUE A REDUCED SERVICE AFTER 6 P.M. XMAS DAY

The CY LAURIE JAZZ CLUB every Sunday night 7.30-11.00

Members 3/-   Guests 4/-   Annual Membership 2/-

CHAPTER 3 - A TASTE OF SHOWBIZ

1954-56 - My Late Twenties

The next all-nighter was one to celebrate the club's first anniversary, and although it did not coincide exactly with the actual date of starting the club at Mac's, it was appropriate to arrange it for the Good Friday, which fell on 16th April 1954.

Featured were Mick Mulligan's Jazz Band, with George Melly, Eric Silk and his Southern Jazz Band, and a couple of skiffle groups, and of course my band, plus another selection of guest musicians. Once again there was non-stop music and dancing in both rooms from Friday evening until 7am on the Saturday. After the session, groups of us used to wander the streets of Soho taking in the early morning sights, visiting the coffee bars, ruminating over the night's musical contributions, and generally winding down and enjoying each other's company.

As a band leader, I suppose I was a bit of a hard taskmaster at times when it came to getting the right sound out of the band as I was so definite about the style that I wanted to play. Nor was it easy, when needed, to get replacement musicians in those days who also wanted to play in the style.

Dave Wood (bass). Johnny Picard (tmb). Ron McKay (drums) Al Fairweather (tmp)
John Potter (banjo). Dick Hughes piano. Self.

General News Features

41

This, and the fact that more and more musicians were forming their own groups (and filching others from the more established ones), led to the personnel of my band becoming quite fluid on occasions and I had to arrange auditions at such times to try to recruit new blood for the band.

It was during one of these periods, probably about the Spring of 1954, that Sandy Brown, clarinet, Al Fairweather, trumpet, and Stan Grieg, piano and drums, came down from Scotland and did the rounds of the London clubs, sitting in when and where possible. They were all good jazz players, in a similar style of New Orleans to my band, and they became regular sitters in at the club during their stay in London where Sandy and I played some very exciting clarinet duets.

Sandy Brown returned to Edinburgh after a while but Al Fairweather decided to stay in London, eventually taking over the trumpet chair in my band when Dennis Field left to join Eric Silk's band. Al and I became close friends and his style of playing was very sympathetic to my own. We would often get together, in my front room working out little duet passages and breaks that we could incorporate in various band numbers.

Cy Laurie blows a "blue-hot" note

Blue-hot, vibrant and yet languorous—that's how maestro Cy Laurie describes the new sound that is filling Mac's Rehearsal Rooms two nights a week and is now bringing fame to this former engineer's apprentice and part-time road-sweeper.

"Blue heaven in a basement" is the title of a really hep article in this week's Picture Post. It tells the Cy Laurie story and gives you some dynamic pictures taken during one of the sessions in the basement Club in Windmill Street.

Meet the band—and the boys and girls who can't seem to get along without it—in this week's Picture Post.

PICTURE POST

ON SALE NOW 4d.

Another valuable addition to the band was John Picard on trombone, another first class player whose style blended so admirably with Al's and mine. John R.T., in his generosity, agreed to stand down in favour of John Picard, who we all recognised as being more suited to the sound of the band.

With an additional change in the piano department, in the guise of Allan Thomas, taking the place of Dick Hughes who returned to Australia, we were able to go into more dedicated rehearsal work.

John R. T. Davies (tmb). Self. Alan Elsdon (tpt). & Carlo Krahmer.
Voice of London Studios   6.1.1955

Ferdman Fotos. London

Now, with the good fortune of having this new line-up, so much more was able to be accomplished in the way of exploring new musical ideas, extending our repertoire, producing exciting new arrangements, and creating an authentic sound without resorting to the carbon copying of the original jazz greats that was so common among revivalist musicians.

It was a line-up which was able to express some of the qualities which, for me, are among the essentials of New Orleans jazz, particularly the thrilling heat that was generated together with the passionate feeling of the blues. It was because of these apparently paradoxical qualities that I decided to call our brand of jazz, "Blue-Hot", a label which has stayed with me right up to the present day.

Within a few weeks, with this new "Blue Hot" formation, more opportunities were beginning to fall into place. Further recordings, concert tours, both in this country and abroad, write-ups in the national and international press, etc.; we were almost be coming near to 'big time'! Weren't we the lucky ones?

Representatives from an international picture magazine, "Picture Post", approached me with a view to doing a story on the club. This resulted in a three page spread in their July issue, entitled "Blue Heaven in a Basement", which brought the existence of the band and the club to the attention of the world. Apart from the atmospheric photographs featured, it included some very complimentary comments on the band and the club, a few of which were;

" . . . nowhere in London will you find players, and playees, more intensely absorbed. There are no non-partisans. The dancers are expert and frenzied. The foot tappers and head jerkers are abandoned - and the band apoplectic in their dedication."

"To thousands, passionately convinced, it is hypnotic, ecstatic, musical experience."

"Debutantes and barrow boys - students, artists, mechanics, incipient stockbrokers - white and black - in narrow trousers, loose shirts, and knotted neckerchiefs - sweat together in the groove."

". . . any one of the limp figures coming out into the street after eleven may as well climb into a monster Bentley as a tube to the last station on the line."

"It is a near institution at Mac's now. Within the first few months there were nearly 2,000 members. On Friday nights there is always a queue of black and blue jeans quietly intent on forcing the "House Full" sign."

"The matter-of-course vigour and enthusiasm of everyone involved hits you as you go in. So does the humidity and heat, the insistent beat and blare of the band, which none but the truest protagonists could withstand - and it's still the newest jazz club in the West End."

So much for that!

On the 14th July, a recording session was set up for the band with John R.T. Davies as recording engineer and, with his expertise in producing the right sound and balance, we cut a number of tracks which were then issued on a ten inch LP (LP's were a new medium in the record field in those days) by Esquire under the title of "Cy Laurie Blows Blue Hot". It became a top seller among the jazz fraternity, and even now is considered quite a collector's item.

An added feature of the record, apart from it being a good example of the type of music we played, was, unexpectedly, the sleeve notes which I had written in an attempt to explain my approach to the music, much of which was often subsequently quoted in the New Musical Express.

For those who may be interested, I include some extracts from those notes;

"Blue Hot - a phrase coined by us to explain our way of expressing a style of jazz, the outstanding characteristics being a combination of 'blueness' and 'hotness'. This is not a contradiction of sound but in fact two contrasting expressions set within one mood.

These days, most followers of jazz are familiar with the origin-forms and early influences of the music; worksongs, spirituals, and blues on the one hand, marching bands, ragtime, etc., on the other. All these forms are known to have merged and moulded into a style of jazz that eventually found its way from the dance halls of New Orleans to the night clubs of Chicago.

The style of jazz at this later period had two predominant influences . . . the first being a feeling for the blues, expressed, not as sentimentality, but as a heartfelt melancholia urgently striving to proclaim itself; the second a contrasting fiery heat, generated by the blackman's whip like rhythmic ability together with his warm tonal qualities and the use of his pulsating vibrato which is, in itself, alive and constantly expressive.

"It has long since been my aim to recapture the atmosphere created by the fine balance of the blue and the hot characteristics in their essential proportions, while at the same time preserving the free ensemble play so necessary to this mode of jazz".

There was more in this vein and, if it wasn't considered an over indulgence of pseudo-intellectual rhetoric by those who were unfamiliar with New Orleans jazz, with its origins and background, it at least showed how seriously I viewed the subject.

However, the outcome of this was that Esquire roped us in for a further recording session a couple of weeks later where the tracks we cut included, "Weatherbird Rag" and "You're Next".

It was a period in my life when events began to speed up for me; my family had moved the premises of their business in the East End to a more suburban area in Essex; I had met Jenny, an ardent jazz fan, a while previously and we were becoming very close;

the popularity of the club was exceeding all expectations; the band was knitting to-gether musically and socially, to all our delight, and jobs were coming in thick and fast, particularly from abroad where our reputation seemed to have rapidly spread.

One of our first very memorable concert tours abroad was our trip to Denmark and Sweden in the August of '54 where we played daily to jam-packed halls of extremely jubilant and enthusiastic crowds. This was not only a boost to our morale but paved the way for further, more prestigious and extensive tours in the future.

A particular highlight of this tour was the opportunity to musically back Billy Banks, an American jazz vocalist who had been renowned since the thirties as the leading "scat singer" of the period. Many of these concerts were recorded and some were issued on labels here in Britain, but as often happens with live recordings of this type, the sound quality leaves much to be desired.

After the success of that tour, further tours were set up in various countries in Europe, as were more recording dates here, a notable one being a live session on the 8th, October, taken during one of our Sunday evening jazz nights at the club.

With the financial blessing of Mac, the landlord of the club, we opened on a Saturday evening in addition to the Friday and Sunday evening sessions, which proved to be a very advantageous move, for the club, for the band, and for the jazz public - and, not least, for Mac.

It was a very busy and enjoyable life for me, gigging most evenings, club sessions at weekends, stacks of parties after hours and mixing with all sorts of lovely people, touring all over the country and on the continent, etc., and life was just great! How lucky can you get?

That Autumn we had everything going for us, the world was beckoning for us to enter into more celebrated professional pastures, the music was becoming the 'pop' music of the day, and my personal sense of elation was more than I had ever hoped.

But then, not for long . . . . Al Fairweather, trumpet, left the band to join Sandy Brown, who had again come down from Scotland, this time on a more permanent basis, and was forming his own band in London. Then Johnny Picard, trombone, left to join Humphrey Lyttelton's band, Dave Wood, bass, and Johnny Potter, banjo, having se-cure day jobs, found that they couldn't commit themselves to the amount of work that was coming in, so they left also, and I had to fill all their places pretty sharpish.

On top of this, my mother fell ill and had to go into hospital, where, to my profound regret, she later died. I suppose it is not uncommon for one, in their later years, to feel that there was so much more that could have been done to appreciate one's parents

and bring them more happiness while they were alive. This has been very much the case with me.

Jenny and I moved in together to a rented country cottage in Essex (such an unmarried situation was in those days totally unacceptable to the conventionally minded majority, being generally considered as 'living in sin'), in an environment that was ideal for the healthy life we were intent on living (Jenny too had become a vegetarian), as well as being well suited for the two pedigree puppies I had bought to accompany us - an Alsatian we called "Memphis", and "Melody", a Golden Retriever. We had some great times there; it was an open house with parties galore and friends coming over to see us at all times of the day - and night.

My quest for a greater understanding of how best to live in accordance with nature's requirements was rapidly increasing. I was learning more about the workings of the body, its structure, the part that the blood, organs, and systems play in maintenance of health, etc., and particularly the vital and fundamental relationship between the type of food that we put into the body, the quality of the air we breath, our life style, our attitude of mind, etc., and the level of health we enjoy.

Being so selective in the food that I ate, it was never easy especially whilst the band was on the road - which was constantly in those days. I was always viewed as being somewhat of an oddity and on many occasions had to deprive myself of the necessary bodily nutriments because they were not available in the food I was obliged to consume in boarding and roadside eating houses. Nor did I smoke, or have alcohol, or the quantity of tea, coffee, and other stimulants to help keep me going, as did many of my fellow musicians. But I was in good health anyway, even if there were difficulties in maintaining it, especially as a vegetarian.

It is not such a problem nowadays as the idea of vegetarianism is more acceptable and widespread. Yet although diet reform is often associated with vegetarianism, one does not necessarily imply the other. There are many who embrace a balanced, healthy diet and life style and who are not vegetarians, and there are others who are strictly vegetarian yet do not keep to a health-giving, sensible programme of living, succumbing, as often they do, to a similar dietary imbalance as many a meat eater.

Of course, there are various reasons for being a vegetarian, either for the maintenance of health, or for keeping the body in a considered clean wholesome state, or for humanitarian motives, in that one may object to the unnecessary slaughter of innocent lives, or for religious reasons, that all God's creatures have an intrinsic right to life, etc. For me, I suppose, all those reasons would apply.

On the musical side, the pressing problem for me at that time was the task of restructuring the band. Young Alan Elsdon, trumpet, who had played a while with me a year or two beforehand until he received his call-up papers and was obliged to respond to the call of duty, now became available. John R.T. Davies once more kindly stepped into the breach on trombone, and, with Brian Munday, banjo, and Stan Leader on double bass to accompany Ron McKay, drums, and Alan Thomas, piano, in the rhythm section, I once again had a full line-up.

Come the Christmas of '54, the band was working full out, and that festive season saw another grand all-nighter at the club, featuring a selection of top name musicians and bands, including Sandy Brown's new band. There were no hard feelings on my part towards Sandy and Al as they both had been friends and playing partners long before I had met them. Besides, they had a good band, and that was important too.

Soho Fair

With my new line-up, we cut some more tracks for Esquire on the 6th January, '55, after which, unfortunately, pianist, Alan Thomas, left to join Sandy Brown's band. His place was taken by Ted Ramm, who had disbanded his own band a few weeks before, in time for another live recording at the club on the 14th of January. The results of this went out on a 12" LP as side two of the previous live club recording of October '54, entitled, "The Cy Laurie Jazz Club". The following few extracts from the sleeve notes may bring a touch of nostalgia to those who were involved in the club's sessions at the time.

"The Cy Laurie Jazz Club began as an informal gathering in a room near Leicester Square, known as the Blue Room. There was no official membership for those who came along because they were usually just friends of the band. Gradually this circle of friends and friends of friends went on widening until an official system of membership became necessary to cope with the increasing numbers. Within a year of moving to its present premises, . . . the club had gathered a membership of over four figures. Also, from Sunday meetings only, the club spread out into two nights a week, then three, until now it is open every night except Tuesday, which is reserved for changing the air, and scraping the chewing gum off the floor, . . .`

"Christmas 1953 saw the inauguration of the first of the All-Night Sessions, such a popular feature of the club now, but an untried venture then. With balloons and streamers, the All-Night session was launched in true Christmas spirit, and with such success that it reappeared next Bank Holiday and is now a regular feature every Bank Holiday.

"On these sides we have tried to bring you as much of the club atmosphere as will be persuaded into a recording made in the club completely informally, and in places, a little inexpertly, as untrained hands twiddled the knobs, and the microphone, twisting around a pendant on its piece of string, refused to record at full strength, or, at one point, not at all. . .

"This 'atmosphere' of the club is created in part by the music, the vitality and firm pulse of jazz which is so good for dancing to, as well as its melodic invention and intricate pattern of inner rhythms and harmonies which make for good listening. It is exciting, varied, and often deeply moving music. But it must not be supposed that the music is the sole ingredient in this recipe for 'atmosphere' for though indeed the main one, there are others. The dancing, for instance, has a great attraction for those who enjoy expressing themselves in movement, for jazz dancing is highly individual. Certain steps ensure that two people dancing together have some harmony of movement, but these are no more than a basic formula for improvisation and invention."

After the Easter all-nighter at the club that year, which featured another array of top class musicians, including the Alex Welsh Dixielanders and Sonny Morris's New Crane River Band, a further change in the personnel of my band occurred. John R.T. Davies, trombone, joined Sandy Brown, as did, I believe, Ron McKay, drums.

Now my band consisted of, Alan Elsdon, trumpet, Graham Stewart, trombone, (who also had trouble retaining the personnel of his own band, so was free), Brian Munday, banjo, Stan Leader, bass, Pete Mawford, drums, and Ted Ramm (who later changed his name to Tony Raine), piano.

I take the trouble to include the various changes which took place in the personnel of the band, not so much for the record, which can always be verified by those interested enough to research the official published discographies of my recordings, but to indicate the general fluidity of musicians as band members and the problem of maintaining a constant, reliable, personnel. Apart from the few who felt that they had found their niche in a particular band, it was a situation which many band leaders were confronted with . . . . . but that's showbiz for you!

Around the middle of July (1955), the band was roped in on a venture promoted by the London County Council specifically to celebrate the artistic activities that were characteristic of Soho. It was an elaborate festival called the "Soho Fair" and it featured a wide variety of presentations, famous people from the entertainment profession, many types of artists, poetry readings, an assortment of musical entertainers - including us, a five-guitar Spanish group, barrel organs, etc. The main site for all this activity was Soho Square, where we were booked to play three or four half hour spots during the afternoon of the opening day on Tuesday, 12th, July.

All this was preceded by a selection of highly decorated motorised floats which made their way through the streets of Soho, ending up at Soho Square where all the fun and games were to be staged. As the floats slowly made their way through the crowds of bystanders, the one which we were on, an all but clapped out old vegetable truck incongruously decked out with bunting and streamers, attracted groups of jiving couples who had gathered behind us.

It was when we started our first set that mayhem began. If I may be permitted to quote from a press cutting I have, the report will give a more descriptive picture of events that followed.

Bomb Site Soho

"A storm blew up in London's Golden Square on Tuesday when the police intervened to break up a street parade involving the Cy Laurie Jazz Band during the Soho Fair Week celebrations.

"The trouble began when the band went on late, owing to a hold-up in the programme. According To Cy himself, he had been invited to play three or four half-hour spots.

"Soon after they had begun their first session, hundreds of jazz fans who had turned up specially for the occasion, started jiving and bopping in the streets.

"A crowd of non-dancers gathered in front of the stand, beating time to the music."The police tried, good-humouredly, to stop the dancing, and the organisers, fearing the worst, called the band off after the third number. This resulted in booing and general uproar from the crowd.

"Then all was quiet for a spell. Eminent actors and actresses gave poetry readings. But Cy thought that the hundreds of fans who turned up for the dancing had a raw deal.

"After police permission was obtained . . . . , the band struck up again on the other side of the square. This time, instead of remaining static, they marched round.

"Crowds of enthusiasts joined in the parade as they played the "St. Louis Blues March.

"But the police apparently had second thoughts about approving the street parade. They intervened once more, and this time succeeded in breaking it up.

"The jazz group were undaunted by this , however, and shortly afterwards, took their followers away to a neighbouring bomb-site in Richmond Mews.

"There they set up their full kit and, watched by more than 3,000 spectators, the fans jived amongst the rubble and broken glass until dusk.

What loyal fans we had!

During these days, I always liked to get around the hall and chat to some of the fans when I could as they were all a very friendly bunch and many eager to know about the music, which pleased me greatly as that was my speciality.

I came to realise that there was a growing number of youngsters among the audience who were learning instruments so that they could play the music themselves. They used to buttonhole me during and after the session wanting to know more about how to go about playing jazz. I was particularly interested in this trend as I, personally, had few to turn to myself when I was an early learner. I explained to them how we got most of our training by listening to the recordings of the jazz greats of the twenties, by playing along with the records, and then getting together with other budding musicians and trying to put into practice what we had learned. I used to emphasise how important it was to get together with others to help develop a technique, to learn to improvise - and above all to learn to 'listen'.

There were a couple of restaurants in Soho where most musicians hung out, one was the Rex, in New Compton Street, and later, the Star, in Old Compton Street. One could always rely on there being a group of us in one or other in the early evenings before sessions, and late night, after sessions.

It was in these meeting spots that I used to arrange times to chat to some up and coming musicians who wanted to play jazz. Some I used to invite to sit in with the band on a Friday evening at the club, but this became a little inconvenient as not only were some of them not up to standard but it disrupted the band's performance, as we had head arrangements for almost every number.

So I thought that if I added another session to the club's weekly offerings and put it on a more casual basis some of these aspiring musicians could sit in and gain experience, etc., it would not only be helpful for them but it would also help spread the music - I suppose I was always a bit of a campaigner when it came to making the music more widely known.

Henceforth, with the blessing of Mac, and the added extra rent for his pocket, I opened on a Sunday lunchtime, principally for sitters-in. In fact, I advertised it as a sitting-in session even though many listeners and dancers frequented the place.

Mezz Mezzrow. Louis Armstrong, Self
1956 Louis first visit visit to Britain

The band generally were not too happy about this after a few weeks. This was understandable as it did get a bit hairy at times because at first many of these young musicians were unknown quantities, and some were decidedly inept, but I felt it was worthwhile to continue somehow. I wanted to encourage these youngsters and give them the opportunity to play with more experienced jazz musicians, which would also build up another generation of players for the future. I eventually decided to book another band for that Sunday afternoon session, and asked my old colleague, Bill Brunskill, who was now running his own band, to take over the spot. I knew that Bill was a very accommodating person who was as keen as I to help budding musicians, and it wasn't long before he established himself as the Sunday afternoon sitting-in band, and Bill's handling of the session was well appreciated by all.

I still have a copy of a leaflet for one of those sessions where the billing for the weekend features my band for the Friday evening session, the all-nighter with, apart from my band Graham Stewart's Seven (Terry Pitts had by that time joined my band when Graham reformed his Seven), Bill Brunskill's Jazzmen, and skiffle groups. Then my band again on the Saturday evening, Bill's sitting-in Sunday afternoon session, followed by my band again for the Sunday evening spot. It was hard work but we all enjoyed it.

It had often been said that throughout my band leading career, I had provided a training ground for jazz musicians as I was so dedicated and "purist" in my approach. If this is true, I am very honoured to be associated with such a reputation, seeing that many now recognised and respected instrumentalists had worked under my leadership.

I often reflect on how things had worked out for me and how I couldn't really believe my luck. When I first started playing as a hobby, it was beyond my wildest dreams that things would have taken off as they did, that I'd be catapulted into the entertainment profession with such speed and success. I was not, by temperament, an extrovert type person as are many who feel drawn to enter show business. In fact, I was quite the opposite, being rather self-conscious and very much on the shy side. It was because of this that I have always been reluctant to give interviews or to talk in public - the most that I could bring myself to do during a performance was to announce the titles of the numbers and to introduce the members of the band, possibly with the occasional comment or quip thrown in when the mood caught me.

I became a little more outgoing in my later years, especially when I was asked by enthusiasts to relate certain of my experiences regarding the origins of the British Jazz Revivalist Movement, which it seems I was considered as being somewhat of a trail blazer. If that is true, it has not been due to any intentional effort on my part to become such. I was just a young jazz enthusiast trying to recreate a specific sound and enjoying doing so, as were so many of us at that time.

There was no question of my being a 'pioneer' and certainly no ambition to enter show business. The fact that I developed a following of any sort was due, I suppose, to being in the right place at the right time. No particular effort was required on my part as right from the start, with lady luck's assistance, everything seemed to fall into place for me. I was just keen on making music, not history - and it seemed to have paid off.

Now I have the great pleasure of expressing myself through playing jazz, and, I hope, able to give others pleasure as well by doing so.

Of late, since I have been digging around in my memory banks, more incidents of this period of the middle 50s have come to the surface, some of which I had thought were now well out of mental reach, especially those where I have been privileged to meet some really true jazz legends. Apart from that memorable get together with Sidney Bechet in the South of France, two other personages stand out in my mind. One being Lil' Armstrong (nee Hardin), the pianist with the original early 20s King Oliver's Creole Jazz Band and former wife of the great Louis Armstrong, when during a trip to Paris around the mid 50s I was booked to play a few gigs as a guest musician with her group.

We became good friends and played together often while I was there. She generously said that she had never heard anyone play so much like Johnny Dodds as I did - what a charmer! As I was commissioned by the New Musical Express at the time to write periodic articles for them, I recall sending them a story from Paris on my time with her - including some pictures of us working together.

Another celebrity I was privileged to meet was the great man himself, Louis Armstrong. It was in the spring of 1956 when, for years before there had been a lot of controversy regarding the British Musicians Union's ban on allowing American artists into this country. It was a decision which not only deprived the British public of being enter tained by some of the greatest talents in the world, but significantly impeded the musical progress of young aspiring instrumentalists like myself by preventing us from experiencing in the flesh what had for decades previously only been possible through records.

However, on this occasion, for what ever reason, the British Musicians Union relented and allowed Louis to enter the country for a limited number of concerts. A few hand picked celebrities and musicians were permitted to welcome him when he arrived at Heathrow Airport - and I had the good fortune to be among them!

In the V.I.P. lounge, surrounded by members of the press and the rest of us in the welcoming committee, he complied with requests to play a little something . . . . Out came his trumpet and, after a few amusing remarks, he then soothingly went into the introduction of his signature tune, "When It's Sleepytime Down South". No sooner had he started, than Diz Disley, the guitar player with my band whipped out his guitar and accompanied Louis on the chorus. On finishing his rendition, Louis looked over at Diz with a nod of appreciation, at which point Diz threw his arms and his guitar in the air, exclaiming excitedly, "I did it! I did it! I did it!"

It was obviously, for Diz, an understandable life-long ambition fulfilled, and a most memorable moment for the rest of us.

At the Press Reception which they later held for Louis at the Savoy Hotel we really got the chance to chat to him and predictably bombarded him with questions about his life, his views on jazz, and the innovative part he played in it - what a thrill it was for us budding jazz musicians at last to have the opportunity to do so.

About this time the lease on the country cottage which Jenny and I had rented was coming to an end and I was in the throes of negotiating the purchase of a more permanent dwelling in the area. I had been scouting around for something suitable on and off for a few weeks before I came across a local dairy farmer (a wheeler-dealer of some considerable repute, I later found out), who said he had some land for sale in a nice out-of-the-way place which he suggested I buy to build a small house on. This sounded a feasible proposition until I heard the exorbitant price he was asking for it, and the fact that, as I subsequently discovered, planning permission for any sort of building had already been categorically refused on three occasions by the local authorities.

However, this farmer, possibly smarting from not having realised a sale for that plot of land, had an alternative suggestion. He had recently purchased a small farm house for his own use and would be willing to sell it to me providing that it was a quick sale as there was a bit of work that needed doing on it before he moved in and he wouldn't start any work if I decided to buy it. Fair enough, I thought.

When he took me to view it, it was, as he had so rightly said, a small farmhouse. What he didn't tell me was it was completely derelict and dilapidated, positioned in the middle of what could easily be mistaken for a Hollywood backdrop of an African jungle's deep interior, well set back from a small and VERY unmade dirt track (which itself was surreptitiously placed on a bend off a B Road), without water, sewerage, gas, or electricity supply.

In spite of it being in such an extreme state of disrepair and neglect (in fact it was really just a shell of a house and our vendor's observation of it 'needing a bit of work done on it' must go down as the understatement of the century), I felt immediately drawn to it, it had great potential and with the three large old oak barns that surrounded the house (I had visions of lots of weekend jazz sessions), the purchase of it was certainly worth pursuing.

He named his price, and I knew by his attitude that it would be utterly useless to try to barter with him, even on the grounds of there being so much work to do on the place to make it habitable. When it came to business matters, I could see he was the type of person who would eat people like me for breakfast.

After consultation with Jenny as to the potential that I thought it had, I asked my brother to talk to the Bank Manager about a loan for such a purchase (my brother handled all my finances at the time as I didn't really want the bother of that side of things). It wasn't that easy to get a loan then, especially for someone who was working in such an insecure profession as show biz. But the Bank had been handling all the family business affairs for years and we were in good standing with them - and on top of that, the Manager was a jazz fan! So I confidently agreed with our vendor to a sale but on the condition that he threw in a bit of the surrounding land which he owned and had a water supply laid on.

After much deliberation, he agreed to my request and negotiations went ahead. He included a small adjoining field to the North side of the house, and the water supply that he agreed to lay on he apparently had already contracted to do for his own purposes before he met me, but now he only had it put in as far as the entrance to the property, which was well over 200 yards from the house!

Be that as it may, I managed to secure the loan and completion finally took place in the summer of '56. It was then, on receiving the deeds of the property, I learned that he had recently purchased some 45 acres of land, together with the farm and other buildings for a low sum. I felt I had really been conned, especially about his lack of integrity with regards to the barns, etc., which he had started to dismantle, but I thought that at least I had the house and some land in my name, for which I was grateful, and that there would never be any need to have any further dealings with the guy . . . . how wrong I was!

A little while after my purchase of the Farm, he contacted me again to let me know that he was going to build a manure silo in another field adjoining the Farm which he owned, on the South side of the property. He expressed his regret

My Band at the Humphrey Lyttelton Club.
Johnny Pickard (tmb). Al Fairweather (tpt). Self.
Photo - Records. London

that I might be inconvenienced by the offensive smell but if I found it too unbearable, he'd be quite happy to sell that field to me for a reasonable price. If I was interested, I was to let him know as soon as possible before he started work on the project . . . . etc. I somehow felt that I had been down this road before and was being taken again.

It was a case of sheer territorial blackmail, but I was cornered. After consulting experts as to the extent of the inconvenience of such a silo, which I understood could be considerable, and checking again with the Bank Manager, I was forced to agree a further sale with him. But this time, thinking I could outsmart him somewhat, and be finally and completely disassociated from him, I went for all the land surrounding the Farm - and some. He agreed, though naturally at an extortionate figure, and I then, after the necessary financial procedures, eventually became the proud owner of a 15 acre Farm, set within its own grounds, which sounded all very posh and upper-class - even though it put me in deep debt for twenty years to come.

I had finally shaken our tricky vendor off my back, yet did he have the last laugh? You bet your boots he did! He stripped the fields of their surface turf and top-soil, for which he received a handsome sum, before final completion of the sale, leaving the fields in such a barren state that it took years before a new top-soil could reconstitute itself.

Anyway, Jenny and I finally were able to move in , heavily laden with stacks of empty orange boxes to use as temporary seating, storage, and table facilities.

It was an in an ideal location for my purposes, nice and secluded, surrounded by fields, and within fairly easy reach of London's West End. In fact, I understood it to be the nearest country area to London.

It was literally only a shell of a place, yet with its oak-beamed charm, I could visualise it as the perfect little retreat for those of us who wanted 'to get away from it all' for a while.

It was reputed to be of 16th Century origin , according to an historian who could date it by the design and cut of the main oak beams. Apparently when the ships of that period were taken out of commission, many of the well-seasoned oak timbers from which they were constructed were used around the country for the building of cottages and houses, and this little homestead was replete with them. Although it had adequate living quarters, the property was apparently used as the bakehouse which supplied the larger estate of the then Lord Lambourne, of which originally it was a part.

With the help of a young local builder, who I employed on a day-to-day basis, it was eventually brought up to a standard of civilised usefulness and suitably modified to help accommodate any overnight guests. For some months the work was an on-going exercise and the builder, who became a good friend and practically part of the 'family', would look after the dogs and the couple of horses I had bought while Jenny and I were away, as so often happened.

By this time, the music was becoming more than well established as being the popular trend of the day. Its fast increasing following, especially among the younger genera-tion, had spread throughout the world and, I'm happy to say, the part my band and club played in this world-wide revival became a very significant one indeed. This, in spite of the pointed reluctance of the BBC, whose extremely powerful influence through its monopoly of the broadcasting medium in Britain, gave the music inade-quate air time.

The national press, on the other hand, were much more generous with their coverage on the subject, particularly so for my band and club, which generally seemed to be considered 'good copy'. Although I must confess that certain aspects of the exposure afforded me at that time was not always meant to be complimentary, as the following front page feature article well shows.

"EASTER MADNESS"

"Teen-age Girls in All-night Jiving Frenzy"

"Over 600 young people - some of the girls were only sixteen years old - took part in an all-night jazz session at a London Club that would have horrified their parents."From midnight on Friday until seven o'clock yesterday morning they dived and jived in a frenzy of excitement. Then, when they took a breather, they kissed and cuddled in corners or slept on the stairs.

58

**Being presented with a Philishave razor by Owen Bryce at the
Woolwich Trade Fair October 3rd 1957**

Tasma Studios. Woolwich.

"MORE THAN ONE DANCER COLLAPSED BEFORE THE END AND HAD TO BE
CARRIED OUT; ONE WAS TAKEN TO HOSPITAL.

"Apart from one squabble in a cloakroom which led to half a dozen youngsters being
ejected, there were no fights. Only soft drinks and tea were served at the bars.

"But the scenes in the crowded room as the night wore on were a pagan ending to the
solemn Christian day that had just been observed.

"For some reason Good Friday night was chosen for one of the four all-night sessions
at the Cy Laurie Club in the heart of London's West End. It attracted an astonishing
collection of youngsters from miles around

"Most of the girls wore jeans or light coloured trews. Scores of the men wore "Teddy
Boy" clothes.

."As the heat and the frenzy grew, girls took off their shoes and danced bare-footed.

Men discarded their shirts and vests. A trombonist played bare-backed.

"Four bands whipped up the dancers to fever-heat with such tunes as "Don't Forget to Mess Around", "Squeeze Me", and "Careless Love".

"Between dances, couples lay on the floor, kissing and cuddling. Others slept on the stairs in each others arms. Two girls went into a clinch and crawled under the piano.

"After six hours the dance-room was like a battlefield, few of the dancers were left on their feet. Bodies were sprawled out along the walls. Another heap lay together in front and on the bandstand.

"Some of the youngest of the girls admitted their parents did not know they were there.

"The youngsters were mostly members of the club (two shillings a year subscription) but they paid seven shillings and sixpence each for the all-night marathon.

"It was the maddest Easter parade this country has ever seen - as stern a warning to parents of teenagers as they can ever expect to get.

Front Page Story. April 1st, 1956

Poor young innocents . . . utterly corrupted!

What with the outstanding success of the club and the almost insatiable demand for the band, the amount of work entailed in organising it all became far more than my brother and I could cope with. So when, (what seemed to be) from out of the blue, Don Kingswell approached me with an offer that he help manage the band and the club, it was an obviously fortuitous and suitable arrangement upon which my brother and I agreed.

It must have been about this time when Ken Colyer had opened his own club in another basement room not too far from our own, just off Leicester Square. I was often asked, as Ken had played at my club on occasions and we had a lot in common regarding our dedication to jazz, if I had any bad feelings towards him for opening on the same nights in opposition, and so near to my club. But this was certainly not the case. Ken had his own following and it never affected my club at all.

In fact, there were now three major jazz clubs going in the area; the London Jazz Club where Humphrey Lyttelton's band played, Ken's club, and my own, all within minutes walk from each other. There was never any question of rivalry as all were attracting healthy and enthusiastic crowds of their own, and the interesting thing was that not only was there no need to compete for custom, as each presented their own particular brand of jazz and therefore their own following, but together they created a kind of 'centre' in the West End, where fans would often go from one club to another to listen to each band. That was good for business, good for the clubs, good for the bands, good for the fans, and good for jazz.

CHAPTER 4 - A NEW DOOR OPENS

1956 - 58 - My Early Thirties

A few relevant incidents come to mind from around this period.

A recording session took place in a London studio which at the time I was hesitant to speak of - I had been approached by a large business company to cut a number of tracks for world wide distribution under their commercial label. Being under contract to another record company at the time, I think it was Melodisc, I had no alternative but to decline their offer, in spite of the attractive amount of money they were prepared to pay for the session.

Shortly after, they came back to me with an even higher offer and, although very difficult to refuse my resolve being sorely weakened, I did once again manage to hold my ground. They then asked if I would consider doing the session for double THAT fee. I said, "Try me!" . . . . which they did. (O ye of little will!).

So, after consulting the band, all was agreed - with the proviso that, owing to the above mentioned contractual reasons, my name was not used for these recordings. that being acceptable we went ahead and did the session. I just hoped that I wouldn't put myself in a similar position to the one Louis Armstrong found himself in during the 20s when he had recorded a session with his Hot Five line-up under another name for the Vocalion label whilst still under exclusive contract to the OKeh company. Immediately after these records had been issued, Louis was hauled up in front of the executives of OKeh, so the story goes, made to listen to the offending recordings and then accusingly questioned as to who Louis thought was playing the cornet on these tracks. Louis replied to the effect, in his inimitable way; "I sure dunno who it wuz - but I promise I won't do it again!"

The line-up for this pirate session of ours was, I believe, Alan Elsdon, trumpet, Graham Stewart, trombone, Brian Munday, banjo, Ted Ram (Tony Raine), piano, Stan Leader, bass, Pete Mawford, drums. It was merely an afternoon's work to cut a selection of standard jazz tunes. These eventually went out on LPs all over the world as; "The Memphis All Star Seven". "The Space Cadets", "Jerry Road and his Dixielanders", "The Mardi Gras Dixielanders", "The Hot Rod Six Plus Two" (mm? interesting this, seeing as there were only seven of us), and probably other highly unimaginative names which were never traceable. They were also issued on a series of 78s most of whose printed tune titles on the label bore no relation to the numbers on the record. Ah well, thats commercialism for you.

Another recording project which is worth mentioning was one with the New Orleans street parade theme. I approach Esquire with an idea which I thought might be worth considering involving a selection of recordings from my band whose titles name some of the streets of New Orleans. The intention was to issue them on 12"LP and include a map of the city, either on the back of the record sleeve or as a separate insert, with a route marked on it which took in all the named streets in an order that a marching band might take. The listener would hear each number, the title of which I would announce and be able to visually follow the journey the band would take.

There would be a familiar linking jazz number entitled, "Walk Through the Streets of the City", which would be interspersed between each tune over which I would describe the various other streets one would pass and the type of scenes one was likely to come across. This would continue until we came to the next named streets on the tune list which I would then indicate, and then the band would swing into the relevant number.

Carlo Krahmer, Esquire's boss, agreed that, being a novel approach, it might prove to be a profitable project. A selection of appropriate numbers were duly recorded on 26th May 1956, and, with Carlo's approval, I spent some time drawing up a map, planning a route, and working out a suitable script, etc. We completed the agreed number of street-titled tracks on a further recording session about a year later on 7th May, 1957, but for some unknown reason, the project never really materialised as envisaged apart from some of the recorded numbers being issue at a later date on 78s - it was a good idea at the time, as they say.

I have a feeling that the reason such an LP was not issued was that Carlo might have been winding up his operations in the jazz field, because from then on we recorded for other record companies, including Melodisc and Parlophone.

At one period we acquired the label of "The Band that Rocked the Albert Hall". We had been booked for a special festival broadcast that was being held there as one of the acts among a whole host of top entertainers, including Frankie Vaughan, The Beverley Sisters, etc. After playing our allotted short spot and wallowing in the ensuing applause, loud repeated chants of "We want Cy!" came echoing from crowds of our fans up in the 'Gods'. This became so insistent after we left the stage that it disrupted the following acts. In fact, each new act that followed was greeted with the same discourteous outburst of "We want Cy!", prompting the compere of the show, the young Bob Monkhouse, to publicly remark, "I want Marilyn Monroe, but I don't go shouting it all over the radio!"

For some time after, the "We want Cy" chant became a bit of a catch phrase in the business. I was told of a radio programme by the Cyril Stapleton Band where the show was continually interrupted by the whole band shouting for their leader with "We want

Cy!" The entire Albert Hall incident provided a source of publicity for the band
which would have cost an absolute
fortune if professionally promoted. Yet,
as inexcusable as such behaviour was,
it was a spontaneous response by hundreds of excited fans who felt our musical spot was far to brief for them - another lucky stroke to enhance our
popularity.

Of course, this boosted the standing of
the band considerably in the public eye
and did absolute wonders for the club
attendance. So much so that subsequently we had to increase the number
of weekly sessions at the club from
three to five, which still wasn't really
sufficient to accommodate the demand.
That meant booking other bands to take
over the extra club nights, and, as our
band was becoming inundated with
work, we needed other bands to fill our
spots at the club when we were away, as well as trying to satisfy the demand for
reliable alternative bands for other promoters who were intent on presenting jazz at
their venues when we were not able to accept the engagements ourselves.

Over the following months much more thought had to go into the whole concern. It
was fast becoming a 'business' and needed to be organised and run as such. I consulted with Mac and my brother, a necessary expansion was put into operation. As
there was now sufficient money in the kitty, I was able to pay the members of the band
a weekly salary as well as finance our intended expansion plans. First off was the
establishment of an authorised Theatrical Agency whose offices were to be situated on
the top floor of Mac's premises - which we acquired by having to add considerably to
Mac's ever deepening pockets.

This office was managed, and often mismanaged, by Don Kingswell and all business
matters supervised by my brother, such as the booking of bands for the various clubs
sessions including the all-nighters, the promotional work in connection with both my
band and the club, the arranging of the band's outside tours, the paper work required,
the itineraries mapped out, all associated hotel bookings, the purchase, garaging, and
upkeep of a band bus, etc. Then there was the promotion of other bands and artists
which the Agency had taken under its wing, the work entailed in organising their
publicity, engagements and tours, and so on!

Although this left me much freer to concentrate on the musical side, it necessitated taking on more staff, not only in the office by the employment of a secretary and an office assistant, but engaging a full time road manager for the band (a position admirably filled by Peter Micky, an ardent band follower). Also hiring more helpers for the club, with a group available to run the door arrangements, under the watchful eye of our young bouncer, Bill Palmer, and his assistant, Ron Buckley.

These latter arrangements were particularly necessary as, sometime prior to this, in the middle of one of our rousing club sessions, we were invaded by hoards of police who insistently brought all proceeding to an abrupt halt, issuing me with a summons and closing down the club. I was utterly flabbergasted, in complete ignorance of what it was all about but having to comply with their demands.

It turned out that Florrie, a friend of the family of long standing who had been taking the money at the door from the club's inception, an utterly charming lady and extremely friendly, the ideal person to greet the fans on entering the club, was at one time too friendly.

It appears one evening during a club session, a couple of youngsters who wanted to come into the club had been refused admission as they were not members. After two or three unsuccessful attempts, they poured some hard luck story on Florrie to persuade her to let them in, which, out of the kindness of her heart, she did. One big mistake!

It was, to my mind, an understandable decision. Compared to so many other clubs in and around Soho, ours was quite a harmless place, with no drugs, sex, alcohol, or anything illegal going on whatsoever - what harm could youngsters come to by en joying an evening of innocent jazz listening and dancing (and possibly a little inoffensive necking under the piano)?

But that was not how the law saw it. These particular "youngsters" happened to be plain clothes police (the sneaky pair!), which, by law, should not have been allowed admission without being members or accompanied by a member. The result was that the club was closed down, although fortunately not for too long, and after extended court proceeding, which we finally and regrettably lost, we were fined Five Hundred pounds plus Five pounds Five shillings costs! . . . . which in those days was near to a Prince's ransom, and quite out of proportion to the 'crime' committed.

This put us in long term debt and set back our plans for expansion considerably. However we finally managed to regain our equilibrium and it was eventually back to business as usual.

I had had little enough involvement in the business side of matters before this current surge in popularity, but I was now even less involved, which suited me fine. I could leave all decisions now to the 'management'. The only time I made my presence felt was in the selection of artists and bands which the Agency handled: I maintained that they had to be musically styled within the idiom of the New Orleans sound.

This put quite a restraint on our manager, Don Kingswell, as he had his sights set on a wider range of talents. From the business angle, of course, he was quite right, but I was still a 'purist' and I didn't want the "Cy Laurie Agency", as it was called, to be associated with any whiff of 'commercialism'. This proved to be very much to our financial detriment, especially when Don wanted to sign up one of our regularly featured Skiffle groups, that of Chas McDevitt and Nancy Whiskey. Their recordings of "Freight Train" and others subsequently went to the top of the charts, resulting in them moving up into more lucrative echelons of the business.

Nevertheless, by 1957 the club business was booming, sufficiently for us to open every night of the week. This, plus Bill Brunskill's Sunday lunchtime sitting-in session made it an eight weekly session club. Not every week night was there a full-house, but more than sufficient numbers attended to make it worthwhile, not only financially, but as a convenience for the jazz public to know that there was a session for them going on every night.

Mac, our friendly landlord, in his financial foresight, decided to install a rear entrance to the club's premises. This was a very ambitious and expensive project and one that took months to complete, but the finished product allowed the club's clientele to enter the premises from a small side street off Great Windmill Street adjacent to the club's main entrance. This side street opened up into Ham Yard, a conveniently sized area which was used as a loading bay of sorts during the day.

Although we were obliged to contribute to the costs of such a radical building operation, the end result was that the hoards of jazzers who arrived early for club sessions, sometimes hours before we were due to start, could queue up in Ham Yard in a more orderly fashion than was possible in the congestion which often occurred at the main entrance in Great Windmill Street.

By this time a further change had taken place in the personnel of my band, which then consisted of; Ken Sims, cornet, Terry Pitts, trombone, Pat Wade, guitar, Stan Leader, double bass, Ron Weatherburn, piano, and Ernie O'Malley, drums. We all became a very close-knit unit, not only musically but also as friends; we had many recreational interests in common, often attended the same parties, dropped in on each others homes when we weren't working, visited the cinemas together, went around in groups, got up to the same boyish pranks with each other, we went through the same phases of humour together, etc.

With Chas McDevatt. Nancy Whiskey. and Jimmy Young.   Bill Francis.

At one time we enjoyed a waterpistol-packing period where we used to revel in springing surprises on each other by a dousing of water, or having shoot-outs behind the seats of our band bus when on the road, and also even backstage at theatres before we were due to go on. Couples of us would often be seen squaring up to one another, pensively steeling ourselves, squint-eyed and snarling, for some fast-draw contest, which inevitably resulted in a drenched pair of would-be heroes.There was one particular little game we delighted in which we dubbed with the majestic name of "Bup". I include a brief description of it not only as a slight diversion for the reader but of its potential to become a popular international competing sport of the future (??). A pair of us would stand side-by-side, facing the same way, with legs apart, hands locked behind our backs, and the outside of one's left foot butting the outside of the others right foot. Using only our shoulders, as contestants, we would thrust and parry, dodge and duck, with the object of unbalancing our opponent. The first to be forced to take a foot clear off the floor would lose that round. The one who secured the best of three rounds would bo announced the winner, until his coveted title would be taken from him, possibly in the next contest. Throughout our many tours during that phase we developed our skills to a fine art in the amusing yet ridiculous manoeuvrings that were required.

In contrast to the increasing success and enjoyment of my musical life, I had suffered a blow in my private life when Jenny and I parted. We had been getting on together so well and had very much in common - except when it came to the question of marriage. She, naturally enough, had her sights firmly set on matrimony and raising a family. I, on the other hand, felt that I was nowhere near ready for taking such a life-committing step. To me, the demands that my future might make on me were then very unclear, and although at the time I was more than happy with what life had so far favoured me, I would not want to jeopardise any greater opportunities I felt might come my way.

As a result, Jenny took a job as an air hostess for which, with her looks and personality, she was extremely well suited. She continued to come home to the Farm on her days off and we still carried on a close relationship, she attending to her professional commitments and me to mine. Apart from that, all was as before - or so I thought.

She apparently had found somebody else to whom she was more attracted which, when I found out, absolutely knocked me sideways. I had been jilted on more than one occasion before, as is not such an uncommon occurrence among the young, and had got over such an experience within a relatively short time, being able to make new relationships through my musical associates to help soften the blow. But this time the emotional pain was more intense and continued for some considerable time.

I found I couldn't concentrate my mind on anything, my eating, sleeping, and other bodily functions were all thrown out of sync. We had become so close and for so long we had shared everything together, particularly our confidences. I just couldn't reconcile her behaviour with the attachment and devotion she had so constantly confessed she had for me. I kept asking myself, "Why? When I thought we were so inseparable?" How could she ever do such a thing?" "Will I ever be able to get over it?" Of course, I did, and although it took some time, the emotional scars eventually healed.

In truth, under the circumstances, it was an inevitable outcome and I should have seen it coming, but as the French would say (if they could speak English); "Those who love are blind".

Nevertheless, I knew that life had to go on, and I was lucky enough to have a creative diversion in my music. Yet the practicalities of now being on my own had to be considered, for, apart from losing a loved one and companion, it also meant having to employ a housekeeper for the Farm to see to the domestic necessities and look after the dogs, etc., as I was so often away.

Then to add to my disappointment, I was also parted from my nine year old niece, Roslyn, to whom I was very attached, when my sister, Marie, her husband, and their children, emigrated to America.

However, by this time my interests in keeping to a healthy regime and becoming acquainted with the laws that govern one's physical wellbeing had taken on an added dimension. I had taken to probing the laws of mental and spiritual wellbeing, which to me was a natural and logical progression.

I had come across some quite revolutionary concepts, which at first I found rather hard to swallow. For instance, the principle of reincarnation, that we have lived here on earth before in other times and circumstances and that there's a specific relationship between our lives today and those of our past - and that all we do in this life has a direct bearing on our future lives.

Then there was the doctrine of evolution, and the intricacies involved in its processes, which proclaims that all living creatures are evolving. It dealt with the subject; not so much from the Darwinian standpoint, but from the standpoint of their developing consciousness. The implications of this, once I got to grips with it, I found quite breathtaking.

Also there's the idea that we are each responsible for our actions and through exercise of our free will, we become the creators of our own destiny, and that we alone should take the blame, or credit, for what we do.

Another proposition was the intrinsic unity of all life, the fact that we are all children of God and therefore are all essentially brothers and sisters, and should all treat each other as such, with the understanding, dignity, and respect that we all deserve - and is ours by right.

. . . . . . .and so many, many, more teachings in similar vein.

I thought if such things were true, how heartening it would be for those without belief, what hope it would hold out for people who were looking for a meaning to life.

With further study I found that all these new concepts were beginning to come together, not just a collection of interesting and inspiring ideas which appealed solely to my intellect, but all part of an integrated and exciting whole, together forming a radical mind-blowing philosophy, one which sheds light on so many of life's mysteries and answered so many of our deep searching questions as to, "Why are we here?", "Where are we going?", "What is life really all about?", "What is the purpose of it all?", "Is this really all there is?", "Is there a God, and if so, why is there so much suffering in the world?", etc., etc.

I would never consider myself as gullible when it came to considering such radical ideas as these and I would always question everything every step of the way, yet at the same time I would try not to be closed-minded and to give each new thought what I considered to be a fair hearing.

When I came across certain unfamiliar statements which, though they might possibly be true, I could not personally verify, I learned not to reject them out of hand but to seriously question them. I was always asking myself things like "How do they know?", "How can they prove such and such to be true?", "How does that relate to the scientific view?", "If there is any truth in them, why is this or that idea not more well known?", etc. In this frame of mind I continued to delve. I explored all sorts of related teaching on such subjects, Buddhism, the Kabbala, Spiritualism, Theosophy, Anthroposophy, the Rosicrucians, etc. I attended various meetings and talks on related subjects, and researched the ideas held by those organisations, societies, and groups who professed similar, and often dissimilar, teachings.

I never really had the mentality of a student of the abstract but through reading and hearing about other people's ideas and experiences, I developed an insatiable thirst for this type of knowledge. After a while, with consistent study, a whole new world of thought opened up for me, with the realisation that there were far more people out there who believed in these things, and had even had experiences as proof of their reality, than we ever get to know about.

As certain of these ideas were professed to be the results of various and independent groups of sensitives and clairvoyant researchers who, with their special gifts of E.S.P., had investigated and documented the more subtle fields of existence, I came to thinking that maybe there is some truth in what they say.

I thought, why should we so readily doubt or reject things others may proclaim, things that may be of help to us, before we ourselves have studied the reason for their statements? After all, we don't have to believe as they do, but by giving them due consideration, it at least gives us the chance to accept or reject from an unbiased viewpoint. Anyway, such was my reasoning and my approach.

Once I recognised the profound significance of such concepts and the elevating effect they were having on my attitudes, conduct, my whole way of life, all my other interests and activities just took second place - including my music. Not that I was losing interest in these other things, I was still actively involved in my many pursuits, and still as dedicated and enthusiastic about my music as I ever was (in fact even more so as it gave me the chance to put these new ideas into practice), but this new way of looking at life soon became an overriding fascination for me - and in time the top priority in my life.

My appetite had been whetted by these ideas and henceforth I couldn't get enough of them. The more I studied the more familiar I became with the whole philosophy, the more I learned the more I realised how much there was to learn, the deeper I went into

70

it, the more my enthusiasm for it intensified. I seemed to be on an upward spiral - and extremely thankful for all my luck in finding something that was so satisfying to my soul.

I suppose to an outsider, it could have been viewed as some kind of spiritual search. Could well be. A search it certainly was, but for me there was nothing 'spiritual' about it all, not in the religious sense anyway (in fact, I came to realise that it overrides all formal religious barriers yet seems to encompass the common essence of them all). I saw it as a way of thinking that promotes a broader viewpoint and an acceptable and practical means of living in harmony with life - which was really my 'thing'. On top of that, many of life's deeper questions were being answered for me.

Yet in spite of my great fortune in being blessed with such an inspiring new philosophy, I would seldom make mention of it. Although I was so enthused that I wanted to share it with everybody, especially my musician friends, on the very rare occasions when I attempted to do so, the responses were either doubting frowns, quizzical looks, courteous tolerance (often accompanied by a glazing over of their eyes), or just out-right scepticism. But did that bother me? . . . yes, it did. Here was I, who had found such

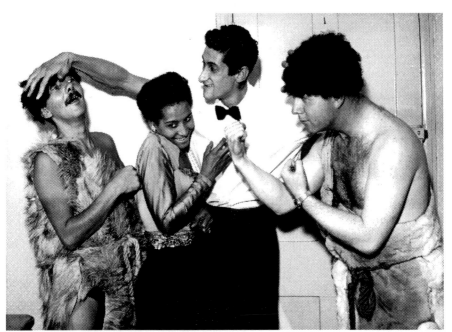

With Stan Leader Maxine Daniels and Ernie O' Malley   Donald Innes

a life-enhancing philosophy, that had opened my eyes to a happier way of living, one that could be of great benefit to others if only they knew about it too, and I couldn't share it with them!

So, being cautious of foisting my ideas on to others, I had virtually to keep it all to myself, which although frustrating at times, was not that difficult for one with my naturally reticent temperament. I just became more and more excited about it all, yet within myself.

To add to my elation, the momentum of the band's popularity was still rapidly increasing, and the band diary was absolutely bulging. We were even fortunate enough to get roped in to play variety theatres around the country, which was quite a breakthrough at that time for what previously had been considered a minority interest. One particular theatre, one of the first which we played, the Hippodrome in Hull, where we were booked for an extended season in the summer of '57, I presented the band, not just as a jazz band playing a series of numbers on stage in nice tuxedos, but endeavoured to stage it in a more entertaining way for the wider tastes of a family audience which frequented such venues. I was always a stickler for professional presentation, providing the music was not compromised. After all, we were in show business.

Tony Raine Stan Leader Ken Sims Self Terry Pitts Ernie O'Malley (drums)

I divided the period we were on stage into separate scenes, each representing a different phase in the evolution of jazz. I think we had the stage for the whole of the second half of the show, as there were other artists on the bill who presented their acts during the first half, including a young and delightful Maxine Daniels.

Terry Pitts would come on stage at the end of the interval in front of closed curtains, well dressed and suave as only Terry could be, to introduce the subject of jazz and how it originated in the African communities of earlier centuries. Towards the end of this spiel, the throbbing of tom-toms was heard behind the curtains which increased in volume as the curtains opened to reveal our drummer, Ernie O'Malley, dressed in a sparse loin skin, pounding away on the said tom-tom accompanied by other members of the band, similarly adorned in such primitive garments, whacking an assortment of other percussion devices while rhythmically chanting at the top of their voices.

After this scene, with the curtains closed, Terry would once again present himself on centre stage to explain the next phase in the evolution of the music. The tabs would again open upon another scene in which we presented ourselves lazing around on bales of straw (we couldn't import cotton bales) on a mock-up Mississippi levee, suitable attired, I might add, in check shirts, dungarees, and straw hats, characteristically frayed around the brims, singing work songs and the blues to banjo accompaniment.

This routine was repeated a few times in a similar fashion depicting various relevant themes until we came to the penultimate scene where we, being casually dressed, were seen drinking and jamming in a piano bar. This was then followed with the grande finale, which featured the whole band on stage in their tuxedos playing out the show accompanied by jiving couples we had enlisted from the Windmill Street club.

It was all really very much over the top, not meant to be in any way an accurate representation of the history of jazz, but more or less a light-hearted parody for amusement purposes only, which it proved to be - especially our panicking efforts behind scenes at the quick change routines. It proved to be very effective, and it was all great fun!

With Maxine Daniels

Whilst chatting one day to Peter Micky, our Roadie, who knew of my attempts at healthy living and trying to keep to a wholefood diet (he couldn't avoid knowing about it, being on the road with us for so long), he made mention of some relations of his in Kent he had recently visited who were also interested in such matters and were growing their own food on organic lines. He spoke of the large and tasty home-grown fruits and vegetables which he had whilst there and what friendly and hospitable people they were.

Apparently these relations were sharing a house with a person who was an expert in such gardening methods. This sparked my interest as, having so much land myself, I had often thought of starting a little organic market garden at the Farm. Of course, being away so much, it wasn't practical for me to do so, besides which I wasn't experienced or even versed enough in the subject to involve myself in such a venture. But if I could employ others to do it, then it might be worth considering. Mm?

With such thoughts in mind, Peter arranged for me to pay a visit to these relations of his in Kent. It was there I duly met Joan and Peter Roberts and their live-in gentleman friend, John Muller. They were charming people and the delicious home-grown food they served up was everything I had been led to expect. But what was more important was that they were all interested in a similar philosophy as the one I was then studying, especially John Muller, who seemed to be the guiding light of the group. I later discovered that he was not only an expert in organic gardening methods but was well versed in the philosophy, someone from whom I could learn very much if he allowed me to pick his brains.

Needless to say he was a learned and willing helper (it is part of the philosophy that one passes on the fruits of one's knowledge and experience to others who are seriously interested), and I thereafter made it my business to visit them at every available opportunity.

The result of this was that further enlightening ideas were acquired, as well as enabling me to develop those which I had already come across. With the additional reading matter that was suggested, together with certain recommended meditation practices, my knowledge of the philosophy, my aspirations and convictions increased immeasurably.

Now more mind-boggling concepts were being imbibed and more aspects of the philosophy were added to the partial jigsaw I had already acquired, each demanding my wholehearted consideration.

I learned of such engrossing ideas as the existence and make up of the Soul, that we all have another self, a higher self of which we are not normally aware in our waking consciousness, an essential part of ourselves which is not subject to the frailties and limitations of our personality life, and that through right effort it can be reached and its qualities expressed in our daily living.

Also that the events in our life and our relationships all have a greater purpose, that the object of our existence is to learn certain lessons and to recognise the kinship which we have with all other lives.

That there are on earth those who have mastered many of their lessons and in doing so have risen in consciousness beyond the stage of humankind, and whose purposes are to help those who seriously aspire to do the same.

And the revelation that the world is entering a new era of understanding and living, which promises to relieve us from the pettiness, selfishness, and injustice which has caused us so much suffering in the past.

All these, and more, were parts of a growing universal picture which was developing in my consciousness, putting my life in clearer perspective and giving it much greater meaning.

It is true that some of these ideas were not so dissimilar to certain religious beliefs I had encountered, but what made these so unique was the wealth of detail involved, often supported by people's documented experiences, that made it all so credible, so much so, that it could easily come under the category of a science.

I found it all so absorbing and uplifting. Compared to this, all my other interests were put in the shade. I loved playing jazz: it was expressive for me, it was creative, and it gave others pleasure (I liked to believe), but when it came to the question of where my priorities now lay, there was absolutely no contest: this new-found philosophy had everything else licked in my book.

I came to realise that it was a philosophy which is not just the result of human deliberations, but from much more profound sources; it is said to be the accumulated wisdom of the ages yet applied to today's conditions. In fact, it was often referred to as the Ageless Wisdom, being applicable to all and every age of Cosmic existence, and for me, the scope, depth, and comprehensiveness of its teachings and the enriched life that I was getting from it was ample proof of this. I was unquestionably well and truly hooked - and that's putting it mildly!

CHAPTER 5 - A CHANGE OF DIRECTION

1958-60 - Approaching My Mid-Thirties

This was the phase when both the club and the band were really riding high. Business was booming on all fronts; the club became a virtual institution in the world of jazz, a Mecca for jazz devotees from all over the world and the 'in' place to go and be seen. It boasted an annual membership numbering tens of thousands - and rapidly growing; the band was now internationally acclaimed, as well as being one of Britain's top jazz attractions. Radio, Television, Records, Stage Shows, Film work, and Concert Tours all over Europe were included in our showbiz triumphs. To promoters and agents the name meant an instant sell-out - success upon success was our happy lot!

One of the recording sessions that we did for Parlophone resulted in the issue of a novel selection of jazz tune titles all loosely related to a jungle theme, such as, "Alligator Hop", "Wild Man Blues", "Jungle Blues", "King of the Zulus", etc., the latter being the number I always closed each of our sessions with, being such a swinger to go out on. My line-up at this time consisted of, Colin Smith, trumpet, Terry Pitts, trombone, Ron Weatherburn, piano, Wayne Chandler, banjo, Stan Leader, double bass, and Ernie O'Malley, drums.

It was very similar to the personnel which subsequently featured in a two-reeler film we did for the Ford Motor Company to help launch their innovative new vehicle, the Transit Bus. The general purpose of the film was visually to demonstrate the efficiency and versatility of their new 'baby'. The actuality of the production proved slightly different.

The film opened with a general explanation of the vehicle and the variety of attributes it had. This was then followed by a visual demonstration of those attributes through a light-heartedly contrived story which depicted members of the band being picked up by the said vehicle and then being driven to a band gig, on the way encountering all manner of hazardous situations which, needless to say, such a vehicle effortlessly surmounted.

The first pick-up was Colin, emerging hurriedly from the front door of his house whilst playing merrily away on his trumpet a little melody which I had previously composed for the film. Then, nipping around the awaiting shiny new Ford minibus, he opened its door, hopped into the driving seat, started the engine and drove off - still playing, even if it was with only one hand.

Then it showed a view of the vehicle with Colin at the wheel driving through the streets of a suburban shopping centre until it eventually pulled up in a side road to pick up Tim Streeton, who was sitting on a stool outside a workman's hut playing his banjo. The bus pulled away after Tim had jumped in the back with the camera following the bus through the streets and then into the country lane leading to my Farm. Here the camera panned to a shot of me, perched atop the front gates of the Farm, clarinet to my lips and pointing skywards, swinging along to the melody of Colin's trumpet and Tim's banjo accompaniment.

Still playing, I jumped off the gate (what agility!), opened the passenger door of the bus and climbed in, just as it was pulling away down the lane. It was all meant to be a double quick operation.

The next scene was Terry, siting on a low parapet wall in front of a large house, playing his trombone with much gusto, waiting for the band wagon to arrive. As soon as it did, he clambered down, jumped into the back of the wagon and then we all drove away, still managing to play our instruments without the slightest hitch.

The wagon drew up by a quayside where, from a barge, Stan emerged with his double bass and ran to the rear of the wagon and clambered in through the doors as it was driving off. This I believe was the second take because, being a tricky shot, Stan didn't make the expected 'clambering in' on the first take without staggering backwards on to the ground as the wagon drove off - minus Stan, and much to everyone's amusement. Trying to board the rear of a band wagon, lugging a double bass which was larger than oneself, was no mean feat. But Stan took it all in good part, as was his light-hearted nature, and the end result was eventually 'in the can'.

Then came the pick up of Ernie who was seen leaning on the railings outside his house, pounding his snare drum to the band's ensemble sound coming from the approaching wagon. He too then jumped into the back of the vehicle with the camera following him and, shooting from inside, it then showed how the whole band had the space to play in its normal rousing manner (believe it if you will).

The final pick up was of a young girl, a budding starlet at the time, caressing in her arms a small kitten, which I think before the cameras started rolling, undignifiedly christened her while she was waiting for the wagon outside a block of flats. After drying her out, the wagon was seen picking her up with her little pet then driving away down the street, with the band still gaily sounding forth, only to be stopped in its tracks by an elderly violinist on the pavement who fired his bow from the violin strings straight into our rear tyre, like an ancient travesty of Cupid.

This was the start of the vehicle's escapades and its versatility in overcoming all obstacles. This first incident showed how easy it was to change a wheel, with our young starlet effortlessly undoing the hub nuts, replacing the wheel with the spare, then retightening the hub nuts, an operation which she performed totally unaided, whilst the members of the band unashamedly looked on - still playing, I might add.

Then we encountered a barrel organist who, possibly objecting to the musical competition in the approaching vehicle, had placed "No Through Road" signs in its path which it readily avoided by turning around within the width of the road, thus demonstrating its efficient 35-foot turning circle.

Following this our unruffled vehicle was confronted with a tip-up truck which had emptied its whole load of 4 foot scaffold poles in the path of the wagon. Although the wagon had no alternative but to run over these poles, the scene from inside showed how unaffected the passengers were, with the starlet's kitten lapping happily from a saucer of undisturbed milk. What effective suspension!

The final confrontation was with a street cellist whose musical renderings were being drowned out by this passing jazz sound. In an irate response, he up-ended his instrument, jammed the metal prong which protruded from its base into the side of the vehicle, thereby scoring the offending motorised monster right along its lower panel. Of course, this was no real problem as all the panels were easily changeable, if the following quick replacement was to be believed. In fact, I seemed to recall that not only was the damaged panel laboriously difficult to remove, but shooting had to be delayed for days until a suitable replacement was acquired from a specialised parts store before it was duly attached, with the aid of two experienced Ford fitters. A typical case of the illusions of the silver screen, my dear Watson!

After a few further examples of the vehicle's manoeuverability, loading capacity, etc., the band finally reached its destination, the stage door of a theatre. The grand finale was when we all trooped out of the bus, yes still playing (we had hardly stopped throughout the whole film), towards a crowd of cheering fans (of specially recruited club members), who ran towards us, and then straight through our ranks, past us to cheer and admire the Ford band vehicle behind us - which after all was the real star of the production.

Such was the triumph of our film career as the finished production was considered a great success. Be that as it may, I never did get that call from Hollywood.

It might be wondered how I am able to recount the above details of the film after such a long period of over 40 years. It is certainly not from any photographic memory ability on my part, but because I actually possess a copy of it - and how I came by that is a tidy little tale in itself.

It came about through a friend of mine, Frank Sharpe, a member of the club and a follower of the band during the 50s. Sometime around the early 80s he turned up again at a jazz club in Lincolnshire where I had been booked as a featured guest artist.

He introduced himself and started reminiscing about the good ol' happy club days, etc., he jogged my memory as to this promotional film I had made for Ford. I told him that I remembered it vaguely but was not too sure about the details of when, where, and what. He then offered to try to locate it for me if it was still in existence, as he was quite keen to get a copy for himself. He kept in touch with me quite regularly after that to keep me up to date with his progress.

Although being industrious and painstaking in his research and probing all likely sources, as was characteristic of him, he seemed to pull a blank at every turn. He related one occasion when, with the distinct promise of success, a copy was uncovered in the bowels of an English Stately Home, it might have been Beaulieu, where some of Ford's film archives were stored. After much persuasive negotiations with a roundabout string of contacts, they eventually sent him a copy of the film they had unearthed.

It was a promotional film for a new Ford Transit vehicle alright, but it was for a later model, and the film featured not the Cy Laurie Band, but Dick Emery. Another abortive attempt for zealous Frank.

However, what he did come up with was the name of one of the cameramen who was involved in the film's production and after tracking him down, discovered that the said cameraman had remembered the film very well as it was one of the first films where a particular new colour process was used for such a project.

With this information, Frank was able to put me in contact with John Waddell, a Managing Director of one of Ford's leading departments who was not only a jazz fan and an ex-Cy Laurie follower, but had sufficient managerial clout to cut through any red tape in locating the whereabouts of the elusive film. John and I subsequently arranged to meet for lunch one day in the foyer of a large hotel where I duly presented him with his requested copy of my latest recording (a likely sweetener?). He told me that he had set wheels in motion to find the film and would let me know if and when anything turned up.

The result was that a little while after our meeting, much to my satisfaction, a video'd copy of the film turned up in the post which I then dubbed to include in a short compilation video of some other clips of my work that I had in my own archives, which I then sent to Frank Sharpe.

An addition to the band personnel at that time was that fine songstress, Rosella Mitchell, whose repertoire extended from the many blues numbers of Bessie Smith and her contemporaries to popular ballads of the thirties and forties. Prior to her joining the band, any vocals we included were either taken by me or one of the other members of the band. But this was seldom required as most of the numbers that I selected for the band were principally instrumental. However, with Ella in the band (she was billed as

Ella Mitchell) changes were made to accommodate her numbers. She was very easy to get along with and always musically in fine form; I particularly enjoyed backing her vocals, endeavouring to adapt my Classical Jazz clarinet phrasing to her more later style material. We also did some very enjoyable light-hearted vocal duets together which, though not strictly in the idiom, were arranged as near as possible.

When Ella discovered that I had an interest in meditation and philosophy, she insisted that she introduce me to a friend of hers, Gertrude Rubinstein, an ex-concert pianist and voice coach who was also interested in such subjects. I duly went along with Ella to meet Gertrude at her North London home. She was a short lady, in her seventies, very fluffy and full of vitality. We got on very well together and had certain philosophical interests in common and from then on I often visited her for stimulating discussions over tea and sandwiches.

In addition, my frequent visits to my philosophy friends in Kent were proving to be a much more enlightening set of experiences than I had ever envisaged. I was now becoming familiar with the deeper aspects of the philosophy, and an avid reader of all the literature on the subject that I could get hold of, much of which had been written in the 19th and early part of the 20th Century, and therefore currently out of print. However, with prolonged and diligent searching of the appropriate second-hand bookshops, I managed to build up a very substantial collection, the contents of which, I might add, were extensive and profound enough to keep me mind-boggled for the rest of my life.

I concentrated on acquiring the works of such authors as Annie Besant, H.P. Blavatsky, Rudolf Steiner, Helena Roarich, Charles W. Leadbeater, Alice A.Bailey, Cyril Scott, and many, many others whose knowledge and insight seemed to stimulate my soul. Certain of these books were quite tome-like in size, and their contents could never be read like a novel, they required serious concentrated study, an ability that was not easy for me to acquire. Nevertheless, with perseverance and the regular discussions that I was able to have with John Muller at his home in Kent, my understanding of such subjects slowly increased, as did my aspirations.

There were also other books of lighter character which dealt with similar subjects but more from a rudimentary angle and were much easier to read and assimilate. A particular set of books in this class was a trilogy relating to the enchanting experiences the author had had in his association with a remarkable and intuitively advanced Soul, which I found especially delightful. It was about this time I came across the first of these three volumes, entitled, "The Initiate". This was written by a student of the philosophy who, apparently wishing to remain anonymous, simply called himself 'a pupil'. It was a work which I often recommended to others who expressed an interest.

My domestic life at this time was practically non-existent. Being on the road much of

Ella Mitchell with the Cy Laurie Band   Landseer. London.

the time and dashing over to Kent in between times, I hardly spent any time at the Farm. It was becoming just like another hotel to me and, to my regret, I was neglecting my devoted dogs. Not that they were not being well cared for, my housekeeper adored them but they were transferring their attachment from me to her, naturally enough. When she eventually decided to move on, she wanted to take the dogs with her as she grew to love them so. She knew that I couldn't give them the care and attention which they deserved and which I knew she would. I was forced to concede that her request to take them would be the best thing all round.

Some little time later, whilst playing a gig in Ipswich, I met Susannah, a girl who was to play a prominent part in my life at that period. She was tall, blonde, and with a figure like a dream. I was captivated by her and it didn't take long before I became infatuated with her. She was not particularly a jazz enthusiast though she liked the music well enough and came to most of my jazz sessions after that, idolising me from within the audience (I'd like to believe). As was to be expected, and hoped for, we later moved in to the Farm together - and so began another period of my 'living in sin'.

It will be gathered by now that I wasn't one to conform too strictly to the conventions

82

of the times, which were far more demanding on one's social and moral conduct than they are today, but what I was strict about was my loyalty in relationships. Yes, there was no question that I liked the girls and in my position, being in the public eye, it wasn't difficult to get to know them (and given the opportunity, I enjoyed light-heartedly flirting with them), but I was never promiscuous or even unfaithful regarding anyone I became involved with. If I had a relationship with a girl I would not consider cheating on her in that way, not only because I wouldn't want to hurt her, but out of the sheer principle of trust. I was definitely no angel, but I did have certain scruples, even if I didn't shout about them.

In general, I suppose I was never really easy to get to know; I spoke little about myself to acquaintances, being, as I've already mentioned, a very private person. This characteristic appeared very evident whenever I was confronted with an interviewer who was trying to delve too deeply into my personal life.

As an illustration, I include an extract of a press-cutting of the time, which may give a more detached viewpoint, not entirely accurate, I might add, of my attitude, my career, my position in the public eye, and of my approach to the music. I quote;

CY LAURIE
The most controversial figure in British Jazz
Cy Laurie is somewhat of an enigma to his associates and those who come in touch with him. In appearance he is a long-legged six footer with dark curly hair and as angular as the clarinet he blows so skilfully.

However, basically he is a man of simple tastes. He loves the open air and spends most of his free time on his farm just outside of London where his dogs and horses respond to such names as Melody and Memphis. His favourite mare, Sapphire, is always ready to greet him with an affectionate nudge.

Invite Cy to have a drink and he will probably order a fruit juice. Reticent though he may be, talk to him about Jazz and he will converse in the devotional hushed voice of a botanist discussing rare orchids, oblivious of time.

Cy was born in the spring of 1926, the youngest son of an East End watchmaker and the only one in the family not to take music lessons. His parents had paid for music lessons for his six older brothers and sisters and they all turned out as musical sledgehammers, so Dad decided, "We are not wasting money on Cyril . . . .". Unaware that his son was destined to be a musician of a nation-wide popularity. Inspired by early recordings of Jazz greats such as King Oliver, Johnny Dodds, Louis Armstrong, Cy bought a clarinet and self-taught eventually became one of the first musicians to revive traditional Jazz in company with other British pioneers as Humphrey Lyttelton, George Webb and Chris Barber.

He was, after leaving school, all set along the road to becoming an engineer and indeed within reach of his Bachelor of Science degree. However he realised that his first love was Jazz and to this end relinquished his career. It soon became obvious that to express his own ideas and interpretations he would have to lead his own group. He took odd jobs from time to time including that of a five pound a week roadsweeper.

His first attempt to form a group of really compatible musicians resulted in the formation of the Cy Laurie Four. His appearance on the Jazz scene quickly brought many recording offers as well as a string of broadcasting contracts.

Eventually, Cy formed a full band of seven musicians. They rehearsed regularly in a basement opposite the Windmill Theatre every Sunday evening. Other musicians would drop in to listen and very often bring their friends with them, pretty soon the friends were bringing their friends and after a very short while a Club was formed. This, then was the birth of the now famous Cy Laurie Jazz Club, which today presents eight sessions every week and has over 10,000 members. Membership is selective and students particularly are encouraged.

The Club is peopled by a set, who enjoy informality of atmosphere and dress, ranging from barrow boys to debutantes. Music playing in the Tabernacle of Jazz is aptly described by Cy as being derived from "Early Jazz influences where worksongs, spirituals and blues were sung on one hand while marching bands and ragtime were played on the other. The two predominant influences being the black man's fiery heat and his feeling for the blues." He thinks that Jazz music reached its most interesting period around the early twenties in New Orleans. A style of music he has labelled Blue-Hot.

The Blue-Hot music with its colourful interpretations is reflected in the clothes worn by the girls who frequent the Club and has proved a boon to journalists and most of the National Daily Newspapers who realised that these youngsters, without doubt, set fashions which have a widespread following among girls everywhere.

Not content with the controversy surrounding Cy and his music, now the Press have drawn attention to his devotees. Photographs, articles, interviews, thousands of words have been printed in all types of publications, such as Picture Post, Illustrated and other magazines the world over, newspapers; all the nationals from the Daily Mirror to the Times Educational Supplement.

Today he has a nation-wide following of people from all walks of life. His band is unrivalled on the whole of the Continent for his particular brand of Jazz. Success has wrought no change in Cy's character and steadfast outlook. Today more than ever he regards his mission to spread Jazz as a serious form of music all important.

Cy Laurie— where is he?

—'NOT IN TIBET'

WHERE is Cy Laurie? That is the question being asked by thousands of jazz fans in Britain, where the 34-year-old trad clarinettist had built up an immense following in his 15 years as a bandleader and pioneer of jazz.

Last December, Cy announced that he was taking "an extensive rest" on medical advice. He was suffering from nervous exhaustion. Since then rumours about Cy's disappearance from the world of jazz have been sweeping the clubs. Among the musicians—many of whom had a lot of sympathy for Cy's fervent ideas on how jazz should be played—there is an air of mystery.

'MONEY LASTING OUT WELL'

Nobody—not even his brother Bonny—knows where Cy is right now. Bonny last had a letter from Cy about a month ago, when the ex-bandleader was in Northern India, and planning to "have a look at the Himalayas."

Bonny told me this week: "I don't really know where Cy is at this moment. I last heard some four weeks ago, when he was in India—the Northern part. He said his money was lasting out well, as things were cheap there. I think he is probably now saving up for his fare back home.

"We are anxious for Cy to return."

Would he return to the jazz scene as a bandleader or sideman? "That's a hard one to answer," Bonny replied. "If I were Cy I would think twice about it. Things have changed so much. For instance, when Cy was playing, Kenny Ball had hardly started. He would find a radical change in the trad scene if he returned."

Musicians shake their heads when asked if they know of Cy's whereabouts.

RETURN

Guitarist Diz Disley, usually a mine of information about jazz personalities, said: "I haven't a clue where Cy is. NOBODY KNOWS."

Terry Pitts, the trombonist who played alongside Cy for years, now leads the old Laurie band under the title of the Terry Pitts Jazz Band. Said he: "We haven't heard anything in recent months. A few months ago we heard he was out of the country.

"I think Cy will return to the British jazz scene all right. It's the only way he can manage—he'd been playing so long.

"There aren't that many people around today who remember Cy in his jazz heyday."

CONFIDENCE

Wayne Chandler, new with the Terry Lightfoot band, played banjo with Cy Laurie for eight months. "I have a pretty good idea where he is, but it was told to me in confidence," said Wayne. "But I can't say. I can tell you he left London about Christmas time on a cruise. But that's all."

Martin Boorman, banjoist, who used to "gig" with

Laurie, said: "It's a mystery. I know he was travelling across Europe towards India, but that's all. I know no more."

Lyn Dutton, who was Cy's agent for more than two years before the group became the Pitts band, said: "The last I heard was that Cy was in the Himalayas."

Asked if he expected him to make a comeback Lyn replied: "I've no idea of Cy's plans. I think one of the reasons for his travelling as far as that was to give himself plenty of

time, under what he feels are the right conditions, to think things out."

RUMOUR

Back to Bonny Laurie. He denied one wild rumour that Cy had gone to Tibet to became a Buddhist monk.

"I WOULD DISCOUNT THAT," SAID BONNY. "SO FAR AS I KNOW THIS HAD NO PART OF HIS TRIP."—R. C.

CY LAURIE, one-time leader of a top traditional band, has disappeared from the British jazz scene. Last heard of, he was considering "taking a look at the Himalayas."

● MATT MONRO

'Monro will click in America'

MATT MONRO and other artists who have had disc successes on the American market should follow-up with personal appearances in the States, according to Arnold Maxin, president of MGM Records.

Mr. Maxin, here on a flying weekend trip, spoke to the MM on Tuesday just before leaving London, where he had been having talks with EMI's Norman Newell.

He frequently tours the British Isles and Europe and has won many ardent fans, who realise that his unswerving musical policy has earned his continued respect and appreciation. Let the following extract from the Evening Standard sum it up:-

" There are many who consider that Cy Laurie is musically barking up a tree that fell down some years ago. In their opinion his music is really Olde New Orleans, Brontosaurus Jazz, Basin Street with the plug pulled out. Laurie the dissenters say has been "Trad" and found wanting, there are silver hairs among the blues.

Yet the sincere flock to hear him in sufficient numbers to make Laurie Jazz brisk business.

THEY MAINTAIN THAT WHILE OTHERS WHO ONCE SWORE ALLEGIANCE TO THE POST WAR REVIVALIST MOVEMENT HAVE SOLD OUT, LAURIE ALONE NEVER RATTED. HERE IS THE MAN WITH THE TRUE METHOD AND IT IS RECEIVED BY THOUSANDS OF BELIVERS." Unquote.

Well, that's one way to put it!

With write-ups like that, how could I go wrong?

How lucky I felt. My life seemed really complete. I had the club which was one of the most popular in the country and still growing rapidly, I had a band whose impact on the world of jazz was quite phenomenal and whose reputation was now being firmly established in many other countries of the world. I had everything that anybody could have wished for.

I suppose it would have been possible to have climbed to even greater heights in the public eye but this would have entailed much social boot-licking to those in influential professional positions, this kind of insincerity I could never have indulged in. In fact, I'm quite certain that if my principles had not been so well formed, I could have achieved a far greater degree of popularity in a far shorter time, not withstanding the increased financial benefits that went with it.

But be that as it may, they were golden years for the club, the band and myself; I was enthusiastic about my music, I delighted in my country home, I was enthralled by this philosophy of life which literally was blowing my mind at every step of the way, and in Sue I had someone lovely to care for and who cared for me. What more could one ask? The future was decidedly rosy and the prospect of ever retiring was never further from my thoughts, I always imagined that now I was established, I'd be playing 'til I dropped.

. . . . that is, until I met Mahesh.

It was in January 1960, I had heard there was an Indian Yogi visiting London who was teaching a special meditation method and that he was holding introductory meetings at a house in Prince Albert Road, overlooking Regents Park. Being a practising meditator myself, though of very elementary standard, I thought I'd go along and see what sort of approach he was advocating. I was aware that there were many different types of meditation around and was always interested in exploring those I came across, so I was quite open to any new method on offer.

On my arrival at the house, I was greeted by some of the English followers of this Yogi who, with one or two others, took me upstairs to join a small group who had gathered in a room on the top floor of the house, duly waiting to be introduced to this Yogi. We were then ushered into an adjoining room where we were confronted with a round cheery faced full-bearded man dressed in white robes with long dark hair hanging down past his shoulders, sitting in the lotus position on a large chair.

He looked very impressive, reminiscent of how Jesus had often been depicted by certain early artists. His name was Mahesh, although he went under the name of Maharishi Mahesh Yogi, and after warmly greeting us, he then proceeded to explain the philosophy behind the meditation method he was teaching, which to me sounded little different from the basic scriptures of the Vedic tradition, with which I was already partially familiar.

In short, he spoke of the existence of a state of bliss within us all which can be contacted through the use of certain meditative techniques, resulting in a complete spiritual transformation of our lives; that the meditation which he gives is a simple and effective one which is suitable for the busy life of those in the Western world, requiring no special power of concentration, no departure from the normal activity of daily life, no study or preparation to obtain sustained results, and takes only a few minutes of daily practice. He claimed that there was no more direct way than his meditation to reach that inner source of spiritual bliss and to eliminate all suffering .

His declared objective was to spread his meditation system throughout the world and thereby spiritualise the whole of mankind. A most noble and worthy aim, I thought, one with which I whole-heartedly concur. I had no problem with the philosophy that he preached nor with his expressed altruistic intentions, but was curious about the professed effectiveness of his meditation method.

So, being ever game to try out all possible means that might help satisfy my inner yearnings, I accepted the invitation to become 'initiated' by him with the prospect of learning first hand whether his claims could be validated or not. After awaiting my turn among those applying for initiation, I was escorted into his room where he, in private, performed the brief initiation procedure in front of me. This resulted in him assigning to me a special personal 'mantra', a monosyllabic word which I was from then on to repeat rapidly and silently, and to practice this regularly for about ten minutes every morning and evening. That seemed easy enough to manage, though in stark contrast to the methods that I had previously come across. Still, as I have said, I was game.

In his efforts to spread his teachings and his meditation method, he had formed an organisation which he called the Spiritual Regeneration Movement, and he took to travelling all over the world, recruiting many followers in the process.

In the following months, I visited him many times during the periods that he was in London, learning more of the Eastern philosophy and working with his meditation method. From what I gathered from his group of English devotees who were resident in the house at Prince Albert Road, he was arranging to return to India at the end of the year to set up a school in the Himalayas where he could train others to help spread his message.

Around the late Autumn, on one of my visits to him, he told me of his intentions to set up a school in the Himalayas which he hoped to have ready by early spring of the following year, 1961, so that he could run his first three-month course before the heat of the summer set in. He said he would be leaving for Europe at the end of the current year (1960) and then go to India - and would I like to go with him?

Needless to say, it was a question from out of the blue and one that hit me right between the eyes. The idea certainly appealed to me, but with so much going on in my life, how on earth could I possibly seriously consider such a thing?

Not being one to completely reject any new notion without giving it due thought, I started turning a few questions over in my mind. Although much of the Eastern philosophy was so readily acceptable to me, certain aspects of it were a bit too 'devotional' for my inquiring mind. Whereas, by contrast, the philosophy to which I then subscribed was more scientific and comprehensive in approach and content. Nor was I wholly convinced that Mahesh's meditation would prove as effective as I was led to believe, being a comparative newcomer to the method and having yet to experience the benefits he proclaimed for it.

He was obviously well versed in the Eastern scriptures, his intentions to 'spiritualise' the whole of mankind was very laudable, and his dynamism in attempting to do so was quite impressive, and I felt that I would like to help such a cause in some way. For these reasons I had come to like and respect him, but a devotee of his, I certainly was not.

For the following two or three weeks my mind was in a complete tiz-waz, one part of me saying, wow! what an opportunity, what a privilege (as nobody else had been asked to go with him). It would be an experience of a lifetime, and even if I found that which Mahesh was working on was not really suitable for me (as I had at times suspected),

I could always travel deeper into the Himalayas where I understood the greatest wise men on earth resided. If that was the case, I would have no compunction in giving everything up permanently to be with such great sages, to learn from them and to work with them.

Yet, another part of me was saying, how can you even think of such things? There was my music, the club to run, the band which relied on me, my financial commitments, the Agency, my family, my friends, my Farm, Sue, my belongings, all that I had built up over my lifetime. I couldn't give up all that!

. . . . or could I?

All such things, although very important and so enjoyable to me, being a side of my life which I always felt had to be lived as much as possible to the full, were in truth of far less significance to me as was the intensifying aspirational side of my life. In fact, with a little further reflection, there was no question of me passing up such an opportunity to go to India. If there was the slightest chance of fulfilling my aspirations, I would go to the ends of the earth - and stay there!

Besides which, apart from all the logical pros and cons of the idea, all mental rationalising aside, I just felt that I was meant to go.

And so, with my mind made up, I had to see how practical it all was to make such a break, how I would go about arranging my affairs so that the minimum of disruption would come from it. There was only a short time to arrange things and also I had musical engagements I was obliged to fulfil.

I explained all this to Mahesh and he was very sympathetic and encouraging, saying that once I had fulfilled my commitments, which took me to at least the end of the year, he would by then be in Italy where I could meet up with him and from there travel with him to Greece, and then, via Egypt, to Bombay.

That being an agreed compromise, I started setting things in motion. I kept the whole thing well under wraps for weeks, telling only those people who would be directly concerned, many of whom, although finding it all very disappointing, were fortunately also very understanding - even if they didn't quite understand. This was especially the case with my family and some of my close friends, and particularly with Sue, who knew full well of my higher aspirations yet gave me her love and her blessings. It was quite a wrench for all concerned, particularly me, but once again luck was with me. Someone 'up there' must have been looking after me as everything agreeably fell into place and all arrangements went as smooth as they possibly could have done.

Sue and I had not been hitting it off too well over the past couple of months and although I still found her attractive, I couldn't see it lasting much longer. We moved out of the Farm into my old room in my family home where my brother was living on his own. I then let the Farm to Terry Pitts and his family for the time being.

In the meantime, Sue and I had become quite involved with the resident group who were running Mahesh's affairs from his London centre. As they had ample accommodation there, we often stayed for a few days and, knowing the situation, they invited Sue to move in there more or less as a resident after I had left, which she was happy to do.

Also my brother and I had discovered that Don Kingswell, who was managing the affairs of the Agency, the club, and the band, etc., had been skimming off the top, as we had long suspected. He was apparently doing such things as paying guest bands and musicians less than he had entered in the books and pocketing the rest - bands were eager to work at the club and possibly accepted the situation of an incomplete fee. There were also similar problems with the Agency and other aspects of the business which turned out to be quite serious. So we had no compunction in asking him to find other employment. I think he wound up working at the 100 Club, in Oxford Street.

However, all that aside, the way became wide open for me to up sticks and leave by the planned date. I thought that by not making the whole thing generally known I could slip away nice and unobtrusively . . . . how wrong I was!

In fact, such a plan seemed to have precisely the opposite effect and sent the whole jazz scene buzzing with all sorts of wild rumours about what had happened to me. Some weeks later, there was a big article in the leading musical weekly, the Melody Maker, headed: "Cy Laurie - where is he?" which included interviews with various musicians and people who might have known of my whereabouts. I quote:

"Where is Cy Laurie? That is the question being asked by thousands of jazz fans in Britain, where the 34 year old trad clarinettist had built up an immense following in his 15 years as band leader and pioneer of jazz.

" . . . rumours about Cy's disappearance from the world of jazz have been sweeping the clubs. Among the musicians - many of whom had a lot of sympathy for Cy's fervent ideas on how jazz should be played - there is an air of mystery.

"Musicians shake their heads when asked if they know of Cy's whereabouts."

. . . . . and so forth.

Apparently, similar articles appeared in various national and international publications, and for some time after there were numerous reports of 'sightings', from the Outer Hebrides to the shores of Tasmania.

But the truth of the matter was really quite simple: although I was deeply involved in my jazz and my life among my friends, relations and the variety of interests which I had, there was that which was of greater importance and more attractive to me which I felt I had to pursue, no matter what the outcome. Whether my efforts would prove fruitful, whether my longings would be assuaged, whether I would ever return to England again or not - in fact, whatever the future held for me - were of little consequence to me. I just HAD to make that trip to India.

After winding up all my affairs, handing over all the business interests to my brother, putting the band in Terry Pitts capable hands (with a replacement clarinettist, it became known as the Terry Pitts Jazz Band and continued with all the contacts and worked at all the venues, home and abroad, as the band had when under my name), I had cleared the decks for my departure.

It was in the depth of Winter when I finally set off on my journey. Dressed in the heaviest of overcoats with a long thick woolly scarf doubly wrapped around my neck, I fondly embraced and kissed Sue goodbye at the Air Terminal before I disappeared through the Customs gate into the unknown future of a new life . . . . . .

Thus was closed the first episode of my eventful life.

EPISODE TWO - SACRED INDIA

CHAPTER 6 - FROM RICHES TO RAGS

1961 - My Mid-Thirties (Part 1.)

I duly arrived in Italy as planned where I was met by a follower of Mahesh who, after helping me settle in at an hotel, took me to the hall where Mahesh was due to give a talk. This was one of the last of many that he was giving in various parts of Europe before going on to Greece for his concluding lectures and then his return to India. I was with him for these remaining talks after which he and I boarded the 'plane from Athens for India, stopping over in Egypt.

As soon as the announcement on the 'plane had told us we had touched down in Bombay and we were free to unfasten our seat belts, I eagerly gathered up my hand luggage, put on my scarf, overcoat and woolly hat (to save carrying them) to follow Mahesh in the queue waiting to disembark. On stepping out of the 'plane, I emerged into a blanket of Bombay's intense heat which literally took my breath away - and me all muffled up in my English Winter garments. I could hardly keep up with the other passengers walking across the tarmac,

Mahesh, still as composed as ever in his white cotton robes, which he always wore throughout my association with him (I had never known him to wear anything differ- ent, no matter what the weather or circumstance), and with me staggering perspiringly at his side, was greeted at the perimeter by a large group of his devotees, bowing and revering him, some even endeavouring to touch his feet. They bedecked him with fresh-flower garlands, they even put some around my neck too - as if I hadn't enough to wear, as we made our way to the airport lounge where while his welcoming com- mittee were honouring his return, I hurriedly stripped off my Winter top clothes before rejoining him.

We were both taken by car to one of his followers' homes on the outskirts of the town where more devotees waited in a large room specially prepared for his welcome. After a further, to me unexpected, and disconcerting, display of adoration, prostrating and garland adorning, we all sat crossed-legged on the floor (I did my best, even if I couldn't stay in that position longer than a few minutes), while food was served up for all - it was the first of many times I would have to eat such food with my bare hands from that position, and from dishes on the floor. Not the most elegant of contorted manoeuverings to behold.

One thing I quickly discovered was that I would have little problem being a vegetarian here in India. The bulk of the population were vegetarian anyway and, I assume, it's still the case these days.

After our stay in Bombay, which lasted about three days, we went on to Delhi where again we were given the same type of adulation by groups of Mahesh's followers. Even I was looked upon in a sort of reverential fashion, everybody was so very friendly to me, treating me as if I was somebody special too (maybe they had seen my film?).

I came to twig that they thought being so privileged to be chosen by Mahesh to accompany him wherever he went, I must be an ardent devotee of his and therefore deserved special treatment. Who was I to dispel such an illusion.

It is true that people in India generally, at that time anyway, looked upon those who are on a spiritual journey in a completely different light than do many people in England; they not only accept them but respect them. Besides which I was British and I gathered there was still a certain amount of regard for the British held by many, probably left over from their past occupation of the country.

Apart from the constant talks that he gave to groups of followers, Mahesh visited a lot of Government offices with the intention of getting permission to build his meditation school on a plot of land in the foothills of the Himalayas. We did a lot of travelling together at that time, all over Uttar Pradesh, mainly by car, until we finally ended up in Rishikesh, a small town in Northern India by the river Ganges.

From there we travelled by donkey deeper into the Himalayas, up the mountain paths on our way towards a small village which nestled in the hills of Uttar Kashi some miles ahead. This journey was my first of many subsequent donkey rides along such treacherous mountain paths where these beasts have an inbuilt suicidal propensity to walk on the very edge of the path - beyond which is often a sheer drop of thousands of feet.

Sitting astride these creatures, whose saddles are of hard wooden construction (the further one travelled the harder the saddles became), one could easily be overcome by the breathtaking panoramic views which only the Himalayas provide, if one wasn't stricken with utter panic at the precariousness of the mode of transport.

When we finally arrived at our destination (I was helped to dismount, albeit stiff in body and limb, not to mention my aching and blistered posterior, by our donkey owner who, incidentally, did the journey on foot to guide the leading donkey that carried our luggage), we were greeted by two heavily bearded men dressed in similar cotton attire as Mahesh. They duly welcomed us with friendly smiles and courteous namastes (a typical Eastern display of greeting performed by a bow of the head with opened palmed hands held together at chest level pointing upwards toward the forehead - an easily acquired custom), then took us to a house where we were dined and comforteds as best the primitive conditions allowed. I gathered that this was the house where Mahesh and his fellow Yogis lived before he started on all his travels from the mid-50s.

I was given a small adjoining outhouse which was to be my room during my stay there, the only furniture being a solitary bed which basically consisted of a wooden frame on legs. Across the frame was bound a network of cloth webbing upon which I was to put my bedding equipment which Mahesh advised me to buy whilst we were in Rishikesh.

It was then that the real culture shock began. First off, there were no toilets. The custom of the inhabitants was to use the surrounding undergrowth to relieve themselves aided by a jug of water which, with their bare hand, they cleansed their soiled rear. Not only could I not bring myself to do this but whatever method I was forced to use, I had to do it in strict privacy.They didn't seem to understand that it was essential for some of us to have our own little four walls where we could satisfy na-

Mahesh Yogi

ture's demanding calls. I explained that such is an essential inbuilt commodity in all modern establishments in the West.

It was bad enough having to squat over the bare ground when it was necessary, but to do it openly, even behind a tree, where someone may easily chance upon me, crouched in such an undignified position, was more than I was prepared to concede.

So what did I do when I had to go? I didn't, I bottled it up. That was my first foolish mistake. I had no hang-ups when I felt the need to nip out for a quick wee, which I conceded had to be done under their conditions, but I did not pass a bowel movement for the whole period of my stay there.

How entrenched can be the ways of our 'civilised' Western culture?

Also on my first night there, on extinguishing my candle and settling down after a long strenuous day's travel, I heard a lot of scuffling in the room. Was there some poor little animal caught in there when I had closed the door? I struck a match to light the candle again only to see a troop of mice scrambling all over my suitcase on the floor. Oh no! I gasped. What on earth could I do to get rid of them? Maybe they were after some food that I had in my case? I had made it a practice when possible to stock up with some food that was more palatable to my taste than the constant curried potatoes, rice, and chapattis that I was obliged to eat at almost every meal, especially in the more remote areas as this was.

I lit the candle again, got out of bed and gingerly moved my suitcase to the other side of the room. There I thought they could scramble away until they got fed up with trying to get into my locked case, and maybe they'd find some other room and other occupants they could scare the hell out of. Dousing the candle again from my bed, I tried to snuggle down with my hands over my ears so that I couldn't hear them. I was so tired.

It was soon after they started their scuffling again that I felt them scampering over my bed as well! Oh my God! This scared the living daylights out of me. Shaking like a gibbering idiot, I instantly threw off my bed covers and, making lots of noise, I relit the candle. There they were, scurrying around the floor and up the wall by my bed. What more could I do? I was practically in a state of terror! I dragged the bed to the centre of the room, and with the candle still burning, jumped back into bed and hastily pulled all the bed clothes over my head . . . . and there I stayed 'til the long awaited dawn.

How often the memory of that night haunts me, especially whenever I sing "O Lord, you made the night too long." It was obviously written with such a night in mind.

All through the following day the thought of having to go to bed that evening filled me with constant trepidation. Came the night, after I got into bed, there started the same distressing scuffling, but fortunately they decided to keep to the floor and although very disturbing, I managed to snatch the occasional wink of sleep. So it went on, night after night, until I eventually learned to accept their presence - provided they kept their activities at ground level.

During the days I accompanied Mahesh on his trips around the surrounding countryside which he was surveying with a group of officials in his search for a suitable plot to start his school project. It was during these times when I slinked off for an hour or two to catch up on some sleep under a tree somewhere in the warm shade . . . . ah, bliss!

This became a daily routine for me until I was warned not to wander too far as these areas are normally inhabited by lethal venomous snakes . . . . . gulp!

Having had a background as a designer draughtsman of sorts, I also got the job of drawing up plans for the proposed layout of the school with its individual dwelling quarters, etc. In addition, I got roped in to write some of Mahesh's publicity pamphlets, and the like, which he used for promoting his lecture tours, etc

The following weeks were spent in a similar manner as we went from one area to another until Mahesh decided on an appropriate location. We then went to Haridwar and back to Delhi so that Mahesh could get all the necessary paperwork sorted which, as is common in bureaucratic circles, especially when it comes to planning applications and such, proved to be quite a prolonged and convoluted exercise. I was familiar with the extreme lack of rapidity in which British officials are known to make their decisions, but this would appear as instantaneous compared to their Indian counterparts who, it seemed, had perfected this ponderous system bequeathed to them by the British.

This was unfortunate as arrangements were already made for a group of Mahesh's followers from America and Europe to travel to India that March to attend his first three-month study course, and so far there was no hope of the intended school in the Himalayas being started, let alone completed, by then.

As a temporary measure, Ram Nagar, a small community about a couple of miles outside of Rishikesh where a sort of boarding school was available which could be adapted to accommodate this first batch of about forty or fifty Western students, was conveniently procured for this required period. Work hurriedly went ahead to set up this building so that it could be ready by the time they arrived, which it eventually was - after a fashion.

I find that I still have some of the literature which was issued around that time relating to those early efforts.

I had now been in India for about two and a half months and was fairly acquainted with some of the problems members of this group of Westerners might face after their arrival. So I was included in a small party which met them when they finally arrived in Delhi. We all travelled by coach to the school in Rishikesh where, after being greeted by Mahesh and a group of his Indian followers, they were shown to their allotted rooms and advised to rest up for a day or two to recuperate after their long journey, to adjust to the local conditions, to meditate, and to prepare themselves for the work of the weeks ahead.

The intentions of the course was to have a daily routine of Hatha Yoga practice (a selection of physical postures to improve and maintain one's bodily condition), lectures (these mainly connected with the Hindu Scriptures and the various established commentaries on them), meditation sessions (in accordance with Mahesh's method - which I gather he later called Transcendental Meditation), and periods for various types of group chanting.

We were barely two weeks into the course when I went down with a severe bout of jaundice. This sapped my strength completely and I was confined to my room for nigh on a month afterwards. In accordance with my Nature Cure principles, I went on a fast for the first week of my illness, consuming only the water in which the rice had been cooked, and the following weeks keeping to a very light diet.

The days were very hot and I spent most of that time in my small room with the blinds drawn in the semi-darkness with just a light cotton sheet across my middle. Food and bathing necessities were considerately brought to me by various locals and members on the course, but apart from that I neither exercised, read, shaved, or attended to any of the normal expected activities of civilised life. I was out flat! And it was some time before I could again resume the vertical position.

Whether the jaundice problem was the result of my prolonged period of self-enforced constipation a couple of months previously, which I have since lived to regret, or to the expected ailments which I understand many Westerners suffer from after their first few weeks in India, possibly due to the unfamiliar food, climatic, and environmental conditions, I never did find out. I had heard, even before I left home, that it is not uncommon for people to go down with all sorts of stomach upsets within the first few weeks after their arrival in India, unless of course, they can avoid the local food and water, etc., which I could never have done in the circumstances,

However, once the condition righted itself, I was back on my feet again and in even better health than before and able to finish the course for the next few weeks. This finally came to an end around June of that year and while all Mahesh's other students packed their bags and headed for home, I had decided to stay around for a while and maybe see a bit more of the Himalayas. I recall being left completely on my own in that school after everybody had left, including Mahesh and his associates, and even the kitchen staff had been dismissed.

Come the day after, it was Sunday, I think, as the Bank in Rishikesh was closed and I couldn't draw out any of my fast dwindling reserve funds, I was caught in a very embarrassing situation. I had no money, there was no food around, and I was starving hungry, with no one around to whom I could turn, and to top it all the school was due to be locked up that evening for the rest of the summer.

I knew there was a Temple a short walk away where it was customary for wandering Saddhus and Sanyasis (holy men who have renounced normal life) to stop over for food and lodging, etc., so maybe, I thought, I could get something to eat there on tick. Being English, they might trust me until I could pay them the following day. But no. When I got there, the kitchen staff, none of whom could speak a word of English, refused point blank to provide me with even a morsel as I was not a Saddhu or a Sanyasi (I don't know how they knew that, my beard and hair were growing a treat), nor did I have any cash to pay them for anything.

Despondent and dejected - I hadn't eaten since the morning before - I wandered into the large courtyard where the huts were located in which these holy men stayed. What a position to be in, no food, no money, nobody around who could speak English, nowhere to stay after that evening, and nowhere to go after that. How short-sighted of me not to have anticipated such a predicament - another of my foolish mistakes.

Sitting beneath a tree, with my head in my hands, trying hard to ignore the unrelenting nagging pangs of hunger, I wallowed there in my plight most of the afternoon. After a while I heard someone insistently calling from the far corner of the courtyard. It took me some little while before I realised that they could be calling me, trying to attract my attention. I looked up and saw this semi-clad bearded Sanyasi in the distance, standing outside his hut beckoning me to come over to him. What on earth could he want? Should I bother to acknowledge him? I was in no mood to be talked at by a local wanting someone to practise his English on, as so often happened. But out of courtesy, I did make my way over to him.

He greeted me with the usual customary namastay and made signs that I should come in to his hut. I politely bowed and did so, he then followed me in, sat me down, and placed a large bowl of rice in front of me, inviting me to eat. I was in no frame of mind to courteously refuse with a "Oh, no thank you, I couldn't really, but thank you anyway," type remark, as I would normally have done. Besides which, he might have taken me at my word, and I couldn't risk that! So with his permission I wrapped my chops around this delicious dish of rice with the eagerness of a contestant in a timed eating competition. It must have looked as if I hadn't eaten for days . . . . well I hadn't.

In truth, I was so grateful for this 'manna from heaven' that it was as much as I could do to keep myself from bursting into tears.

I don't think I had ever enjoyed a bowl of rice so much before, or since, as I had enjoyed that one. I think I could have shifted another ten of them, but to this desire I wouldn't let on, although I did doubly emphasise how much his generosity was appreciated - as if he didn't suss this anyway.

He seemed a very kindly man and, in his easy to understand English, he spoke to me for about an hour of his interests in the various Indian Saints and their teaching, etc. What wasn't mentioned was how the heck did he know I was so hungry that I would eat in the middle of the afternoon, nor did I even enquire where he managed to get a bowl of rice at that unusual time of day when most of the population were luxuriating in their customary afternoon siestas. These ascetic hut dwellers never had their own cooking facilities, their food was normally supplied from a central kitchen. Did he have his own allotted ration put aside from his earlier meal in case there was someone around who needed it? Or was someone 'up there' still looking out for me?

Now, with at least something nourishing in my tum, I returned to the school to pick up my things, a few personal belongings and my bedroll, etc. Before doing so, I spotted a young Sanyasi wondering around in the grounds outside the place. He approached me and made polite conversation in his broken English, introducing himself as Ananda and explaining that he had come down from the higher reaches of the Himalayan mountains near the source of the Ganges River where he had been living with his Master. He seemed a pleasant young lad, maybe about 20 years old with a very clear complexion and dressed in the traditional Sanyasi get up, a saffron coloured cotton robe wrapped loosely around his body. I invited him into my room and we chatted a little while I was getting my things together.

He described how calming and spiritual the atmosphere was up in the remote levels of the mountains and how he was devoted to his Master, etc. I casually asked him why he had come down from such peaceful heights into the more populated area of the foothills. Imagine my astonishment when he replied that he had come to look after me, and that his Master had given him that special mission. . . . . What? Hey hold on a minute, I thought. How did he know about me? Or even more to the point, if what he said was true, how did his Master know about me.

I didn't pursue the subject at the time as I wasn't sure whether he was pulling my leg or not and didn't want to embarrass him by cross-questioning him. Little did I suspect that he would be my constant companion for the next six months or more.

As the school premises were on the point of closing down for the rest of the summer and the remaining caretaker was expressing some impatience to bolt and bar all the doors behind us, my Suddhu visitor took me to a small nearby Temple for the evening where we ate and then bedded down for the night, my mind was turning over all sorts of questions. How did that first Sanyasi know I was hungry? Where did he spirit that bowl of hot rice from? How did my new acquaintance know I was in need of assistance? How come that if he had come down from the mountain tops 'to look after me', a good three weeks journey or more, he had arrived just at the time of my worst predicament? How could his Master foresee such a situation, possibly weeks before hand? What sort of people was I dealing with? Or was it all just a series of coincidences? Or just another case of my exceedingly good luck? There was much for me to ponder on.

The following morning, my new found Saddhu friend suggested that while I was in that area we take a look at some of the holy sites together, which was totally agreeable to me. From then on, in the company of my young companion, I took to the life of a wandering Saddhu (in Western garb), traveling mainly on foot, all around the Northern Province, visiting many of the abundant Shrines, Temples, Sanctuaries, which are a common feature of that region. They have a system of Dharamshalas there, available exclusively for their roving Saddhus and Sanyasis, where accommodation and food is provided free of charge for a maximum stay of three nights.

These facilities were normally located either within the grounds of a Temple or some similar place of worship, or more remotely situated yet connected to a local religious community. Some were extremely primitive in standard and the fare supplied very basic, whereas others were less so, but all were offered in good faith and all decidedly welcome after a long day's trek through hard country. With the aid of my companion, I was generally regarded as a fellow pilgrim and therefore also able to take advantage of such hospitable privileges.

Our travels took us through a wide assortment of environments, from mango groves, forests, jungle areas, through gently flowing streams and raging rivers, some of the latter only to be crossed by primitive and perilous rope bridges, to the rarefied heights of the glacier-clad mountainous regions. We encountered a wide variety of Yogis, Saints, and holy men, some living in mud huts, some in caves, some in jungles, some cloistered in Temple annexes. Most were scantily dressed, either in light cotton dhoti's (a kind of wrap-around skirt), or merely strips of cloth that only just covered their privates, and some were completely naked!

All were very friendly, especially those who were able to speak a little English, which varied from the fairly accomplished to the totally incomprehensible. Mind you, some didn't even speak at all, having remained in silence, in some cases, I understood, for many years. There is a prevalent belief among a large section of holy men that lays great store in the value of a period of prolonged silence, that is, not speaking or relating to anyone. It apparently diverts one's expressive energies towards the inner side of one's life, enabling one to contact and explore the more subtle areas of their being. It is a practice which is said to deepen, enrich, and strengthen one's spiritual existence. Well, I mused, if that is so, I wouldn't mind having a go at that myself sometime.

On our travels we ventured into a variety of differing atmospheres and traversed over all sorts of terrain, my friend in his bare feet and I in my Marks and Spencer's leather sandals. There was one time when walking down a very unfriendly stony and craggy hillside, the strap on one of my sandals snapped - and we were some miles away from the nearest village where a repair might be possible. As evening was drawing in and there was a Temple near the village where we could stay the night, it was less than advisable for us to delay reaching there. So there was no other alternative but for me to hobble to it on one bare foot.

Of course, would you believe, the strain on the surviving sandal was too much for it to hold out after that, so that went also. I won't describe the condition of my blistered feet and the sheer agony I was in by the time we reached the Temple, but it took me days of tortured limping before I could discard the wooden staff that I used to help keep me mobile.

During those months we travelled many miles together, from the panoramic heights of

Uttar Kashi in the Himalayas to the Eastern area of Banaras (later renamed Varanasi). It was shortly after we left Banaras, around the Autumn of 1961, that my young Saddhu companion came down with a fever. Possibly because his constitution was not suited to the warm climatic conditions or, and this more likely, being among people and-subject to the adverse psychic environment of the more populated areas proved to be too foreign to his system. Whatever the reason, he said he needed to go North again to recuperate, which we did.

By the time we reached Nainital and were once again in the foothills of the Himalayas, the climate was becoming more bearable. Nainital was a beautiful little town, built around a mountain lake, with a bus station, a nice little shopping area and a couple of small hotels. We trekked up the hill to a Temple about two or three miles outside of the town where we had planned to stay for a couple of days before we moved on further North. The Sanyasi who was in charge of the Temple greeted Ananda and I on our arrival by writing his welcoming Namastays on a slate, explaining, in scribbled English, that he was undergoing a long period of silence and to excuse him if he didn't speak. He wrote that it was not the type of silence which required isolation as he had the affairs of the Temple to see to and in that capacity he could therefore arrange to provide us with the customary food and accommodation.

The following day, our Sanyasi host invited us to dine with him. Through his slate writing, he introduced himself as Baba Har Das, and explained that he had been in silence for many years on the advice of his Master, who he called Babaji, who was a great Rishi (spiritual being) yet one who was constantly travelling around India helping people who were treading the spiritual path.

I was rather taken aback when he explained that his Master, Babaji, was due in the Nainital area in a week or two, he was asked to pass on a message from Babaji to me when I turned up that he would like me to stay at the Temple until he arrived so that he and I could meet. This time I didn't hesitate in enquiring of my silent acquaintance how this Babaji would have known I was going to be there. "Babaji knows everything!", was the reply. Oh yeah, I thought, another gullible devotee. It was obvious to me how cynical I was becoming; it appeared that the whole culture was influenced by a Guru-orientated tradition which, although very sound in principle, seemed also to spawn many an unquestioning naive adherent, so much so that I had come to take a lot of apparently outrageous statements with a pinch of salt.

Yet also there was a part of me which treated certain pronouncements with a degree of respect, being not beyond the bounds of possibility. After all, hadn't I experienced unusual 'coincidences' with regard to my dealings with certain holy men, my meeting with Ananda being no exception.

However, I consulted my young companion on the idea of staying for a while until

Nainital India.

Babaji arrived and he said that although he himself had to move on up into the more refined atmospheres of the higher mountainous regions, he recommended that I should stay on there, and that it was right for me to do so.

When I thanked Baba Har Das for his offer and that I'd like to accept his invitation to stay there until Babaji arrived, he said that Babaji had told him that I could stay there for the rest of my life if I so wished, and that all food and expenses would be supplied free. Ouch! What had brought on such a generous proposal of hospitality? I felt quite flattered. I humbly expressed my sincerest thanks and said that I was very appreciative and privileged that he should extend such an offer to a stranger in his land, but would welcome the opportunity to stay at least until Babaji arrived, and we could then see how things went after that.

In the meantime, apart from my fare money home, I still had some funds that I could use for my keep for a little while longer. I kept these funds in reserve with the intention of getting myself some new clothes as the little that I had brought with me to India had been discarded long ago, all that I had by then was a change of underwear and the shirt and trousers that I stood up in - and rather tatty they were too by that time. So I thought I could forego such niceties as new garments and, if necessary, rig myself out with a dhoti and its accessories (the simple cotton 'ensemble' that other Temple occupants wore), so that I could then draw on these meagre funds of mine for present necessities before I decided to make my next move, and maybe if and when there's no money left, I might then consider taking Baba Har Das up on his offer to extend my stay. He agreed that that was a sensible approach.

I also felt that if I could afford it, the chance to settle in for a period would be welcome as not only would I be able to assimilate the experiences of my travels, but I could write home and maybe catch up on the news there. Although I never really felt home-sick, I did feel that I would like to know how things were going with my family, friends, Sue, the club and the band, etc.

The following day, I bade my young Saddhu friend a fond farewell, wishing him a speedy recovery to full health and thanking him for his kind and helpful companionship. He departed with a a very touching remark in his slightly improved English, saying, "I will always remember you with the core of my heart."

EPISODE TWO - SACRED INDIA

CHAPTER 7 - MY LITTLE HIMALAYAN KUTI

1961-62 - My Mid-Thirties (Part 2.)

For my stay at Hanuman Garh, I was allotted a little mud hut, which they called a 'Kuti', situated within the Temple grounds yet completely isolated, about two or three hundred yards from the main buildings. The hut was basically squarish, delicately perched on the side of a steep hill yet with the added luxury of a narrow balcony which faced on to the valley. There were two doors in this single roomed hideaway, one for the entrance situated in the middle of one wall and the other, positioned directly opposite the first, which opened on to the balcony. This was a very practical arrangement as with both doors open it afforded a through draught which could be quite a life saver during the very hot days.

The only piece of furniture which occupied the otherwise austere white-washed interior was that which served as a bed, being composed of a few wooden planks nailed together and mounted on four legs. Well, I suppose, it was an improvement to sleeping on the floor, as I had so often done during my recent journeying.

However, the scene from the balcony was out of this world, being over 8,000 feet up, I could see to my left and sweeping round to the front of me the breathtaking contours of the snow covered Himalayan Peaks; to the right steeply sloping away from the balcony was a forest area densely populated with a vast array of wild life, from an assorted selection of monkeys to the varied species of highly colourful birds. It was practically a heaven on earth, and for this alone it was worth all the journeying, difficulties, and deprivation.

From the Temple compound itself, there was a winding hillside road leading down to Nainital and for the following week or so I made several hiking trips into the town to get the layout of the area and to stock up on necessities. Baba Har Das had introduced me to a young man from the town who was a local Temple follower, another adherent of Babaji, who seemed quite happy, and even privileged, to be assigned to me and help me settle in. Being able to speak English somewhat, he was also able to translate my needs to the locals when necessary.

Apart from the need to find a suitable private place for me to attend to nature's calls, which had been the bane of my days whilst travelling around, the main drawback for me to this idyllic existence was having to eat the food as served up by the Temple occupants which, though not out of the ordinary as the basic local diet goes, was now becoming more than a little troublesome for me. For some months now I had become practically allergic to a particular spice they commonly used called 'jeera', as it was served to me in large quantities in the food I had to eat during my first couple of months in India, whilst staying in Uttar Kashi. Although I invariably had been obliged to eat it, principally because I was hungry, when it was included in my food during my travels with Ananda, he was always at hand to help me steer clear when such food could be avoided. I knew that although something would have to be done about it, for now, it wasn't really an issue, I was too impressed with my good luck to be where I was to concern myself with this question - in these paradisiacal surroundings, such a minor problem withered into insignificance.

It was about early November, 1961, approximately 10 days after I had first arrived at Hanuman Gar that my translator/helper came to my kuti to inform me that Babaji was in the area and he would like me to visit him. Fair enough, I thought, let's see this guy, see what he had to say and maybe then I can decide where my next port of call should be. Apparently Babaji had only recently arrived in the area and had not settled in any particular place, but was resting at an undisclosed spot up in the local hills. It was a good five or six miles walk away and even my guide did not know exactly where Babaji was until we met another follower of his while we were walking up a narrow path through the forest. It was then we were told to climb up the hills through the forest to a clearing where Babaji was awaiting us.

On reaching this clearing, we came across a group of people, about a dozen, I suppose, who were seated on the forest floor around this Indian gentleman who was also seated. This was Babaji, I assumed. He beckoned me to come through his little gathering of listeners and to sit in front of him, which I did. My first impression of him was one of bewilderment: he was quite ordinary looking, a man in his fifties I would have thought, with a roundish , smiley face, very unshaven, a closely cropped haircut, and, what looked like, no front teeth. He seemed to have a rather stocky frame from where I was sitting, around which was a loosely wrapped blanket - certainly not my idea of a great Saint!

I suppose I expected an imposing, long-haired, full-bearded, highly dignified looking person (and there were quite a few of them around), adorned in either saffron coloured or lily-white robes, who, Jesus-like, spoke words of wisdom with every utterance. Not this guy, he didn't even speak a word of English! And he was casually chatting to his small band of followers as if they were all enjoying a nice little tea party.

He spoke to me, through my interpreter, asking my how I was getting on in my little kuti, did the mountain atmosphere agree with me, how was I coping with the weather there and the food, etc., and many other more mundane questions - not a hint of a word of 'wisdom'. I asked why he had tucked himself away up here in the forest, many miles away from anywhere, when I gathered there were so many of his followers waiting eagerly for his 'darshan' (to pay their respects, to bathe in his aura, and to receive his blessing), all around the area. It appeared that it was precisely because of this that he wanted to be in such an isolated spot for a while, and that he would be practically mobbed if everyone knew where he was. Seemed logical enough. But why was he so revered?

I put this question to my friend on our way back to Hanuman Garh (after a short and not particularly impressive first meeting with Babaji). I was told that there were so many stories surrounding him of the miracles that he had performed; that he could see into the future, could read peoples' thoughts, had been seen in more than one place at the same time, helped people overcome their problems, particularly those of a spiritual nature, etc. Well, I thought, I suppose such things should not be so hastily dismissed as being impossible, but I couldn't accept anything like that on the say-so of easily-believing devotees, I had come across too many of them.

Babaji

Within the space of the following week, I met him three or four times at various obscure locations, during which he seemed very chatty and amiable yet still not especially out-of-the-ordinary in any way. Maybe my interpreter was not that accurate in his translations, his English was never strikingly proficient, but I must confess that nothing particularly profound was conveyed to me. What Babaji did try to make known to me was the desirability for me to spend a period in silence, and that if I thought the idea agreeable, I would be more than welcome to stay at Hanuman Gar in my present kuti if I wished. That was nice of him.

I tossed this proposition around in my mind for a few days afterwards and although in general I was not averse to trying out such a radical departure from the norm, there were certain practical considerations which needed to be sorted out. Without going into too much detail, I mentioned this to Babaji on our next meeting, before he was due to leave the area to visit other localities, and he told me not to be concerned about anything, Baba Har Das would help meet my needs .... and that was it!

I left that last meeting feeling rather disappointed, to say the least. He had said nothing obviously tangible or significant that would help me assuage my inner yearnings. But then, if I was honest with myself, although my wanderings, the people I had come across, and the experiences I had passed through, etc., had been of great interest to me one way or another, no matter who I had met or what I had done, I still had not been able to satisfy in any way the need that I felt in my heart.

It had been nearly a year since I set out from home and I felt no further forward now than I did before I left. Nevertheless, I did think that if I undertook a period of silence and seclusion, it could not be that bad a thing, and it would give me a bit of an opportunity to think things out. With my mind more or less settled on the matter, I was feeling a bit more positive about the idea.

That afternoon when I returned to Hanuman Garh, I was greeted by Baba Har Das with the slate-written information that he had built a small enclosure made from corrugated iron sheets in the forest, about 100 yards down the hillside from my kuti, where I would be free to attend to nature's necessities in strict privacy. Also that he was in the process of laying on a piped water supply from a mountain stream to my kuti that would give me the convenience of fresh water from a tap fixed to my balcony, and that the job should be completed within a couple of days. In the meantime, if I would like to go into the hardware store in Nainital to pick up a small paraffin stove, a chapati plate, one or two cooking utensils, etc., of my choice, they will be expecting me.

I couldn't believe it!

How did he know what was required, I had only just decided about a couple of hours or so ago, before I reached the Temple, to try out Babaji's suggestion of staying there longer to go into silence, yet he had built this little toilet for me, ordered and had delivered piping and fittings for my water supply (and to get anything delivered promptly in India is in itself a miracle), and was halfway through running it down to my kuti - and on top of that had arranged with a shop in Nainital to furnish me with all the necessary cooking items.

Even if Babaji sent him a telepathic message to get all these things done, how did Babaji know what was needed? I certainly didn't go into any detail when I mentioned to him that there were some practical difficulties to my staying on. Verree weird, to say the least.

In anticipation of this period of seclusion, I stocked up on supplies like chapatti flour, ghee (a kind of clarified butter), cooking oil, paraffin for my new little cylindrical cooking stove, toilet paper, chalk and a slate for writing on (as per my host), pen and ink, paper, stamps, and envelopes, as well as a few airmail letters, for writing home. I was soon all set to go - or really to stop, which would be more appropriate. It was arranged that they would send someone daily to my kuti to check up if there was any written message I had placed outside my door for any additional needs. Also I cultivated a tame shop-keeper who would supply me daily with freshly uddered milk (Buffalo, that is), rice, vegetables, and other such comestibles, which he would leave outside my door. What more could an apprentice Sanyasi want?

So it happened. From that day on I had to adjust to my new mode of living; I would see no one, speak to no one, and communicate only through the written word when necessary. I would do all my own cooking, a simple enough chore seeing that all I lived on was Buffalo milk, rice, chappatties, and boiled vegetables; I would do all my own washing, an even simpler chore as I wore the minimum of cotton wrap-arounds, which was all that was required, the weather being so hot, and which also eliminated the need for lengthy drying times.

I had placed a thin cotton filled mattress on the wooden boards which served as my bed, a couple of cotton sheets between which I would nightly slither, and a double sized over-blanket made from Tibetan Llama wool (a 'prasade', or gift, from one of Babaji's devotees) if and when the nights became cold enough to warrant its use.

Thus did I settle in.

I was to spend nearly a year in my kuti under these conditions, with the exception of a month during the spring of the following year when I was obliged to travel to Delhi for a while.

Well, one might ask, how did I cope? How did I occupy my time? Wasn't I lonely? Wasn't I bored? Didn't I long for home, my family, my friends, my music, my old prosperous and happy life, and the loving arms of Sue? Yes, there were without doubt times when it wasn't easy to bear, when being alone and having to fend for myself, which was something I had never done before, became difficult and at times even arduous for me, but if it would help me to satisfy my aims, then I would suffer such deprivation. It certainly would not be a form of existence that would suit everybody but on the whole it was a valuable experience for me, one which I wouldn't have missed for the world.

At first, it was novel to live in such a way and I viewed it as a bit of an adventure. I got down to writing letters almost immediately, the first that I sent (on completion, my outgoing mail was picked up outside my door and duly posted) was one to my brother, putting him in the picture as to my present situation and requesting him to send me a parcel of selected books from my bookcase. That done, I then wrote to the various members of my family, including those in America, and also to Sue whose letters had somewhat diminished over the last few months from about two a week to once every month or so. She still confessed much affection for me but had moved to a flat in town and was now mixing with a set of new friends in London and living a rather hectic existence, what with her work as an assistant to an antique dealer (which she wrote me about) and the constant round of parties, socialising, etc., she did therefore not write too often. I could appreciate that; she was young, very attractive, and loving, it was a natural outcome that she should find such a new life for herself, especially with me not being around and now with no immediate prospects of returning.

During that initial period of kuti-dwelling, I took time to reassess my thoughts on Mahesh's system of meditation and my responses to it. Although I found the Vedic doctrines upon which he often based his talks a very valuable and an inspiring presentation of the spiritual side of life, it did not seem as appropriate for my type of mind as was the Ageless Wisdom philosophy which I had previously been following. As to his meditation system, I came to the conclusion, after some months of conscientious practice and serious consideration, that it was not as suited to my temperament as the system I had been practicing for some years prior to meeting Mahesh. I therefore felt that now, under such new circumstances, it was opportune to revert back to my former meditation method.

Once my books had arrived, which took nearly a month, and I had got into a routine of cooking, study, meditating, writing letters, compiling notes on my studies, etc., and even trying my hand at a bit of poetry as well as a little sketching, the days simply sped by, and before I knew it, Christmas was upon me. Not that such a festive season was ever celebrated in that part of the world but it was an occasion for me to send out another round of letters as well as answering those which had arrived. Being now in the 'depths of winter', it was possible for me to get a little early morning sunbathe on my balcony before the sun became too hot, which will give an idea of the weather conditions at that period. What must it have been like on the plains?

I did have a little incident when we were experiencing a cold snap during the January of 1962. One morning, the temperature had fallen well below zero and the hillside was covered with a solid sheet of ice. Unusual, but seeing how high up we were there was nothing particularly untoward in that, I thought . . . . not until I attempted to walk down the narrow pathway that I had made in the grass on my daily journeys to my toilet enclosure.

No sooner had I set foot on the path than I realised there was no grip for my feet, I slipped over, fell onto my rear and clumsily slid down the hill on my back, gathering speed until I became completely out of control. The hill was so steep that I knew that if I could not slow myself down somehow, I would cannon into a tree further below towards, if not a certain death, into a very mangled English Sanyassi. The nearest bush was way out of my reach and all the grass and surface growth was under ice, but as luck would have it (there she was again!), a small piece of corrugated iron sheet from which my loo had been constructed was lying discarded, protruding from the ice yet held firm by it. My descent was increasing rapidly but in a mad frenzied effort, I managed to roll myself over towards it to make a grab for it as I sped past. I was successful, in as much as it halted my fall, but it tore the palm of my hand to shreds in the process, which took weeks before it healed. It was not an experience that I would recommend, even to the foolhardy, especially when one is heading for the loo, toilet paper in hand, and rather caught short, at that.

From then on, until the weather became more friendly, I made sure that my journey loo-ward took a circuitous route through the surrounding forest where I could descend the hill moving from tree to tree in a more dignified manner.

Apart from such mishaps, life was very comforting for me, there being no demands on my time or energy, no deadlines to meet, no pressure to live up to the expectations of others, nor having to indulge in small talk with anyone, etc. I was becoming very happy about my little life of luxury. However, as attractive as it had become, it was not my objective to travel halfway round the world just to have a comforting existence. True, I was gainfully occupying my time by studying, meditating, doing a lot of thinking and trying to sort things out a bit more, but couldn't I do that sort of thing at home at the Farm?

When I next saw Babaji later that month (an occasion when I broke my silence for half a day), I naturally thanked him for all the conveniences which he had arranged for me and explained how I was getting on, that I was very happy in my little kuti with things as they were, but I did wonder how such an existence would help satisfy my inner longing. I also questioned how long I would be able to continue without becoming lonely and bored. (I took this line of approach thinking it might elicit from him some specific spiritual practices or some definite routine for me to follow, as so far, I had had no concrete feedback from him that would enable me to assess his wisdom in these matters.)

He seemed very understanding regarding my position and said that I knew I was welcome to stay as long as I wanted, that the period of silence should be profitable for me, and that whenever I felt that I needed to move on, I should just let him know. In the meantime if there was anything further he could do for me, I had only to ask and he would arrange it . . . . and that was how it was left. No instructions from "the Master", no wise injunctions, no profound utterances or such. Just that!

As I had no specific plans in mind, it was the easiest course, at least for the time being, to take up his generous offer to stay. So from then on I resigned myself to continue wallowing in this "luxurious" existence until, as he himself had said, I felt that I needed to move on. It is interesting to see the way things worked out from around that time. Rather than narrate the turn of events leading up to my trip to Delhi in the forthcoming April, and also to help give a broader picture of my thoughts and feelings during that period, I feel I can do no better than to include certain relevant extracts from some of my roughly scribed efforts home of that time - if I might be excused the lack of literary expertise and the feeble attempts of humour.

This first one was a missive to my brother Bon, sent on 9th February, '62 from Hanuman Gar, Nainital.

".... As for me becoming increasingly interested in "home news" yes, I am fully aware of it and will briefly explain to you the reason for it. You see, I'm really a simple sort of bloke (uncomplicated, I mean, not moronic - although I'm not really convinced about THAT either) and for such a bloke to "up and leave" everything and everybody that has for him been his whole world and environment for such a long time, as I did, can't but expect any other reaction than to miss these much ingrained habits, people and suchlike to, what might appear, a very considerable degree."

To sever all as I have done with the intention of returning within a few months was in itself some form of consolation and especially as the thought of gaining what I wanted most out of life dangled carrot-fashion before my nose. But then, I'm forced to admit,came disappointment after disappointment and I found myself trudging half India looking for "I don't know what" to help justify my existence - not being at all satisfied with all the "I do know what's", that life has so far offered.

"So after exhausting my desire for trudging this undesirable country (and that has been a very prominent factor towards my present state of mind and body; the food, dirt and filth, the poor people, and everything about this country, is all so contrary to my way and past standards of living. What I have put up with and I'd even go so far to say torturingly suffered, physically, mentally, morally and spiritually, I would never tell - but I'd do it all ten thousand times again and MUCH more if I thought that in doing, it would bring me even one iota nearer to that unknown what-ever-it-is that I so ardently long for), I naturally took advantage of the opportunity to remain here for a while. Being rather (though many would think fanatically so), at the moment one pointed in my aim, I have endeavoured to accept whatever comes my way, be it hardships, horrors or dangers (and some of a very real nature too) until I at least either reach my aim or reach the conclusion that all my efforts are useless.

"This being the case, anywhere on earth - as I have previously told you - is as good as any other place, though the more congenial, the better (and I doubt if there could be a less congenial one than this country). And at this address, though I'm quite contented and taking life fairly easily, it would be surely expected that my mind, having nothing else to do, constantly flits back to home and all "homey" connections. So it really amounts to me not having what I'm used to - not having, or even knowing, what I'm looking for - thus a sort of frustration on either side with plenty of boring moments to realise my loss of the past, even though temporary, must give rise to such desires as a news-from-home-hunger-itus.

111

"So I guess you've got some inkling now of how welcome all your letters are (as well as my own unexpected outburst of literary talents which have been inflicted upon you of late).

"Whoops! After rereading that little diabolical discourse of the past couple of pages I'm sure you may think I'm moaning about things! This is not the case or my intention - I've brought it all on myself and just as easily I can take it all off by becoming "normal" - but I won't take it off until I must! I'm putting it all down to experience which, though difficult, is at least philosophical and have accepted everything so far (but accompanied with much chewing of bottom lip) and will try to continue to do so even to the extent of returning home in a few months as empty, if not more so in many ways, as I left - and to do what? - I don't know.

"Fortunately, the anxiety of the future doesn't seem to be one of my characteristics as I've only myself to feed and fend. I guess all this must seem a very precarious and foundationless way to live one's life but it's that faint glimmer of hope that makes even the "Doomed" navigate a leaky boat. Though I'm sure you can understand it to a certain degree - I hope! Me homesick? Of course not (says he bursting forth with 73 choruses of "My Bonny lies over the ocean". [Note: Bonny is my brother's nickname.]

". . . . For your information, Buffalo's milk (or so I'm told that's what I'm getting) has a slight taste of goats milk about it, sort of animally and seems much more watery than cow's milk (though they could water it down before it comes to me - nothing would surprise me) yet possibly more fattier, though certainly not creamier. I find the glass, difficult to clean because of the residue of fat left after I've drunk it. I doubt its value compared to cow's milk but I don't really know. No, there's no cheese available, only in small tins (Kraft process) at about 15/- (75p) a tin! Camel's eggs, I'm afraid are off these days and I haven't had any form of eggs since I arrived in India - it is considered non-vegetarian food here and not easy to obtain, apart from in larger cities.

"I got someone to purchase a small tin of Ovaltine for me (as a sort of night drink over the Christmas period - a little self-indulgence I permitted for being a good boy). It only cost me about 13/6 for a small tin!!! So I spend the whole day gazing wistfully at each beautiful gem-like grain. I put about three grains in front of me before placing them on my tongue at night, like a miser with his gold dust!!"

There were more such comments in that vein but I trust sufficient has been given for now to afford the interested reader a general idea of my life style at that time. For the following weeks I continued luxuriating in this favoured existence, fruitfully occupying my time by studying, medding, (meditation) writing, sketching, and as I've mentioned, even firing off an occasional salvo of poetic verse. Two attempts at this latter, the drafts of which I have now unearthed from my well disorganised archives, will give an indication of the talent, or lack of, which lay hid deep within the bowels of my unconscious (no facetious comments please).

The first was in Valentine form, abundantly peppered with arrow-pierced hearts, in response to a very tender and loving letter from Sue,

"14th, February, 1962.

To Susie - (not just) My Valentine

"As is the custom of our land to speak of love to those
Who on this day will understand thro' poem or thro' prose

Custom also doth decree and to this I must abide
Maintaining my anonymity though hints I cannot hide

But clues must surely give away the author of these lines
That make a difference in display from your other Valentines

How obvious each clue is shown and not left you in the dark
The distance that these words have flown and the tell-tale postal mark

But there's one very subtle clue in case you're still in doubt
Within each word a fondness true of every line throughout

'Tho this you're sure to recognise, who else can feel the same
My affection knows no compromise, it must reveal my name

This day of joy to hearts so dear all lovers
feel entwined
But to just one day in every year my love is not confined

Throughout the year I've thought of you altho' you're far away
My mind is filled with my sweet Sue for thirty hours a day

To woo you 'neath a million stars I leave to other beaus
My fondness doesn't need guitars ' cos in each word it shows

Nor do we need a moon above or ribbon'd pink bound flowers
A small and Valen-tiny love is dwarfed compared to ours

But while we're many miles apart 'tls well to sond this sign
To show you're still within my heart and not JUST a Valentine."

113

Ah well, that's love for you.

Here's another sample I thought I might inflict upon you, dear reader, written to my amusing young nephew, Lee, accompanied by appropriate sketches, and aimed to arrive for his birthday on April 1st - which he was always being ribbed about.

" A NITTY DITTY FOR THE PRETTY WITTY"

"Those born this day seem to regret
That people make at their expense
Much ridicule lest they forget
They've been endowed with little sense
Yet this we know is not the case
Nor do exceptions prove the rules
The greatest even of our race
The world has dubbed as April Fools
Yet really 'tis but only they
The foolish fools one always find
Who indiscriminately say those born
This day have addled minds

The truth is that in days of old
But few could say amusing things
A fool was he who could unfold
A Royal jest to please the Kings
He filled their hearts with priceless fun
No wonder he was loved by all
And prized was he by everyone
So proud to be the King's prize fool

Liked and loved for miles around
For all the joy that he'd transmit
Through him much happiness was found
His humour lacking not a wit
He made the world a happy place
With his rare gift that pleased all folks
By cheering with his sunny face
And sharing of his jolly jokes

A catchy phrase, a merry quip,
His precious gift would cheer the heart
In truth a Fool is not a drip
In fact, in fun he's twice as smart

This day's ordained by Gods of Mirth
Allowing only those they pick
To be entitled to take birth
Those smarter ones whose wit is quick
So let foolish people ridicule
'Cos really then the fools are they
Not smart enough to be a Fool
To take their birth this treasured day

Now you know this day's true worth
To spread to all your sunny rays
As granted by the Gods of Mirth
Your very witty turn of phrase
So fill your life with laughter loud
Until your sides are fit to burst
May all your days be joy endowed
Examples true of April 1st.

Afterthought

"Talents nil I'm forced to use
Trite rhymings so well worn
Poet Laurie-ate - mm? begs excuse
This abundance of utter corn!"

Now there's a couple of justifiable specimens of poetic license - or liberty.

By about mid-March of '62 time was beginning to drag and the original novelty of it all was wearing thin. On speaking to Babaji again when next he was in the area, I tactfully made it known that boredom was beginning to set in and I was undecided what to do

about it. He asked me if I would be willing to allow the occasional local visitor into my kuti to sit at
my feet and ask me questions, etc. I told him that I'd be quite happy to welcome anyone who wanted to see me for a chat at any time, providing it was convenient and I could ask them to leave when I saw fit, but certainly not to sit at my feet! How demeaning!. He smiled and suggested that I put aside the last day of each month to receive people and use my slate to converse with them if I felt I wanted to . "O.K", I agreed, "We can start from the end of March".

The following series of extracts were from the next of my literary forays, this one to my brother completed on 27th, April, 1962, from the Birla Temple in Delhi.

"Dear Bon,

"Well, as you can see, I've finally shown my bony, pale face once again in the outer world, and what a very noisy outer world it seems after all those months of peaceful ness. Or maybe it's just one of the over-emphasised characteristics of this particular country, its noisiness, I mean.

"Baba Har Das, my late host, has kindly arranged for me to stay here at this Temple for free for a while, so once again I'm able to live on about a few shillings a week, with Temple grub thrown in (when I can stomach it), though in spite of this, the extras that I buy here, (milk, fruit, etc. the recent visit to the local Western Vegetarian Restaurant and the fare to get there and back) are making quite a drain on my financial residue, but I'm fortunately better off than I anticipated, though as I said, Delhi dwelling is more costlier than my late mountain shack so being better off doesn't really amount to much.

"It certainly is hot here now and this I'm told is only the beginning of summer! To give you an idea of the heat in my room, I washed a towel yesterday and forgot to wring it out - I just put it down soaking wet and all screwed up and about half hour later I saw it lying there waiting to be hung out to dry, so I thought, I picked it up and was staggered to find it was bone dry! There wasn't even a trace of water where it was lying. So this morning when I washed a few things I just left them lying around wet - they were all dry within the hour! Its literally like living in an over-heated airing cupboard - almost impossible to sleep nights. I have an overhead fan but all that seems to do is to blow hot air in my face. And it's even worse outside because one is exposed to the heat and sun, even the wind is a hot treacherous enemy! What must it be like further South in the Summer? I daren't think!

[Note: As a favour, I had brought into India a few items for Mahesh when we first arrived in Bombay, including a camera and tape recorder, which were entered in my passport and which I was deemed responsible for. I agreed to this not knowing that if they remained in the country beyond six months, Customs Duty would be levied. I had lost all recollection of such items until the Officials tracked me down and demanded the money due (at least, it seemed the Civil Service functioned . . . how odd!) - and, as far as I remember, no amount of letters to Mahesh's organisation relieved me of that responsibility.]

" . . . . . You know, I really can't remember a thing from one minute to the next - and I seem to be getting worse! I went to the Customs Office a couple of days ago for confirmation about this camera duty amount and, of all things, I forgot my own name!! For quite some time I panicked staring into space, my mind was an utter blank! I mentally went through all the names that I thought sounded familiar, hopelessly trying to grasp something that might remind me of my own. The Officer who had asked me was getting most impatient as pen-poised he was waiting to write it down - I felt such a closet! I had to stall him off by trying to pretend I couldn't hear him and he was only about six inches from me! I obviously didn't fool him, just made myself look a bigger twerp! How about that for a dunderhead of a brother? Anyway in spite of this particular incident and after chasing from one department to another I have finally got a con cession from 600 Rupees to 200 Rupees. I thought this was quite an achievement knowing how tough officialdom is, even though I spent almost two whole days doing it! 200 Rupees is about £15 . . . ."

"Now about my home-coming, it's possible that it will be delayed for a while. What has actually happened is this; before I left Nainital there were many people coming up from the Plains, being the beginning of the tourist season, and I had a visitor, who had come to the Temple, who went through all the normal questions that the majority of the over-inquisitive Indians asked me and he told me that whatever I was looking for, it couldn't be found in India it would more than likely be found in TIBET because that was a very sacred country before the Chinese had invaded it.

"I had more than once toyed with the idea of Tibet over the past few months but never took the matter seriously because not only did I have no cash for any further expeditions but knew how impossible it would be to get permission from the Chinese Govt. to enter Tibet.

"As you know I have been more than disappointed over this whole Indain trip and, also as you know, that though disappointed, still undaunted and not discouraged, so I thought I might at least try to apply for permission for Tibet. So I spent my first few days in Delhi chasing from one Embassy to the other - British, then Chinese, then Indian then back to British and again to Chinese - you know the sort of thing - I knew it wouldn't be an easy thing to apply for but didn't think I'd have so much trouble.

"Anyway, eventually, after becoming very Embassy weary, I made my application which was as good as refused by the Chinese Embassy - they were most uncooperative (even the office staff) even when I insisted that they refer the whole matter to

Peking Ministry. They said they would but practically assured me that there was no hope of permission. I have been told by various people that the Chinese have killed all the Lamas (holy men) and destroyed the Monasteries, but never-the-less, I'm quite determined to have a go at getting there and I'm hoping that you'll bear with me and try to understand how I feel about all this business.

"I'm sure you've surmised by now that to me, life as I know it is really just not WORTH it, and although preferable to its opponent - death, is as far from satisfying for me to warrant the excepted existence as a means of passing my time here on earth. No, I feel there must be something more to life than what I've been led to accept; what that something is, I don't know! Where can I find a someone who will help me? - that I don't know either! But there is one thing I DO know, that I can never stop looking until I'm satisfied in, not only what it is I'm looking for but until I have actually found it! - or die trying.

"I won't say any more for fear of you thinking I'm being too dramatic about it but whatever you may think, please try to understand, which I know is a hard thing to ask you knowing, full well that I don't even understand it myself! We have all heard of stories of people who felt they have some sort of calling in life and have gone to many lengths to satisfy this, but believe me Bon, whether you'd class me under this type or not is not really my concern - all I know is that the urge in me is so strong that I'd willingly devote my whole life - or SACRIFICE it - to fill this immense hole in my heart!

"As you may know I was, even in England, looking for help and guidance for many years but there, and here, has been merely a series of disappointments, would you blame me for wanting to have a "last fling" in Tibet before I came home? Although it's practically certain I won't be granted permission (I'll try my darndest) - I'd hate to think now that I left the East without at least trying to get into Tibet, the once most sacred place in the world, don't you agree? I hope you do because you know how I value your opinion in these things and although you may think I'm carrying things a bit too far, I feel that sometimes you've got to deal the whole deck before you turn up the Ace!

"So please forgive me if I don't come home when I arranged - I'd like to, at least, wait here a little longer 'til I hear from the Chinese Embassy. Then I'll let you know what I'll be doing if I don't get the permission I'm hoping for. I really don't know on what terms the British are with China but I doubt if they're very good, but you'd probably know more about that than I because I haven't seen a newspaper for months, besides I never did have any concern in politics, as you know.

"Now whatever happens, whether I get permission or not, I'll still wait here in Delhi until I know for certain one way or another, which means that I may have to break my tightly adhered principles and ask you to send me some cash. I have skimped and scraped in my endeavour not to have any more money sent out here than I originally planned but soon I'll have to break into my fare money. If I don't go to Tibet (which is the most likely event) I'll only spend a little of my fare in living here waiting, so I could either return by boat or you could send me the extra for 'plane. But if I go to Tibet then I'll probably need every penny I have. If that is the case, could you please see your way clear to put by about £150 to £200 for me for my fare home. I won't need it now but only when I return from Tibet and am ready to come home, I'll then write you to send it to me (this is all in case I get the nigh-impossible permission) but if you can, please try to put it by soon, just in case.

"In very many ways I feel very disappointed in this new and unexpected idea of mine because as you know, I was really getting over-excited at the thought of being back home with you all again. But now this Tibetan idea has been growing very strongly in my mind during the past three weeks or so, I feel I want to see it through - one can never tell where it may lead (says he, clinging to the last straw like a drowning man). When I try to view the idea objectively, it appears so futile because even if my application bears fruit it would be hellish to cross the Himalayas, specially for me who's never even climbed an ant hill let alone a mountain! - and the highest range of mountains in the world, at that!

"Then there's all the trekking in the snow plateaus of Tibet - it's all above 12,000 feet and apparently the very rare village one may come across consists of only about three or four tents! - the people live a nomadic life except in the two or three cities like Lhasa or Gyantse (which I'm told have a population of about 10,000 people) - food is scarce, travelling is difficult, mules are costly, the only means of carrying supplies), and the temperature is seldom above freezing point.

"All this and more, because I don't know where to go or what to look for and the whole country is overrun with bandits, and guerilla warfare is continually being waged - it is considered quite a troublesome place these days with a very low boiling point.

"So you see, the chances of me being successful are slimmer than the edge of a razor blade and any sane person wouldn't dream of it, but I guess my dreams are of a different weave to those of the sane, and I'd be willing to make an attempt no matter how conflicting the circumstances were.

"Foolhardy, reckless, and irresponsible? . . . . or committed, steadfast and true?"

Photocall London Cy. Acker Bilk. Jimmy Asman. V. Laurie.

100 Club   Cy & Acker Bilk 1983 V. Laurie.

Re-union with Joan & Peter Roberts   Bude - 1988   V. Laurie

CY with Alan Elsdon   1989   V. Laurie

120

Jazz in Duketown 1989 - Den Bosch - Holland
Cy & Harry Gold

Jam Session. Golden Tulip Hotel.
V. Laurie.

Whitney Bay. 1994   **Hugh Rainey. Cy. Monty Sunshine. George Webb.**   V. Laurie.

121

CAN slay the fans anywhere and at any time. He and his band were playing in the open air at the famous Soho Fair when the audience started to jive in the streets. The next number was 999—somebody sent for the police to break it up!

YOU can hear Cy and the boys play their real-gone music at their club at Great Windmill, London, W.1., six times a week and twice on Sundays!

LOVES the open air—has a farm in Essex.

ALL-PROFESSIONAL band has cut discs like "Cy Laurie Blows Blue Hot" and "Cy Laurie Jazz Club" (both Esquire L.P.'s), "Clarinet Rondo" (Esquire 78 r.p.m.) and recent E.P. "Jungle Rhythm."

UMPTEEN outfits have been put on the right road by Cy's own band agency.

RIDES a horse called Sapphire and has two dogs—an Alsatian and a Labrador.

IT'S for sure you'll want to know how old Cy is—he was born 31 years ago in London.

EVERYONE who digs Cy's music can join his fan club by writing to the Great Windmill address. There are around 10,000 members. Students may join free.

Cy Laurie

| NEXT WEEK | CHARLES McDEVITT | ✳ |

Printed and Published in Great Britain by D. C. THOMSON & Co., Ltd., and JOHN LENG & Co. Ltd., 12 Fetter Lane Fleet Street, London, E.C.4. Registered for transmission by Canadian Magazine Post. © D. C. THOMSON & CO., LTD., 1958.

With Helen Gould at Farm Photo Session
V Laurie

My favourite photo of Ronnie -- Greece 1986   V Laurie

With Beryl Bryden Owen Bryce & Iris Bryce   Soho Photo call 1996

With Ronnie Denmark

EPISODE TWO - SACRED INDIA

CHAPTER 8 - FURTHER LETTERS HOME

1962 - My Mid-Thirties (Part 3.)

One early morning during my stay at the Birla Temple in Delhi, I spied a little sparrow who seemed to be in trouble in the corridor outside my room. It was having some difficulty in its attempts to fly. When I approached it to take a closer look it just fluttered its wings, half hopped, and half wobbled about six inches forward. I noticed that the little thing had a length of black cotton tied around its legs, the result no doubt of some unfeeling mischievous children. In my concern for the little creature, I managed gingerly to round it up and take it into my room where I placed it, scared stiff (both of us that is), on the table. There was hardly anything of it, it was so frail, and if it wasn't that its eyes were half open, I'd have thought it was quite dead.

The cotton around its legs was fixed with a few knots and tied too tightly for me to try to undo them with my fingers, so I had to resort to other more precise means. I had a needle handy which I used to try to unravel the knots, which proved to be a very ticklish operation, as not only did the little thing keep jerking its legs from my hand, but such delicate thin legs would so readily snap at the slightest undue pressure if I wasn't careful, also I feared sticking the needle into its unsteady kneecap.

It was really a job for someone used to handling such creatures, (which I was not), as I was almost as distressed about the whole affair as was this little mite. The disturbing thought in my mind was that its life and wellbeing depended on how successfully I was able to cope with the situation, and I felt a heavy responsibility.

More by luck than skill, after much picking, poking, and prodding, I finally managed to free the cotton from its legs without damaging its stiffened body. I gently prised open its tiny beak and dropped some water down it but there was no sign of response. I repeated this every few minutes but still nothing so I just had to leave it in the lap of the Gods. What a shock it must have suffered, probably as much by being handled by me as by the original perpetrator of its predicament. About a half hour later, it shook its head a couple of times and blinked its eyes - at last signs of life. I administered the water treatment a few more times and then its wings began to flutter a little. Slowly it revived and even started drinking from a little saucer of water I had placed underneath its beak. Success at last, I thought.

It eventually tottered around the table top trying out its wings until finally it took off onto my bed where it sat for a while trying to regain its composure. It then flew around the room a couple of times before flying out through the doorway into the corridor and then out through the open window there. I followed its flight from the window only to see that it had perched itself on a nearby rooftop where it was instantly surrounded by a group of other sparrows. I assumed this must have been some form of protective ritual to help enable the little guy to recuperate from its ordeal. I watched this display for a good half hour until the whole group of birds finally flew off. What a rewarding sight - I was as pleased as Punch with myself.

I stayed in Delhi for about a month to sort out the possibility of entering Tibet but the waiting became too tedious for me, as did both the financial and weather conditions. So I returned to Hanuman Garh, as the following extracts from the next letter to my brother explain:

Written on 24th, June, '62 from Hanuman Garh, Nainital.

"It didn't take long for Delhi to become far too hot and expensive for comfort for me. After much careful consideration I thought it best to return here while I await a reply from the Chinese Embassy. I reasoned it this-a-way, that the fare money to return to Hanuman Garh from Delhi being about £1.00 by the cheapest route would be my only expense, apart from my daily milk here, during this waiting period. Whereas by remaining in Dehli, that same £1.00, and possibly more would be absorbed in a few days of living in that hell-like furnace-type City (if the term "living" could be applied to my type of existence).

"So taking all facts into account I eventually decided to suffer the journey which, by-the-way, I paid for dearly at the high cost of an excruciatingly painful headache on my arrival at Nainital. But as it turned out it was a move to my advantage - I think! It didn't take me long to settle here again and to adjust myself to this relaxing scenery and the pleasant cool mountain breezes.

"I'm not sure if I've told you before but I have been sharing my room since last Autumn with a large variety of the most obnoxious looking insects, including the ugliest of spiders, some almost the size of a baby's hand and, worst of all the most uncongenial room mates one could wish for - scorpions! During the Winter months of December, January and part of February, these demons seldom made an appearance but otherwise there's at least one or two of these dreaded scorpions who favour me with their unpleasant company, normally between dusk and dawn. Soon after I arrived back here in May one horrible little specimen decided that my bed was more comfortable than the floor (altho' I can't say that I fully agree with it) and in the middle of one night victoriously stung me on my thigh.

"Fortunately scorpion stings in this area are not fatal, although they can give one intolerable pain two or three days on end but, if such a thing can be said in the circumstances, luck was with me as this particular monster must have been a small one, probably out on experimental manoeuvers, and though it gave me much pain immediately after the sting, it only resulted in an irritating wound for a while afterwards. But to make up for its lack of complete success, not a week had passed before one of its class mates got me on the ankle, but once again it was luckily a small one (about one-and-half-inches from tip to tip) leaving a similar result. Oh! once again to tread that green and pleasant land!

"Anyway, I tried to take a philosophical view of it all by thinking that things could have been worse - and it wasn't long before they were! I did one of the most foolish things imaginable. I have told you that I was doing all my own cooking which incidentally, I find positively tasteless and almost unpalatable (I certainly would never want to marry ME), well, during one of my gastronomical endeavours I cleverly upset a pan of boiling ghee (clarified butter) over my right hand. This sheet of paper would immediately disintegrate if I tried to explain the flow of words that followed this incident, so I leave it to your imagination as to how I reacted. I spent the following 48 hours on my bed with my walnut-sized blistered hand dangling painfully in a bucket of water (which I was told at the time was the worst thing I could have done) and wincing with every painful throb, feeling extremely sorry for myself.

"Fortunately my body heals fairly quickly and after a few days the pain subsided considerably, and apart from my fingers being completely out of action and my hand looking like a bunch of ripe hot-house grapes, it troubled me little and by now the only indication of the event is a speckled-pie-bald effect of the new and old skin. The result was not only to prolong the pregnancy period of this letter but it has completely put an end to my house-keeping career (thank goodness), though, needless to say, if I had the choice I would have ended it by far less torturing and less dramatic methods. It was arranged for someone to do my cooking for me while my hand was healing.

"Now although all this sounds rather disturbing, I was surprised to find that I took it all quite well on the whole and didn't feel the least bit brought-down by it all. Even not hearing from the Chinese Embassy, which I'm forced to take as indicative of their refusal to grant my Tibetan application, didn't worry me that much, for I really expected it to be turned down.

"But as the sunshine follows the rain so I feel that, after my little collection of troubles, I have possibly made the contact that I've been waiting for, though in these matters it's very difficult for a novice to be too certain, as there are so many fakes and phonies.

"At this time of year many people who can afford it come to this area to escape the heat of the plains and about three or four weeks ago an elderly man arrived in a little village about a half dozen miles from here. I heard about him from some of the locals and decided to pay him a visit.

[Note; This information was not strictly accurate as I had not before ventured to mention my contact with Babaji in previous letters, a contact which really took place for the first time in the November of the previous year, as related in the former chapter].

"He seems to understand my "problem" as to why I'm here in India and gave me the impression that he could help me. Altho' I've met many others of similar nature, I feel that this man may be genuine - at least I've nothing to lose by trying. Whatever the drawbacks and disadvantages of this country, one prevalent trait to be found is that they respect, honour and support those in search of a higher life and this particular man seemed to take me under his wing. I have explained my financial position to him and he has told me not to bother about money as he will supply all my needs and I should have no occasion to spend even a pieyce (less than a farthing).

"I have been seeing him most days recently and I only hope he really may be able to help me in my unusual quest. He - they call him Babaji, as far as I can gather it's a common name here of fatherly respect - he has said that I shouldn't bother about chasing around visiting Tibet, etc. for the time being and suggests that I should stay here at Hanuman Garh for the rainy season.He'll be leaving in a day or two and has said he'll be returning in either August or September to see me, when he hopes to give me a little more information as to what he thinks it's best for me to do. (the rainy season is from approximately June 15th to 10th September).

"Meanwhile he has arranged for my fooding which, although not of home-cooking quality, is far better than I've been getting here in the past. I'm also taking advantage of the wide variety of fruits which are available here during this season, and this alone is a satisfying change for me. Mangoes, peaches, apricots, pears, plums, apples, berries of all sorts, sweet corn, etc., all very cheap and in much abundance, so my food problem has very much diminished. He is now paying for my milk and has offered to supply me with shirts, trousers, shoes, etc., those of which I've been using for the last 18 months being seriously afflicted with an overdose of tailoring surgery really should have been submitted to the local crematorium long ago.

"I can't think of much else to tell you except that it's as rainy as a hundred Manchesters right now, and for a fraction of the day the clouds are right outside my door. Though it's not the depressing sort of weather that normally accompanies such rain, in fact apart from intermittent attacks of home-sickness, I feel comparatively contented here and even slightly optimistic now."

A selection from the contents of the next epistle I sent to my brother, about a couple of weeks after the above, on the 5th July, '62, will give a clearer idea of my situation at that time and indicate the beginnings of an added complication in my life.

"I don't quite understand this letter from the Indian Customs, they told me when I was there that all my liabilities are cancelled and they wrote the same in my Passport too.

Anyway, there's a lawyer friend of mine in Nainital, I'll ask him to help me write a letter explaining things . . .

"I'm glad you've seen more of Sue recently, what was her trouble to make her come to see you for treatment? Nothing serious, I hope! (my brother was a practicing Osteopath and Physiotherapist).

"I would like her address please, as I'm not sure if the one I have is her latest or not. If there's the remotest possibility of my staying here for some time I'd like to let her know as soon as possible because I'm not too sure of her attitude and feelings towards me (her infrequent letters are not very informative) and I wouldn't want her to waste her time waiting for me (though I'd really doubt if she'd do that), and fond as I am of the little screwball it would be quite unfair of me not to clarify my present position to her and the possibility of me not returning for a few years, don't you agree?

"Could you have a chat with her about it and maybe ask her to write me a nice long letter in the very near future. If not, then I'll write to her when you send me her present address. You can tell her I was very disappointed in not seeing her when I had hoped at the end of April, that I hope she's happy, and that I'm very fond of her . . .

"A couple of days after I last wrote to you, this man I have told you about, Babaji, presented me with two summer shirts, two undervests, two pairs of light grey trousers and a couple of coloured handkerchiefs thrown in - how about all that! And when I thanked him for it he said it was unnecessary because he knows how I feel. I was quite overcome. Even my food now has surpassed all expectations.

"To give you a f'rinstance, I have just wrapped my stomach around a soya bean soup, a mixed salad (consisting of grated carrot, turnip, tomatoes and mint) which I get daily now, boiled potatoes and ladies fingers (bindi), chappaties, yoghurt, and rounded off with a grated coconut custard - a very pleasant repast compared to what I used to get, eh? (tho' not a patch on home cooking, a sample of which I am very much looking forward to).

"This afternoon I intend to partake of the large quantity of mangoes, apples, peaches, etc. that are squatting so comfortably at my right elbow accompanied by a tall glass of milk - and all this drains my purse by not one cent! Tell me, my good friend, how are the poor people faring these days? Ho-hum! (says he using his travellers cheques to pick his teeth), "Life is just a bulge of bellies."

"Talking of teeth, do you remember our dear friend Strausberger once mutilated my upper set by fixing in a bridge which turned out to be the most unfixed bridge that ever was fixed? Well one of the front teeth (which was one of my few real ones - joke??) that he used for the fixing broke off at the roots last week. The gum is growing over the broken part of the tooth that is still embedded and I fear that it is in the process of rotting within the gum. So it won't be long before I'll have to get it seen to, methinks.

"It'll be quite a big job as I think the whole bridge will have to be taken out somehow, also I fear an operation to extract the broken part in the gum. Not looking forward to it in the least, 'specially as the Dental Surgeons here could be rather primitive in their methods and they have no Health Scheme, so it'll probably cost me quite a packet too. Maybe they'll give me a concession on the price if I supplied my own pliers, rasp, brace and bit.

"So far there's no pain, only a happy little dungeon in the gum, so I may be able to hold out 'til this man returns in a few weeks, maybe he knows of a good Dental Surgeon, he seems to have many followers. Just before he left last week he did say that he might return in about two or three weeks time but that's not very definite, anyway. I'll let you know as soon as I know a bit more.

"I was very pleased, ever so, ever so, with your fatherly sympathies regarding these hare-brained desires of mine to stay out here longer. God knows how tough it is for a pampered kid like me who's had everything easy for all his life to battle alone with all these darned uncongenial and inconvenient modes of existence. I would have felt it a hundred-fold if your voluntary sympathies were not with me. You know that, don't you? And I'm sure you know how much I appreciate your attitude about being with me in spirit until I return, I was more than very touched by your remarks. I would like to say, that in giving me your understanding sympathy I think you've omitted much of what I really would like to have and that is your opinion.

"I don't think it's normal for a bloke like me to chase around the globe on such a vague and seemingly futile quest driven by an urge who's strength seems to increase with every hardship, towards an unknown goal which in itself could eventually be found to be non-existent. Ask me what its all about and I'm ignorant of it all as was that scatter-brained, spoilt, good-for-nowt' youngster named Cyril Laurie of 25 years ago with whom I frequently endeavour to reconcile myself, with a most unsatisfying result."

By this time, although the letters I received from Sue, as pointed out to my brother in the above letter, were far less frequent than they were the previous year, the feelings that she expressed for me in them seemed not to have diminished in the slightest. In fact, she confessed that they had intensified. How sincere this really was I couldn't judge, but who was I to discourage a little bit of ego inflating, which at the time was very much missing in my life?

I was always very honest with her as to my situation, that my stay in India was quite open-ended and that there would be no chance of me ever thinking of getting involved now, not at least until I could determine the direction that destiny might have in store

130

for me. Of this I knew she was fully aware and that I should therefore not hastily reciprocate her expressed endearments.

She apparently was living a very full life, doing the social rounds, living it up with moneyed friends. Yet the way she constantly expressed her affection for me in her letters was not just extremely flattering but quite overwhelming, so much so that it would be far too personal and intimate for me to repeat here.

What I can do though, because it is so relevant to my story, is to quote from a letter I received from her whilst at Hanuman Garh on the 23rd of July 1962, possibly in response to the chat which I requested my brother have with her.

". . . perhaps it's an understatement when I say the only thing of importance is this. May I drop in for a visit soon, as soon as I receive the personal invitation which is urgently needed?

"Pick yourself up!! and after you have examined your feelings upon the subject, let me know soon.". . . .

I shall probably fly as the boat takes too long. I won't be able to stay more than a week, and want the go-ahead as soon as possible.

". . . I feel I must come and cannot fully stress how pleased I will be when I know I'll be welcome"

Yipes! What an unexpected bombshell to have dropped in my lap! Before she took it into her head to do anything impulsive, I immediately replied in the following manner.

"Dear Sue,

"Wow! What a most unexpected request!" One thing about you is that you're never dull, always full of surprises - boy! this one certainly takes the cake!

"Now let's just sit down and relax, and try to consider this thing logically. I will try to consider it first from your point of view.

"Firstly, my pet, what on earth could have possessed your pretty little head to decide to venture into the jaws of the dirtiest, inconvenient, and oft times unbearable monster that goes under the title of 'India'? Surely if it's a holiday you're seeking, the Continent offers much nearer, cheaper, and more congenial circumstances.

"Secondly, this would be the very worst season to come here, if it isn't unbearably hellishly hot then it's as wet and humid as can be. One either bakes in the heat or boils

131

in the dampness and rain. The rainy season is definitely not for newcomers, and it won't finish 'till mid-late September.

"Thirdly, for anyone, but a member of the idle rich, to consider travelling halfway round the planet and to stay for only a week must be completely looney! To spend all that hard-got cash then to limit one's stay to a few days is the most extravagant waste I've heard of since the Boston Tea party.

"Fourthly, why the devil spend all that ill-afforded dough (£250 return I think, at least) to travel by plane when you can do a good class ship passage for less than £150 return, leaving you with over £100 extra to spend, which amount alone would allow you to live many, many weeks longer here at a first rate hotel, or many months in a less 'luxurious' environment, if you'll pardon the misuse of the word.

"Now from my point of view, I'd undoubtedly do my nut at the thought of seeing you but, as fond as I am of you and as pleased as I would be to see you, I feel that it wouldn't be right for me to condone this mad hare-brained scheme of yours, at least not at such short notice, namely for the following reasons.

"Firstly, I am here as you well know, for a specific purpose and until quite recently have been very disappointed, disillusioned, and disheartened, as you probably have gathered. But I have now, at last, contacted someone whom I hope will be able to help me so, on the strength of that possibility, I have temporarily placed myself in his hands. He has kinda' taken me under his wing and, as I have no cash to spare, he is providing for all my needs (all details regarding this I have recently given to Bon). In view of this, I would not want to do anything for the time being, without his consent, otherwise it may jeopardise any help that may be forthcoming from him. He isn't due in this area again for maybe two or three weeks.

"Secondly, it has been my policy whilst here not to partake in anything that is not directly pertaining to my purpose and feel that I would be very bad, dull, and possibly exasperating company for you. F'rinstance, Nainital is a popular Indian holiday resort being comparatively high (about 6,500 feet) and cool with all sorts of interesting attractions, i.e., horse riding, yachting, women company, etc., all of which are very mouth-watering for me, living the austere type of life I do, but I would not venture to take advantage of it for the stated reasons.

"Thirdly, although it has not been easy for me to resist all these enjoyments of normal life, here at least, I have so far succeeded. But if there's one thing that would strain my resistance it would be your presence and wonder if all the advantages of my existence out here (even the word existence is a gross understatement, seeing how tough I have found it) would be completely nullified by meeting you at this stage.

I have recently written to Bon to have a chat with you as soon as possible about your future intentions, and have asked him to tell you to please write a long detailed letter to me immediately, because as I have now made this contact, it's possible that I may not be returning to England for a few years yet -anyway, I've been told by this man that I should be prepared to remain away for a few years - and it's possible you may not fully realise how, above ALL else in life, I am eager to achieve the object which first brought me out here, nor do I know your views and feelings on the subject these days. So in view of all this I wrote to Bon giving details from my end and asking him to speak with you - he's a very understanding person regarding these things - and let me know either from him or, preferably, a nice long letter from you that I can answer as soon as possible to clarify the position for both of us.

"Now if, in spite of all the foregoing, everything worked out favourable for your trip here, meaning of course, if I get a favourable answer from this man (he's expected to return to this area fairly shortly) and if you still wish to come after we've exchanged two or three letters, and you're prepared to spend a longer time here than a measly week, and you're willing to wait 'til the weather is more congenial (possibly by the middle of September), then, I'd meet you on arrival at Bombay - I wouldn't dream of allowing you to unnecessarily waste your cash by coming by 'plane, it would have to be either ship or swim, so there! And I'd be ready to welcome you with a large bouquet of kisses and cabbage leaves. Incidentally, I'd also want to send you a short list of things to bring for me - but more about that in my next letter, after you've spoken to Bon.

"I take it that you're not relying too much on your London job or else such wild plans as this could not be considered if your job demanded you back in a short while."

I then made a few practical suggestions as alternatives to making the trip to India, but not knowing too clearly what her situation was, I reserved many of my opinions.

I also hastily wrote a letter to my brother, to apprise him of Sue's unexpected request. This went off on the 26th, July, 1962, and included were the following ramblings.

"They tell me here at the local Post Office that ship postage should only take three weeks and when I told them that all my ship mail has taken at least double that, they just laughed! Stupid lot!! I think the Indian Govt. must employ the overflow from the asylums here. Especially the bunch from Customs because on that Court Order for the tape-recorder duty they threaten to take the money that they have already got! Anyway this Lawyer friend of mine (who turned out to be more Lawyer than friend) has sent off a very official letter telling the Customs people that the money they want (which they already have) is too excessive. Whether he did it intentionally or not I can't say, but in their Indian way there're demanding what they've already got, and in his Indian way he's told them it's too much to ask for and they can't have it, so everybody 's nicely confused and tied up in knots, when really the matter was settled with the tape-recorder over a year ago! I'm now awaiting an answer, though I doubt if they'll send it before consulting the clowns from the local Circus, tra-la-la!

"Next comes the Sue subject. Yes, I did get a short letter from her though as usual, no news. But what she did say made up for everything that she could've said. I almost had quintuplets when she said she was flying over to see me next week!! How about her.

"Within ten seconds I had recorded the most dissuading remarks that ever flowed from a pen in a hurried letter in reply to hers. Anyway like the inconsiderate brother that I am, I passed the buck and told her to see you before she made anything like such a move as THAT! The little pinhead wanted to fly here and only stay for a week! What a waste of dough!!

"Anyway, I've asked her to write to me about how she feels about things, but you being more tactful than your sister's youngest brother, I would still prefer you to talk with her to explain how single-minded I am these days in the object of my trip here, and that at the moment nothing else in life is so important to me, which leaves my future very undecided and nebulous.

"I'm sure you can put it to her better than I can, but in any case I've given her a general idea and may possibly hear from her in the next few days. But there's no denying that her last letter 'fair gave me a turn, it did'! As pleased as I would be to see her, it would make things very awkward for me to keep to my austere and non-indulgent regime.

"I've explained to her in my own inimitable way that for the time being I've put myself in the hands of this man and wouldn't want to do anything that could possibly spoil my chances of his help, at least, not without his consent, anyway.

"So if you can smooth all this out for her, I'd be very grateful, everso, everso.

"About two or three weeks ago I braved a visit to the local Dentist and as soon as I saw his equipment, the water on my knees splashed over in fright! I was quite undecided whether to suffer the pain of my broken tooth or to let him extract it and live on liquids for the rest of my life. His assistant helped me decide, by sitting on my chest! But it didn't turn out as bad as I had expected, the most difficult part was gripping the tooth with his fire-tongs; the extraction itself was quite a simple operation - he only dragged me around his surgery three times before the tooth came out!!

"The result of it all was that I spent the following week in bed, mumbling insanely to my four walls with a face like a distorted barrage balloon. It's all gone down now, especially my opinion of Nainital's Dental Surgeons. On top of all this, I had one of my bouts of diarrhoea (with which I am occasionally inflicted) so I went on a few day's of milk, then milk and fruit. Am now on plain boiled vegetables, milky rice and yoghurt, the diarrhoea has nearly gone (and my intestines with it) but the skin on my face is very blotchy and I've only just twigged why. It's due to a couple of tablets I took to help relieve the pain of the tooth extraction - the bloke wanted me to take about six a day!

I took two on the first day and that was all.

"I've been to him a couple of times since and he has "dressed it" for me (whatever that means). He keeps giving me boxes of drugs to take - I've never known a bloke so drug conscious - I keep telling him I'm allergic to drugs and injections, so after much arguing I've finally compromised by taking some Vitamin B Complex tablets to help me "heal quickly and build up my resistance." I heal quite fast as it is and nobody would think my resistance needed building up if they knew how well I resisted his pill taking persuasiveness.

"My weight was quite normal before the fast of the last two weeks, though I don't know if I told you but after my illness last year my equatorial dimensions increased quite considerably, possibly due to not breaking a prolonged fast properly - in other words, I'm now in the possession of a bit of gut! I've tried some exercises but they don't seem to help much, it's not that bad really, my waist is now about 31" instead of 28".

"The Dentist is really quite friendly, he's invited me to tea next week, and I won't be surprised if he serves me up Penicillin pastries and Morphine biscuits, "Would you like a little more M & B or Streptomycin in your tea?"

"He has quoted me 100 Rupees for fixing a new tooth in the gap on the broken bridge - it's too much for me to pay at the moment because it's only for show, but Baba Har Das said that he'll treat me to it because Babaji (this man I told you about) would want me to have it fixed. I've refused to let Baba Har Das pay for the time being and maybe I'll speak to Babaji about it when he comes, meanwhile I'll keep my big mouth shut!

"I sent off my answer to Sue's letter on the day I received it, and almost by return of post (if you can call 10 days 'return of post' by the standards of efficiency one expects from the snail mail of India), I received a reply from Sue with the following comments.

"Dearest Cy,

"Thank you for your prompt reply. I guess I shock myself sometimes, but then I'm used to it. Now firstly I'm pleased that there is at least some possibility that my proposition may work

."... I have saved and been left some money .... Now I was faced with this dilemma, shall I save it or .... [then followed a selection of alternatives open to her]. So I dismissed all thoughts but furthering my spiritual education.

"But all through these thoughts, which went on for months, there was one thought which pervaded all others, Cy 'Enigma' Laurie, and India. I want to see you. I have never stopped dreaming about you so perhaps I can break the dream!"

I wrote back to her asking "why do you want to break the dream"????? Prophetic!?

EPISODE FOUR

CHAPTER 9 - SUSAN'S ARRIVAL

1962-70 - My Mid-Thirties (part 4.)

So much had been happening at home whilst I'd been away that much of the content of my family's letters to me was connected with certain personal concerns. My brother was good enough to see to my financial affairs, settling my outstanding income tax demands, making sure the payments for the Farm were kept up, collecting any musical royalties that were due, chasing the Lynn Dutton Agency for a set of master tapes of the band which was left with them for issuing, and another set in the hands of a German Agency, being a recording of a concert of our last tour there. He also had the bother of getting new Farm tenants after Terry Pitts and his family had left, and then consistently having to extract the rent from this new family, who turned out to be very unreliable payers. This latter chore proved to be quite a headache for him as they apparently fell into dire straits, so he understood.

During this period he also married a girl who lived a few doors away from our family house, and about six months after, in his letter to me in the August of '62' he announced that his wife, June, was pregnant and was due in the following May. The family business of watch and clock repairs, etc., which he had been running, was becoming financially unviable, and he was having to rely more and more on his secondary and part-time income as a physiotherapist and osteopath, which he found, though ethically worthwhile, a great drain on his vitality.

My elder sister, Ethel, also had a very ailing retail business, and an even more ailing husband, who together could not adequately financially support their family, and she was worried stiff as to how to cope with such a situation. She had tried to sell her shop to pay the bills but was unable to attract a suitable buyer willing to offer an acceptable price. I asked my brother if I had enough cash left over in my bank account after all other expenses were sorted out to treat her to a trip to the States so that she might spend a few weeks with Marie, my other sister's family there. This was eventually arranged and it turned out to be an enjoyable and helpful break for her.

Meanwhile, I myself was free from such worldly problems, yet I had my own series of difficulties to cope with, but far less serious in nature. A particular incident occurred one early evening prior to my retiring for the night which, though comparably minor in itself, turned out to have very significant consequences upon my future attitude. From the corner of my eye I caught sight of a very large and unpleasant specimen of scorpion climbing up the wall of my kuti near my bed (which was now always strategically positioned at least eighteen inches away from any wall).

The chances of it being out for my blood were small as unless it decided to ascend a bed leg or climb across the ceiling to drop on my bed, which fortunately these creatures had not been in the habit of doing, I was in little danger by its mere presence; besides, I believed that they only attack humans when threatened, which was, I suppose, as good as pretending that they didn't exist.

Although he seemed well out of harm's way, the mere sight and thought of him (or her) occupying the same Planet as myself filled me with revulsion, especially after my previous encounters with its younger relations (this might even have been one of my earlier adversaries grown up!). Responding to my fear and urge to put him in his place, I gingerly picked up one of my sandals and,leaning over from my bed, gave him one good hefty clout on the noggin. Bang! That'll show him whose in charge around here, I thought. It was a direct hit and he instantly fell to the floor, not quite dead but writhing in agony, his sting-weaponed tail flailing in all directions in a wild effort to inflict the utmost damage on his unseen protagonist - me. Should I give him another clout and make sure that he wouldn't be around to sting another day? Or should I let him lie there to die as all obedient lethal scorpions should do?

It was in that moment of indecision when I had a complete change of mood - I felt a great wave of compassion come over me. There was this little creature, who obviously was suffering intensely in its death throes because I had taken it into my head to inflict that fatal attack upon it with hardly any logical justification at all. Why? It wasn't doing me any harm, even though it had the capability to do so, but then so had all the others I had reluctantly been sharing my little home with for these past few months?

I then decided to administer that final blow, not out of loathing or fear of the little creature, but out of sorrow that I had been responsible for its unnecessary distress and its eventual demise.

From that day on, I vowed never knowingly to kill any other of God's creatures, unless it be either in self-defence or to relieve it of its agony.

And so it has been.

To continue with the events leading up to Sue's arrival in India, the following quotes from my letters home describe the manner in which it came about.

On the 20th of August, 1962, I had written to my brother saying:

"This man I told you about, Babaji, came here about two weeks ago and I put the proposition about Sue coming over here, explaining how it would expose me to very much temptation seeing as I haven't seen any Western girls for such a time, or even met any Indian girls come to that!

"But he said it would be quite alright if she came and it would be a good change for me, and as far as the temptations were concerned, I must be like a Lotus, immersed in water yet above it, when a drop of water falls on the leaf of a lotus it rolls off leaving the leaf dry. An excellent metaphor but how difficult to apply! Scientifically the water on the lotus leaf finds a grip owing to the surface tension, but even that's beyond me too.

"So I've written to Sue to come as soon as she likes and Babaji told me to go to Bombay to meet the boat. He also told me not to worry about spending my money and that I should live without skimping myself. Although I have deprived myself of the pleasures that India has to offer, indulgence being possibly detrimental to my original purpose, I intend to make quite a pig of myself whilst in Delhi and Bombay by living in hotels and gorging on as much suitable food as I can lay my gullet on!

"As for the other pleasures like riding, boating, films, etc., I fortunately have no desire for such things, although I don't doubt for a moment I will be attracted to them when Sue's around, that is provided she decides to come.

"So I'm very much looking forward to this slight respite that I've surely earned, and as I have already broken into my fare home, I feel that I might as well live a little "luxuriously" (and I use that word in a very comparative sense) if one can call the use of an indoor lavatory (and I'm lucky if I get a seat-type one instead of the hotel squatter), shower bath (and not a bucket of cold water and a dowsing mug - tub baths are completely unknown here and hot water is as rare as cows wings), plates, cups and saucers, (instead of dirty half worn, greenish brass platters, and an even greener spoon - can't eat with my fingers as is the custom here), knife, forks, and even a table cloth (instead of the floor which is "cleaned" ONLY with cow dung - they say it's healthier to use cow dung for cleaning floors but, but . . . but . . . . - what do YOU think???) and even a waiter to serve me (do these things really exist?!!?), and if one can call these things 'living luxuriously', then I'm gonna do me a Rockerfeller for a week or two, at least!

"I have asked Sue to bring me a few things that may help quicken my dreary days here and I'll include a short list that I intend to send her at the end of this letter, for your information.

"Yes I did clarify the position with Sue about my future being undecided but feel that it may not soak into her mind - as you know some people would rather think what they'd rather think and ignore what they've been told to the contrary.

"Quite honestly, although I like her as a girl (of which there are many that I like for the same reason), as a close companion . . . ., I'm not sure if we would be that compatible. But seeing as we've had such close associations in the recent past, I naturally feel more sympathy towards her and also, I believe, she likes me very much, which is

138

something I miss greatly these days, i.e., having someone around to love and to love me in return. So in spite of my strict regime out here (or maybe because of it), I'd do my nut if she does come, it will be great for me right now as for the past few weeks I've been going through quite a difficult period due to home-sickness, lack of interests, bad living conditions, etc., etc., all of which seem to be piling up on me and I'm afraid to admit, slowly defeating me. I think Babaji is aware of this fact and maybe has agreed to allow me "out on probation" because of it.

"By the way, I have a new enemy these days: they're leeches! As you know, I use the open forest when going to the toilet and during the rainy season leeches abound. They're nasty little horrors that transfer themselves from the greenery to your body (mainly legs) when one brushes past them. They range from about half inch long to about 3 or 4 inches long and these larger ones are nearly a quarter inch in diameter, that is their normal state, but they stretch into long thin thread-like things that crawl through one's cotton socks, trouser seams, and they seem to be quite partial to shoe-lace eye holes as an entrance to reach one's flesh, attach themselves to it and suck blood 'til they blow up like grapes, when they fall off on their own accord leaving the wound to bleed deep red blood for hours after (I think they first inject some sort of anti-congealing substance into the wound) and it's impossible to get them off once they bite, even if they are cut off the head still goes on sucking, and the whole trouble is one doesn't even feel them, crawling or sucking!

"So these days I go to my toilet all muffled up as if I was going walking in a typhoon rain-cum-hurricane storm! Anyway it's just another pleasantry to add to my list of "why I don't like India" reasons.

"But getting back to Sue, I think you can now understand why it's difficult for me to write her exactly as I feel for fear of offending her, though as I said, I've told her my future is quite undecided and I may stay here for a few years, etc., but I'll clear everything up that is still foggy for her when and if I see her."

Sue did finally arrive towards the end of that September and I met her at New Delhi Airport (the 'plane was eventually the favoured means). I had arrived the night before and finding no hotel accommodation available spent a sleepness night in an office at one of the temples. I was so very pleased to see her, she looked lovely. She didn't quite recognise me at first among the crowds at the Airport as I was fairly tanned and sported a beard and shoulder-length hair, which I don't think was expected.

What happened after that I related in a subsequent letter to my brother written from Kashmir: (extracts of which if, dear reader, you will continue to bear with me, I again include here.)

"Babaji (my friend and "sponsor") came to New Delhi while we were there and met

Sue. As she had expressed a wish to see Kashmir he suggested I bring her here. It's supposed to be the Paradise of India and I've always had a hankering to come up here myself so I was pleased when he made the suggestion. We reckon on being here for ten days before we return to Nainital, and if there's no hitches I'll be there (Nainital) by about mid-October. We arrived here last night after two days in transit and I fear that either the Indian bone-shaker buses or the food has claimed another victim because Sue's now in bed with stomach trouble. I had the Doc to her today and he suggested lemon juice for her for the day (which I was quite pleased with) but he also gave her some pills and medicine.

"He said she'll be alright tomorrow but the poor kid is rather disappointed to spend her first day in "Paradise" confined to bed. Anyway providing she feels O.K. tomorrow we intend to see Srinagar "tourist style", then we'll move on to Pahalgam for a few days, then probably Gulmarg or Sonamarg; these places being considered the high-spots of the local natural attractions.

" . . . . I think we've discovered the cause of the trouble, it was possibly due to the last lap of our journey from Pathankot to here, about a 15 hour bus ride ('plane was too expensive) from the hot climate to the cooler one without a change to heavier clothing (our clothing was in our luggage all securely tied on the roof of the bus), and because we arrived late at night when it is at its coldest, I think Sue caught a chill in her stomach."

The next letter to my brother was from Hunuman Garh, Nainital, around mid-November from which the following quotes are taken.

"Dear Bon,

"Have once again settled back at the above address [Hanuman Garh, Nainital,] after a few weeks of journeying Kashmir-wards and back. We had a very enjoyable time though we both feel rather travel-worn at the moment and on top of that Sue is having trouble with her back these days, ... But apart from that I think she's enjoying her stay here so far.

"She's staying in a friend's house about ten minutes walk away and comes to see me in the morning and after staying with me and cooking some really knock-out meals, leaves in the evening - that's the routine these days, but if I was anything of even a passable chronicler, I wouldn't start telling you of what's going on now but would tell you what went on since I last wrote . . . . and try to recall (chronologically) travels up to the present time.

" . . . Now, as to our adventures of the past few weeks, Sue was in bed with much stomach trouble when we got to Srinagar in Kashmir, as I think I told you when I dropped you a note from there. She was in bed for about a week and had hardly eaten.

140

"Anyway, when she felt strong enough to make the three hour bus trip to Pahalgam we quickly packed up and only gave the Srinagar hotel an hour's notice before we left, arriving in Pahalgam in the night where she went to bed again for the first couple of days. We stayed in a pleasant hotel and took advantage of the "treks" into the near interior

."... seeing as Sue was still in a state of convalescence and I'm lazy by nature, we did the treks by what are known as "Dandies". These are reclining-type chairs fitted to horizontal sticks and are carried by four or six men to each "Dandi". Rather an expensive way to travel but ideal for loungers who want to be carried and to see the Himalayas in a princely manner. Anyway, these treks were absolutely the mostest and Sue has taken some photographs which I'll try to get her to send you.

"After Pahalgam we returned to Srinagar to live for a few days in a knockout house boat on one of the local mountain lakes. The peacefulness and serenity that this sort of living induces could never be put into words - it's really the last gasp in relaxation. The only shadow on our lake-dwelling calmness was the inevitable shopping that has to be done because Srinagar is famous for its Arts and Crafts (the whole of Kashmir is, come to that) and prices far below the considered value of the articles - we sent you and June a hand-woven carpet from there, a reminder that we thought of you, you should be receiving it fairly shortly as it was sent by surface mail .... We have bought two or three more little trinkets for you both but Sue will take them with her to give to you personally.

"We then left for New Delhi and the hotter climes where we stayed for a few more days. Sue was having a lot of trouble with her back and hip, in fact she wasn't really free from it throughout our whole trip, in Delhi we saw a doctor who was recommended by our hotel but he only wanted to administer handfuls of drugs, he said he'd been suffering from the same trouble for 15 years himself - how's that for an admission!!

"We finally arrived at Nainital where Babaji (my friend) had previously arranged for Sue to stay in an hotel, though I'm afraid after a few days she found it impossible to remain there owing to the food by that time (apart from the better-class hotels that we stayed in) the Indian idea of English food was getting her down, seeing as there was little variety from vegetable cutlet made with mashed spuds and spices, so we arranged with one of the local followers of Babaji to put her up near here and now she's more than happy coming here in the mornings and staying until night.

"As I told you, she's cooking some really breathtaking grub for me, can you imagine my excitement to have nut-cutlets, braised carrots, cheese on toast, vegetable soups, etc., placed in front of me daily. She's been a real brick to me, sometimes spending practically the whole day in preparing grub in all manner of varieties. She says she enjoys it but I guess I'll never be able to understand how some women can spend hours and so much energy making something that takes about 10 minutes for a pig-guts like me to devour. Ah well, it's a jolly good job they don't think like that otherwise I'd never be the consumer of mouthwatering dishes, would I.

"Unfortunately, she hasn't got that much scope to work with; I'm not eating eggs until I get back to England, cheese is very expensive (about 24/6 per pound tin, and very rubbery cheese at that), the Barmene that you sent is treated like gold dust and is nearly used up. I only have two small paraffin oil stoves for her to cook on and there's hardly any of the accepted cooking utensils available - we have one knife and fork, two spoons, and a bent tea strainer for cutlery (and cooking work) for both of us.

"We have discovered a highish-class restaurant in Nainital that makes us whole-wheat bread at a very reasonable price, which obviously ads to that "at-home" feeling these days. So though we're living quite extravagantly, I'm enjoying it to the full.

"Oh yes, we also have another mouth to feed now, because a few nights ago I had my footsteps 'dogged' by a little black mongrel puppy when I was coming from seeing Sue to her place of rest. It's a poor, thin, frightened little thing so I've tried to feed it but it hardly eats more than a slice of bread a day, if that! It's shivering practically the whole day, poor ol' dog, but now I keep it in my room at night (strictly against my principles but I feel that it needs lots of warmth, food, and loving) and hope that it will regain its health fairly soon. It 'hounds' us wherever we go now and Sue has become very attached to it, but dogs in this country generally have very little future because there are so many of them homeless and most of them are ill-treated - you can't try to stroke them without them ducking from your hand as if they're used to being clumped!

"So don't be surprised if Sue arrives back with a four-legged companion next month.

Here is another letter to my brother sent towards the end of November;

"Not much to report since last wrote apart from our trek to Pindari Glacier. It was a knockout experience to go right into the interior (well, they call it the interior even tho' it's only at the foot of the "monster" mountains like Nanda Devi, etc., but really it's another 10 day trek to the real deep interior from Pindari), and the biggest thrill for me was that I was only about 30 or 40 miles from the Tibetan border, though of course, that short distance, which could be well covered in under an hour on the Southend Arterial takes over a dozen days over these snow-covered colossi, as well as carting all the essential equipment of tents, ice picks, thermal clothes, spiked snow boots, safety ropes, dozens of sherpas and a whole caravan of necessities and provisions, etc.

"Maybe I'll get around to it one day if the Chinese ever become well disposed towards me - what a hope!"

It was during our time in Srinagar, a good three weeks after Sue had first arrived,

142

whilst we were enjoying living on the house boat on that delightful mountain lake I succumbed to her sexual charms. In spite of her constant proximity, the perpetual opportunity, and her patent willingness, I had held back.

It is commonly an accepted notion among those who are treading the path to enlightenment, particularly in India, to remain celibate whilst undergoing such spiritual disciplines. It apparently is a means of conserving one's creative forces so that one may refine and utilise one's energies to help attain one's higher goals, possibly in a similar manner as is a prolonged period of silence, but obviously far more radical. Although I had made no vow of celibacy, I was quite prepared to see if an abstinence of sexual expression would prove favourable to my aims (living as I was, chance would have been a fine thing, anyway).

However, although such an ascetic approach might be necessary for some, I have long subscribed to the idea that for others, there are certain additional factors to take into account. For instance, providing that such an act is not solely for selfish reasons, but is an expression of the love one feels for another, one aims at the achievement of mutual satisfaction. The energy then involved is of a higher quality and therefore its expression is to a degree justified.

In the case with Sue and myself, in the short time we had become re-acquainted with each other, which amounted to just over three weeks, I felt increasingly attracted to her, to the point where it might be considered that I was 'falling in love' with her, which was an unusual experience for me. Although I was overtly free with my show of affection for her through an abundance of hugs and kisses, it was becoming painfully obvious to me that my lack of any deeper intimate contact was causing her much distress.

There was a conflict raging within me which had been building up over those past weeks. Should I continue to try to restrain myself or to give way.

I reason it this way;

It might have been to my eventual benefit to discipline my feelings this way, but then what of her feelings and her happiness, surely that was an important factor to consider? What sort of love is that which can cause suffering to those one has a love for? Was I demanding too much from myself and expecting too much from her?

I had for years been guided as to the extreme importance which the principle of love plays in life by a comment in the Alice Bailey books, which runs;

"Love is the life expression of God Himself, love is the coherent force which makes all things whole, ... and love is all that is."

Now, all my ideals as to the nature of love, that it is the basic essence of life, were being sorely tested. I had for some time held that love, of whatever degree, requires to be expressed otherwise its energies become congested. To withhold it from those who need it is in direct contravention to the very essence of love, which is to 'give', but where this lack of givingness' is motivated by one's own gain, is it therefore a subtle form of selfishness?

Whether my reasoning was valid or whether I was deluding myself, I was at pains to determine clearly. But it all became quite academic in the end.

One late evening whilst we were staying on the houseboat in Srinagar, we took a small boat out on the lake, it was the time of a full Moon which, reflecting romantically in the ripples of the lake, was a sight to behold and the sense of deep tranquility that was present was so overpowering that you felt that you could practically have embraced it. When we returned to the houseboat the inevitable happened.

Babaji was fully aware of this recent phase that had taken place in our relationship as he referred to it on more than one occasion, and not always that subtly either (unless we were receiving only the interpreter's version). Whether he condemned or condoned it, or even sympathised, I was never able to ascertain, but his attitude towards me certainly never altered. He was still as generous with his gifts as ever. He was good enough to arrange for Sue and I to visit various cities in and around the province, providing food and accommodation free from his various followers wherever we went. It was really like a paid touring holiday for us, seeing the sights of Agra, Bareilly, Banaras, Lucknow, Haldwani, Allahabad, Ranikhet, etc., and staying in some of these places for weeks on end - and without it costing us a cent! He just couldn't do enough for us.

Sue had originally planned to return to England about three weeks after her arrival in India, but as so much was happening, she kept extending her stay week by week, eking out her money when and where she could, finally deciding to get back home by Christmas of '62. As for my reserves, they had all but vanished, including that which I had sent to me from home and my return fare which I had broken into long ago - on Babaji's encouragement that we should enjoy ourselves together. Come Christmas, Sue's intended return never happened, nor did it for some months after; due to Babaji's generosity we were still doing the rounds, using Nainital as our base from which we did our various explorations.

It must have been around the late spring of 1963 when Babaji broached the subject as to whether I would like to return to England with Sue. I was not overly enthusiastic about the idea, I had no money to go back to England with, nor did I feel that I had fulfilled the purpose in India that I would have liked. On the other hand, I was rather homesick and a bit weary of my disappointments, and in a way, the idea of returning home had its attraction for me. After much serious thought, I had come to accept the fact that I would go back. On Babaji's instructions, one of his followers offered me the money for my return fare which he said I should accept as a contribution from 'above', and that money should not be an obstacle to this way of life.

So, resigning myself to the fact, Sue and I prepared for our trip home. We booked ourselves a steamship passage from Bombay to Tilbury and I then wrote to my brother of our impending return. I sold my typewriter, telescope and watch and purchased the necessary trunks and packing cases that would accommodate all the books that I had accumulated (my personal belongings were practically nil) and we bought a few trinkets as gifts for members of our families.

The farewell meeting with Babaji and his faithful followers was a very emotional affair, and the amount of gifts bestowed on me in token of their feelings towards me was very touching indeed, to say the least. Whatever impression of me Babaji had conveyed to all his devotees throughout the region since I had been connected with him must have been very favourable for them to have responded so.

We finally took out leave from Babaji and his group, very reluctantly on my part, and made our way to the Bombay docks. I visited the barber shop to become separated from my scalp and facial hair, an operation which had not taken place for over two years! Sue had her hair done and we had our photograph taken together. The departure went according to plan and the boat sailed on the midnight tide - I was on my way home at last.

Yet somehow, as we drew away from the shores of India, I felt a deep heaviness in my heart.

Believe it or not, I really had a great love for the country. I had been so saddened by the squalor, dirt, poverty, and primitiveness in which its peoples lived and which was so evident, no matter where I went. Yet the sense of spirituality which seems to permeate the psyche of the country was everywhere to be found, if one had the sensitivity to detect it through the outer materialistic veneer.

For me it had been a country of vast extremes; I had stayed in the best of hotels and had eaten from and slept on the dirtiest of floors in squalid little vermin-ridden mud huts; I had been snowed under until I was stiff with cold and had been smitten by sunstroke at a temperature of over 125 degrees in the shade; I had been stifled by the overwhelming humidity of the rainy season and had been almost breathless through the lack of air at heights of over 14,000 feet; I had been absolutely entranced by the magnificent expansiveness of the Himalayan Peaks and had been as depressed as hell imprisoned in a small, empty, white-washed walled enclosure for months on end; I had been full of energy and brimming over with radiant health and had been in intense pain with a fever of over 105 degrees; I had travelled in the most luxurious of cars through spotless streets of its modern cities and have had to walk bare-footed through the roughest of territory until the blisters on my feet were over an inch in diameter; I had spent months alone without seeing or speaking to a soul and had been squashed by mobs of people in the dangerously overcrowded 3rd class trains and buses; I have had the stimulating companionship and bountiful generosity of many of India's holy men and had been conned by the cunning practices of some of their devious traders; I have had the joy of seeing the majesty of trained elephants and other such beasts cooperating with men in their work and their colourful celebrations and have had the stark fear of being bitten by the many poisonous snakes, scorpions, spiders, etc., which abound in every crack and crevice.

I had come across men who had withered limbs and mutilated bodies through mis-guided so-called Yoga practices, Fakirs who performed magic tricks, who lie on beds of sharp nails and walk on red-hot coals, sword swallowers and snake charmers, and the pathetic beggars who cut off their limbs to enable them to extract more money from sympathetic tourists; these as well as many others with horribly twisted and deformed bodies, such as incurable lepers, many of whom overtly use their infirmity for financial gain. There are those types who would slit your throat for a few annas, then there are the many Saints of much learning and wisdom who guide and work to alleviate the many worldly troubles and suffering that afflict their people, men of great compassion and kindness who have abandoned their worldly pleasures for the sake of helping humanity.

I had seen highly fertile areas with an abundance of fruit trees, an apparently never-ending harvest of rice, sugar cane, bananas, etc., that grow so prodigiously that they sold for less than a halfpenny each, and sweetcorn that would cost anywhere between two and three shillings each in England at that time could be purchased there in the streets, freshly roasted and salted, with lemon and butter for under one penny. In addition there was the copious produce taken from the mango and coconut groves. Yet in stark contrast there were vast red desert-like areas where nothing seems to grow at all, where I gather famine is rife and water is as precious as diamonds.

It is a land that harbours all the pairs of opposites one can imagine, from princely to poverty, pollution to purity, petty to profound, purgatory to paradise - what more of a mixture of hell and heaven could there be?

In spite of all this, in an inexplicable sort of way, I had acquired an affection for the country and was rather melancholy that I was now saying farewell, not knowing when I would return - or even if!

Although I was now at last on my journey home, and very happy about it, what of the future? I had no money, no means of earning any (I hadn't touched or seen a clarinet for over two and a half years), no prospects, and no idea how I would continue in my spiritual quest.

So once again I was heading into an unknown future, and once again another episode of my life had come to a close.

EPISODE THREE

CHAPTER 10 - HOMECOMING

1963-66 - Approaching my Forties

The weeks that Sue and I spent on the return trip home proved rather troublesome as the basic incompatibility between us, which was the cause of our drifting apart before I left home in 1960, was again making itself strongly felt and had in fact surfaced a few weeks after her arrival in India, disrupting the atmosphere which was so conducive to my being there in the first place. It became so serious that, by the time we arrived in England, I felt quite determined to end our relationship. How come the deep feelings that I had for her just those few months ago could have turned so sour in such a short time? What sort of love was there between us which must have been so vulnerable that it had withered that easily?

I knew that it was not uncommon for couples to be madly in love at one stage in their relationship, even to tie the nuptial knot and vow to love each other forever and never to part, etc., and yet to be at each other's throats with a rage and vindictiveness bordering on hatred at another stage of their relationship. Is it not possible for two sensible people to keep that original love alive, that it may sustain them through the inevitable difficult periods? I certainly would not want to encourage an affair which had the seeds of such serious dissent as was then beginning to appear once more between Sue and I.

It all cast an unpleasant shadow on the enjoyment of the sea voyage, which in itself could have served as a holiday. The boat stopped off at Aden and Suez and, for the added pleasure of his passengers, the Captain, who was a friendly cove, took us for a trip up the Bosphorus to the mouth of the Black Sea, which was an interesting unscheduled addition. We then docked at Marseilles for a while before calling in to Barcelona as our last stop before reaching Tilbury - and then home.

My brother and his wife June, met us at the docks and, apart from being held up at the British Customs, who went through every inch of my luggage only to find stacks of inoffensive books and papers on abstruse subjects, the homecoming was a joyous one. Sue and I settled in for a short while in my old room at our family home, which I always felt was my prerogative, but as my brother and his ever swelling wife (the baby was due shortly) were using the house as their home, I began to feel our presence there was becoming an intrusion, so I therefore had to rapidly consider alternative accommodation.

My position now was not an enviable one: I was not only without money, without a job, without any future prospects, but I had now nowhere to live, the Farm being still occupied by our friendly but non-paying tenants. It was then timely I thought to make the agreed break with Sue, whose elderly father had become ill and she was required to return home.

With the last scrapings of my bank resources (apart from that which was put aside for the Farm mortgage payments and which I definitely refused to touch), I arranged to take a furnished bed-sit in the East End of London.

Sue and I had a long and soul-searching discussion as to how we could sort out our personality differences: she professed a deep love for me and that she would never want to be without me, and I too had very strong feelings for her, which I had made no effort to conceal. So in spite of my previous resolves, we agreed that we should have another try and that we should move in together into this furnished bed-sit that I had paid a deposit on.

It was not the most salubrious of lodgings, having to share bathroom, kitchen, and all facilities with others who were not as hygienic and congenial as we would have wished. Nor were the general living conditions much to our liking either, even though the rent I had to pay was quite excessive, far more than I was charging the tenants for the whole of my Farmhouse and grounds - and not getting.

After spending a short time together in these not-very-agreeable East End digs, and with funds again fast seeping away, I had thought of trying to convert one of the old barns at the Farm for us to live in. It was a good idea at the time (as they say), but it didn't turn out to be wholly successful, I decided to make some alterations to the house by portioning off the rear extension area, which was not being used, and adapting it to provide a separate flatlet, leaving the main part of the house for the family who were renting the place - without paying! They were way behind in their rent even though they were both working and I was sure that they could afford to pay me, but as they had four children and nowhere else to go, I really had no choice but to let them remain, which I did, although on the understanding that they would catch up on their arrears within a specified time - and I was now on the spot to see that they kept to it.

But did they? Not on your Nelly!

They eventually moved out with many empty promises of paying off their debt as soon as they got themselves settled again, etc., but nothing was ever forthcoming.

Sue and I then moved into the main part of the house, leaving the flatlet available to let. This proved easier than I thought as there was an immediate response to my local advert and within a week the flat was occupied, and providing us at least with some sort of an income which, although small, was adequate to keep us supplied with basics in eatables. Also being by then the height of the Summer, I was able to let out some of my land for grazing which not only supplemented our income but enabled us to save up for an old motor car.

The financial problems my sister and her family had with their retail business were reaching ruinous proportions. She was in deep debt owing to a major and prolonged slump in the trade, her husband had fallen ill and had to go into hospital and, as much as she tried, she couldn't sell the shop with its upstairs accommodation at a reasonable price which would allow her to purchase another property for housing her family. I came up with the idea, which I put to my brother, that if I could get a loan from our 'nice' bank manager to purchase a house in which my sister and her family could live and which also had a couple of extra rooms for letting, my sister could then sell her shop at a lower price than she had been asking, move on to this new property, and we'd have the rent from the extra rooms to help pay off the loan to the bank.

After doing our sums, my brother and I then put the proposition to our 'nice' bank manager.

On the strength of my previous professional reputation, with the Farm as collateral, and the fact that I had proved a reliable payer for the Farm mortgage, I was able to borrow a large enough loan from the bank. In addition, with the long-standing reliable reputation we had regarding the family watch repair business, we both, as a joint venture, purchased a largish house in the London suburb near to where we had previously lived.

After making the necessary alterations to the property, my sister and her family moved in, we let the spare rooms as bed-sits, and we were able to more than adequately meet the mortgage payments from the income - with a little left over for our pockets. So we were not only helping our sister out but I had an added amount of cash on which to live.

I was not exactly back on the road to prosperity, but now, within a year of my return to England I had become solvent again, living in my own home, able to eat more regularly, able to support Sue, able to run a little car (we had managed to purchase an old Morris Minor convertible for a few pounds), and able to be classed as a 'Property Owner'. Having this little run-about of a car enabled us to get around more and particularly to take trips into London to attend group meetings on philosophical subjects.

However, I realised I was now being sucked back into the flow of everyday living again, and it wasn't much to my liking. The thing that struck me quite forcibly was the obvious difference in the values which I held and those of the majority of people that I came across. They seemed to place so much importance on issues which I had come to consider of little significance in life. So many seemed to be living on life's surface, wholly centred around their own concerns, which invariably seemed to me to be quite petty and often to the detriment of others. Was there any justification in these observations of mine? Was I becoming a bit out of touch with the world as it was?

For years I had been trying to cultivate the qualities of harmlessness, goodwill, a sense of love and harmony in all my relationships, especially those which involved myself, but I suppose, being away from society for so long, I assumed, albeit somewhat misguidedly, that acquiring such qualities was the aim of others also.

This was obviously not always the case. There was a glaring need in my eyes for people to understand themselves better, to appreciate why there's so much dissension in the world, and how they could intelligently work to resolve and even prevent such problems. In my naivety I was to find how prevalent was this lack of concern towards encouraging harmonious relationships, even among the participants of some of the small group study meetings we were now beginning to attend - who, I thought, of all people, should know better. I obviously had a lot of readjusting to do.

Someone Sue and I had been chatting to at the end of a public lecture one evening mentioned that they knew Cyril Scott personally and, in acknowledgement of our enthusiastic response, said that if we were that keen to meet him, they could arrange an invitation for us to attend a dinner where Cyril Scott would be speaking . . . . . Wow! Not 'arf'!

It was at this dinner that we then had the opportunity to meet this great man, the author whose works on Diet Reform and Modern Occult Philosophy we both so much admired. After a friendly little chat together, he invited us to pay him a visit at his home in Eastbourne, to have tea with him and Marjorie (Harston-Scott) and to discuss some of the ideas he had written about.

What a charming man he turned out to be. Not only was he an author of deep and original philosophical substance but also a pianist and an innovative classical composer of renown. What a thrill for Sue and I.

During our time with him and Marjorie, he mentioned that there were some friends of his who lived just outside Tunbridge Wells who occasionally ran small group meetings which we might find of interest. He then gave us the address of Nancy Magor and Michael Eastcott of "Sundial House" and suggested that we pop in and see them on our way back to London, which we did.

We arrived at 'Sundial House', a large detached property bordering on an expanse of local farmland, and were warmly greeted by Nancy and Michael who invited us to join them for tea in their large attractive garden. They were very much followers of the type of philosophy which Sue and I were attracted to and apparently ran a series of meetings on various topics connected with it. Before departing, they invited us to attend their next gathering which was their annual summer conference, consisting of a fortnight's series of talks, meetings, and meditation sessions. Of course, we jumped at the chance.

It was during this summer conference that we made many interesting contacts, one of the most important being Dr. Roberto Assagioli (Dr. Sag / the Doc) a professional psychologist and a student of the famous Carl Jung, who not only was the founder of the innovative psychological system which he labelled "Psychosynthesis" and was the principal of the institute of the same name, in addition to being the author of a host of books and professional papers on that subject, but of greater significance to me, he was also an associate of Alice A. Bailey, an author whose profound writings were a great source of inspiration for me and were to continue to be throughout the following years of my life.

He lived in Florence, Italy, and was only in England for that fortnight to give a series of talks during the conference, he was also kind enough to chat to Sue and I privately on a few occasions as well. He had a vast store of knowledge and a very clear and agile mind, in spite of being nigh into his 80s at the time and rather deaf, and although he was an Italian his command of the English language was impeccable. We also made many other helpful contacts during that fortnight conference and, on the suggestion of Dr. Assagioli, in cooperation with others there, we subsequently started a young people's group in London to study Psychosythesis.

In addition Sue and I became involved in various other groups such as the Young Quakers, Young Theosophists, Anthroposophical Study Groups, etc. where we got to meet many other people with similar inclinations, although unfortunately, not the same philosophical approach. Still, as always, each to their own.

We had arranged to meet Dr. Assagioli again by attending his Psychosynthesis Conference in Switzerland the following Summer of 1965. In the meantime, we continued doing the rounds of the study groups, attending various meetings, lectures, and courses, not to mention the residential conferences we frequented at places like Tekles Park, in Surrey, Attingham Park, in Shropshire, and similar venues.

We started running small study and meditation groups of our own which provided an opportunity for me to discuss the particular philosophy that I had been studying for many years. It included a series of concepts which, at that time were not that widely appreciated. So for the most of those involved with these groups I was practically treading virgin ground and, I gather, it proved very helpful to many.

Although I had been meaning to keep a diary relating to these group activities and my experiences in these fields for some time, I never really got 'round' to it until we met Dr. Douglas Baker in the Summer of '65, when he was lecturing at a conference in London. As he was expounding certain concepts which were very similar to those we held, we made it our business to make his acquaintance. We often visited him after that at his North London flat, where on one occasion he showed us a few pages of his personal diary.

From the nature of some of the entries in this diary, he appeared to have certain psychic abilities, some of which he described quite graphically in these pages, and which I found exceedingly fascinating. He stressed how important it had been for him to keep a diary of his spiritual progress and he would always encourage others to do the same. Was that a little prod for me?

As much as I have always tried to steer clear of any type of writing work, I seemed to be constantly faced with a need to use such a medium in whatever work it seemed there was for me to do - and here it was again! It must be something to do with my Karma.

So, once again, overcoming my aversion for literary composition, I started my diary which, I must add, has proved to be of great help, not only in providing me with a means of recording my trend of thinking and my changes in attitude over the years, but also enabled me to detect some form of pattern to my life - as well as comprising a helpful reference work for compiling a section of this present effort!

Another person we admired and had the good fortune to become friends with at that time was Clara Codd, an authoress and lecturer of high Theosophical standing. She must have been in her seventies at the time and lived at Tekels Park with her sisters; it was a great delight when we visited her for tea or dinner to be served by her and her sisters in the old Victorian way, with exquisitely prepared fare served on delicate bone china, as was their custom.

We were also fortunate enough to make the acquaintance of Sir George Trevelyan, who ran the Wrekin Trust, which did such fine work in catering for those interested in genuine New Age subjects and the promulgation of altruistic ideas. We were able to work with him on various projects which we saw as being vital pioneering work in that field.

August and September (of '65) we took ourselves off to the Continent, first to spend a couple of weeks in France at a camp site for an international gathering of the Young Theosophists, then on to Switzerland, to Ville nouvelle, to attend Dr. Sag's (Assogioli) Psychosynthesis Conference. We stayed on with the Doc for a week or so after the conference for the small group meditation and study work which he supervised, all of which we found very stimulating.

On our return we were all fired up and raring to continue with the assorted groups with which we were then involved.

So that was the general trend of our life for that period, attending study, meditation, and discussion groups, as well as lectures, meetings, and conferences, running our own groups, etc., and generally establishing ourselves with our acquaintances as keen adherents of such subjects.

The lectures, meetings, and conferences, were, on the whole, centred round one or a series of speakers who presented ideas on a relevant subject and then threw open the remaining time to their audience for questions. This seemed to work quite well except for the more reticent types like myself, who felt restricted when wishing to inquire further. Nevertheless, the atmosphere created at these get-togethers was often very conducive for renewing or making new contacts.

By contrast, the small groups which we were involved with were much more personal in nature, enabling each member to relate more easily to the others. Yet, in spite of their obvious advantages, they also had their down side which effected their efficiency as vehicles for progress.

The discussion groups generally consisted of one or more of the members putting forward their ideas on a theme and the others duly responding to them. Sometimes there was someone who took charge of the proceedings, but whether there was or not, invariably tension was the outcome when opinions were forcibly imposed. It was an eye-opener to me how the balance of a group could be so easily disrupted by one unsuitable person.

The study groups, on the other hand, were usually based upon some written work, invariably drawn from an author connected with a particular organisation, society, or school of thought, whose statements were discussed and either dissected, criticised, supported, or merely just acknowledged, through a group exchange. This again pro-vided fertile ground for wayward arguments if allowed to get out of hand, which often happened if there was no one present with a strong enough personality to maintain a semblance of order.

The groups who got together for meditation work were generally less particularised in their procedure, this was because there are so many differing types of meditation methods, it depended very much upon which one the majority of the group members had assembled for.

Most of the personnel of these groups continually fluctuated in numbers, people coming for a while then leaving, possibly due to the subject matter proving unsuitable to them or that more dominant members often tended to override the others, no matter what the chosen subject matter. The smooth working of a group, I found, was where the members had a common purpose and were able harmoniously to adhere to that purpose without constantly digressing, as was so easily done with the above type groups.

We kept our involvement in each of these groups completely separate and it was intriguing to see that, although each had their own group individuality, so to speak, there were many characteristics which they appeared to have in common, such as flitting from one subject to another week after week, or after taking a vote on the preferred subject matter or procedure when agreed and adopted, many who were originally in favour never turned up any more.

As ear-bending was never a prominent trait of mine, with most of these groups I was often partly an onlooker, making my presence known only occasionally when I felt it would be helpful or necessary to do so. My reticence was due not only to my inherent reserve in such situations and my inclination not to unduly impose my ideas on others (although I made them known when I thought appropriate), but also because of my interest in the way certain participants handled situations and their apparent reluctance to avoid any possible conflict. I found observing in itself an important study of human nature . . Sue adequately made up for my reticence, being far more outspoken than I at these sessions.

We continued to attend such meetings on and off for some years, not only because we were naturally interested in the subjects dealt with, but also to help support their efforts and to keep the numbers up, because most of those we met were genuinely searching for some better understanding and way of life, even though few really seemed to be on our particular wavelength.

The groups that I ran enabled me to use a different approach. The primary purpose in our coming together was either to study a specific yet relevant pre-selected topic, be it the basic principles of Psychosynthesis, using the writings of Dr. Sag, or some aspect of the philosophy or meditation method with which I was familiar, or topics selected from the works of certain source authors, such as, H.P. Blavatsky, Annie Besant, C.W. Leadbeater, Alice A. Bailey, Cyril Scott, etc.

This encouraged us to maintain a mental focus which helped minimise disagreements and the intrusion of extraneous digressions. This also proved to be a more useful way to keep the group together and on an even keel, as well as to increase our understanding of the subject chosen. In a way, this also enabled the group to be self-selective, as those whose interests were not compatible with the predetermined group study work naturally moved on to other fields more suited to their aims, leaving our group much freer to pursue its specialised topics.

In a similar way to the other groups, each of the groups which I ran were normally kept separate from the others, mainly because each was concentrating on a different aspect of the philosophy, which helped keep the study work contained. No group was ever meant to include more than seven members and this enabled them to be more friendly and easier to work with.

We made a point of meeting regularly one evening a week (which when running, say, four groups, meant four evenings out for Sue and I) in a room provided by one of the members. We would use as a theme for study something taken from literature which was considered as originating from a high source, and which I had previously found helpful for myself.

Sandwiched between each evening's study work were two periods set aside for a meditation, one to start the meeting and the other to close it, the theme of each meditation being synchronised to the particular astrological phase through which the planet was then passing. After the closing meditation we had refreshments and a little socialising. A similar pattern was employed when we had the occasional meeting at the Farm, but these were usually extended into whole day affairs.

The subject matter chosen for study would generally be one which the majority of each particular group felt suited to their interests, and of which I had a smattering of knowledge so that I could help guide the line of study.

For instance, if the subject preferred was, say, Evolution, I would recommend and use some study material that dealt with the various facets of that subject, such as: the formation, development, and destiny of the Planetary Kingdoms; man's place in the scheme of things; the various human races and the phases through which they have passed, and how man has reached his present point of development; that we are now entering an age where man's progress may be vastly accelerated, etc. These facets were approached not so much from the angle of academic science, although that was naturally taken into account, but more from the occult scientist's point of view.

Among other subjects used for study were; Reincarnation, which dealt with man's cyclic return to earth, the pre-birth and after death states; an analysis of subtle existence including his emotional and mental life; the reality and role of his higher self, or Soul (which all possess); the workings of the Law of Consequences (or Karma, as it is sometimes referred to); the means of release from this continual re-embodiment process, and so forth.

Then there was the very relevant issue of Discipleship, which proposes that we are all on earth to learn certain lessons which, when successful, will enable us not only to handle and govern our lives more efficiently, but to become more effective in helping others; here emphasis is laid on the development and control of our mind and emotions and the acquisition of such personal attributes as understanding, compassion, integrity, peace, patience, tolerance, and other virtuous characteristics, as well as how these can be more easily attained through specifically applied disciplines, and further enhanced through group effort.

Then again there were those who wished to study the Energy aspect of life, which covers the fundamentals of universal substance, visible and invisible; that all which exists is, in essence, a form of energy and how the various streams of this energy influence the life and make up of the whole Cosmos, from an atom, to man, and to the Solar System, and when wielded correctly can be used to create, to help, and to heal.

It is not difficult to appreciate that each of these subjects, and the many others, have vast implications and would need lifetimes of study to master properly, but as it is, there exists more than enough information to keep us going - for this lifetime anyway.

It might well be asked that if such things are so, where does all this information come from and how would one know if it was true or not?

If one can accept the premise that there exists much more to life than we at present are generally aware of, it might be more acceptable to appreciate that, without stretching the questioner's credulity too far, much of the knowledge studied is drawn from results of research undertaken by certain investigators gifted with extra-sensory abilities (which apparently we all have in potential), and who, working through a system of group exchange, have been able to check and cross check their findings and thus verify the reliability of their information. In addition, those great sages who have learned life's lessons and have passed on to the higher stages of human development, have dedicated their lives to helping others, and possess this vast knowledge which they make available to those people who have developed the necessary intuitive sensitivity, have also confirmed such findings.

These days the study of such subjects would not seem so outrageous to the public mind as they did in the 50s and 60s, and those interested in studying them would necessarily have needed to have been of a certain type with a special leaning towards such subjects, as I obviously was. For most of us involved in the type of groups I had started to run, such study was found very rewarding and the format adopted seemed to be successful for our purposes.

However, it was slowly dawning on me that, although each of these groups was specialising in a particular aspect of the philosophy, and therefore working mainly with literature that dealt with that aspect, there was a need eventually to synthesise all aspects. After all, if it was really a comprehensive philosophy, originating from the source of all wisdom, as I had always believed it to be, then it should be able to be presented in that context without being slanted towards any special school of thought or associated with any particular 'isms'.

There were many books written over the past century or more, specialising in various facets of the subject, some of them quite deep, which in themselves, I found extremely engrossing and ideal for concentrated advanced group study, but, as an understanding of each aspect requires some appreciation of the other related aspects, I felt

157

there should be some presentation available linking the most relevant aspects together. I wasn't aware of any work that addressed this requirement, that dealt with the salient concepts of the philosophy and their essential interrelation. This was continually brought home to me when queries arose during our study of one aspect which could far more easily be dealt with by a knowledge of others.

What I felt was needed was a summary of a selection of the philosophy which would give an overall picture and would also help students decide which particular aspect they wished to work on.

I was well aware that to produce such a summary would entail quite a lot of work and would be far beyond the scope of someone like myself, who was still comparatively only scratching the surface: it would really require a dedicated group of students to tackle such a project.

What I felt could be within my scope was the gathering together of a few people I knew who had an understanding of the various topics and were interested enough, as a team effort, to compile such a summary, relating each of the dominant aspects of the philosophy in such a way that would not only help put them all more in perspective, but would act as an introductory offering for those less familiar with the concepts. Once a preliminary understanding was acquired, through the study of such a compilation, prospective students would be able to delve deeper into their chosen field, and then together, possibly collate all the results of their findings for the future use of others.

It may have been a bit ambitious but not altogether an impossible task. It also had the advantage of enabling us to learn to work together and, as a group, to develop those higher values which such a philosophy advocated.

A compilation of this nature would certainly help meet a need, and we wouldn't be required to go into too much detail with it at first. If I attempted to organise such a project, I would need first to present the idea in an understandable form to all those I thought might be interested and available. But then, wouldn't that entail more written work? Well, I thought, if that was the case, maybe I'd consider it - at some future date.

In the meantime I suppose I could at least jot down a framework of what I thought would be needed, even if it was only for my future reference. So, once again, tentatively putting pen to paper, I made some notes on what I thought might be required which would help clarify my thoughts. I mention all this not only to give an idea of the way I was thinking in those days, although somewhat idealistically at the time, but because it has a bearing on a future project which I launched.

I made a point of speaking of this idea to Dr. Sag when we met him again at Sundial House in August of '66. He was not backward in encouraging me to attempt such a project, seeing as Sue and I had been working with groups and were more able to assess what was required. But, as much as I respected his opinion, even his encouragement was not a sufficient kick up the rear to get me to start such an undertaking.

Our work with our own groups became very satisfying in as much as people seemed to be gaining something helpful from them, not only in acquiring knowledge and, I hope, an elevated sense of values, but we were able to bring those who had similar interests in touch with each other, which always adds help and support to one's efforts. For myself, it was to my utter delight that I could be so involved with such philosophical matters - and with people of like mind.

The big fly in the ointment throughout this whole period was that the trouble between Sue and I was becoming impossible to resolve. It was a sheer case of a conflict of personalities which, as neither of us were capable of handling, dragged on through the years. It all seemed to come to a head toward the end of 1966 when I discovered that she had recently been with other men during the times when she had stayed out overnight. That did it! We finally decided that it would be best all round if we parted. I had asked her to leave on occasions but my attachment was such that she stayed against my better judgement and had then taken advantage.

It had always been a stormy relationship ever since we left India, but now it was far too damaging to both of us for it to continue. Here was I advocating such high-minded qualities as tolerance, understanding, love, and harmonious relationships, yet as much as I tried to apply them to my own affairs I wasn't successful.

In the early part of '67, as we both respected his opinion, we wrote to Dr. Sag and explained our problem, how serious it had become, that it seemed insoluble without us breaking up, and asking if he could give us the benefit of his advice. After a couple of exchanges of letters, it was agreed that Sue should go out to Italy and stay there with him for a while.

I had become so involved with her over the years, sharing my whole life in all its intimate details with her, and in spite of our extreme incompatibility and the constant state of conflict that existed when we were together, it literally tore me apart to be without her. My whole world had fallen apart.

For months after I couldn't think straight, I couldn't sleep, I hardly ate anything, I seldom left the Farm, and only for bare essentials, I pulled out of all my activities, including my groups, and withdrew into my shell at the Farm, alone, confused, depressed, and utterly heartbroken.

Little did I realise that it would take many years before I could regain some semblance of stability in my life.

. . . .'twas over thus.

CHAPTER 11 - TO ITALY AND BACK

1967 - My Early Forties

In trying to make an effort to shake off the intense loneliness that now engulfed me, I thought it would be a more positive move for me if I could concentrate, as best I could, on putting the group research project I had considered into operation. If I could establish some regular meetings for the proposed group research, it might give me some incentive to rouse myself a bit and help alleviate the slough of despondency I was wallowing in. But as fate would have it, those whom I contacted to help me get the project off the ground, though all seemingly keen on such an idea, for one reason or another, were not available to involve themselves at that time - or so they said.

Well, I thought, maybe I'll try another tack. As most of the literature which we studied as a group presupposed certain elementary concepts, which I invariably was asked to enlarge upon, I'll draft a series of papers myself which, as ill equipped as I felt I was for such a task, could be used to present the fundamentals of the philosophy to others less familiar with it than I - and I could offer the use of the Farm as a base for its study. I knew it would mean having to get down to writing again but I was desperate to occupy myself and thought that tackling it in this way, I would not only be able to start on my project but have people coming to the Farm as well, which may have been part of my motivation.

But before I was able to put such a course of action into operation, another set of events unfolded.

It seemed that every letter that I wrote to Sue in the weeks after she left was filled with deep remorse, and her short and sparse replies only accentuated my state of solitude and self-pity. I asked her if she would mention to Dr. Sag how intensely I had been affected by the whole affair and would it be possible for me to come to Italy for a week or two to see him?

I eventually had a reply from her saying that, yes, he would see me but she wouldn't be there as she was going to stay with a fellow in Switzerland whose house we had both stayed in a couple of years previously. He was a bachelor, living alone, and he never tried to hide the fact that he was attracted to her - and now to be told by her that she was going there to stay with him certainly didn't make me feel better.

A date was set in early April of '67 for me to make the journey to see Dr. Sag. After some days of frantic scurrying around to purchase my rail and boat tickets, plus all necessities for the trip, and to bid farewell to family and friends, I locked up the Farm and took myself off to Florence, Italy, not knowing exactly what to expect or how many days, or possibly weeks, I would be allowed to stay with the Doc. I knew he was a man of much experience and with his knowledge of Psychosynthesis and the Ageless Wisdom, I was sure I could benefit greatly by being with him, no matter how long or short a time, even if nothing really came of it, it would at least provide some sort of diversion for me.

Before leaving, I had purchased a small tape-recorder which, I thought might come in useful if there was anything particularly profound and relevant that the Doc might have to say and I would want to keep for posterity. A 'small tape-recorder' in those days consisted of a box-like unit about the size and weight of an economy-sized cornflake carton - filled with lead. The recording medium for this particular machine were 3" reel-to-reel tapes (audio cassettes, I gather, were yet to be invented), a goodly number of which I armed myself with before setting off.

After a wearisome three day journey, I arrived in Florence at Dr. Sag's residence, dirty, tired, and hungry, only to find that my poor host was unwell and confined to bed and therefore unable to see anyone. Eda Pallombi, his efficient secretary, helped me settle into a room allotted to me in a building adjacent to his residence, which also housed his offices. After a bath, a little grub, and a short nap, I was feeling much better and more able to discuss with Eda the general layout of the area and how I should go about getting in stocks of food (I was required to cater for myself) and any other items I might require.

There was no word from Sue when I arrived, as I would have dearly hoped, nor did I hear from the Doc for the first couple of days until one evening he invited me into his bedroom for a preliminary chat. He said he was feeling much better and that as soon as he was up and about, possibly in a day or two, we could start our work together . . . . . what on earth was that supposed to mean?

It wasn't long before I found out - to my cost!

In spite of his age and frail health and being extremely deaf, he put in a good ten hours a day of solid work, as a practicing psychologist, presiding over the activities of his Institute of Psychosynthesis, organising conferences, lecturing, writing books and articles, he also ran study and meditation groups, in addition to fitting in private one-to-one sessions with people like myself who were eager to explore the more esoteric side of the Ageless Wisdom, his knowledge and experience I recognised as being far in excess of mine.

After a day or two of periodically chatting to him about my present situation, general background, interests, my work with groups, aspirations, and intentions, as well as my relationship with Sue, a pattern in our association began to take shape. The typical routine which we settled on, and followed throughout much of my stay with him , was we would get together most mornings and afternoons for about an hour where he would view and help me interpret the free-drawing work which he recommended I should carry out at least twice a day (a very potent Psychosynthesis technique), discuss the causes, and the possible solution, to some of the numerous problems that effect so many people (being a professional psychologist, this seemed a major interest of his), expound upon certain facets of the philosophy (which was the major interest of mine), and generally give me the benefit of his knowledge and experience. His manner was always very courteous and his desire to be of help very evident, not so much from a fatherly standpoint, but as a genuinely interested and supportive friend and confidant.

Dr. Roberto Assagioli

At his request, I recorded most of our discussions which I would then transcribe so that I could build up a record of much that went on between us for future reference (of course, that meant more writing for me).

In addition, he would ask me to check over some of his notes he had prepared for his forthcoming lectures, to write down my comments on them as well as my response to some of the points he had made and then make suggestions for improvements, (even more writing!)

He would also recommend passages from certain books, and even whole books, for me to study, as well as some of his own essays on specific, relevant subjects, requesting once again that I duly take notes on them and include my considered comments, (and yet still more writing!).

Also, knowing that I had knowledge of the philosophy, he'd ask me to give him my written interpretation of, and even expand upon, some of the topics he had touched on in his essays and lectures, etc., with a view, with my permission to include them in some of his work etc., which he would acknowledge, (if he was intent to force me to overcome my aversion to writing - he failed abysmally!).

And on top of all that, most lunchtimes, and some evenings, he would hold group meditations, to which I was invited, sometimes they turned out to be fairly long ones too. What other activities he was engaged in he never actually vouchsafed to me, but there were certain little indications which he occasionally let slip. But however he

162

occupied himself each day, for me it was all go, I was lucky if I could squeeze in time to prepare and eat the food I had stocked up on! As for writing the occasional letter home in answer to those I had received, that was practically out of the question. Well, if it was a diversion I was looking for, I had certainly found it in Dr. Sag!

After about the first three weeks or so, we had a little 'how-are-we-doing?' conversation; was I was happy with the way things were going? was I coping with the work he'd given me? could I handle any more? would I like to ease off a bit? would I rather try a different approach? and so on.

I replied to the effect that, from my side, I would like to take as much advantage of his knowledge and experience as possible, if he found that acceptable, I would be open to suggestions if he thought we could work in a more productive manner. Otherwise, if he was agreeable, I would be more than happy for things to continue as they were. . . . like a lamb to the slaughter!

He said in view of his age and state of health and the demands on his time and energy, he too would like me to take as much advantage of him as I could and that he found my efforts very helpful to him and, therefore, he couldn't see any reason why we shouldn't continue going on as we were for the time being. Of course, this brought up the subject of how much longer he wanted me to stay.

I had no need to emphasise my keenness to learn, I had already made that quite clear, but I did let him know that there were certain commitments in England which I had to attend to. When I explained to him what they were, I was surprised how much I had become entrapped in the whirlpool of such worldly liabilities, something which I had made a special resolve to avoid.

I include my remarks to the Doc on this issue because it is so relevant to my intentions to be as free an agent as I was able, and not to be too restricted in pursuing my primary aims, which were of course of a spiritual nature.

"I have two main commitments in England, one being a house in the suburb of London of which I am half owner, . . . this is divided into bed-sitting rooms that we let out and it's my province to make sure all is running well, to collect the rents each week from the tenants and do the few handy-man's jobs around the house. . . . . I had a letter from my brother last week and he tells me that the rooms are vacant now and tenants have to be found. This is also my province and one of the most necessary and time-consuming of them all. My other main commitment is my Farm, in which a flat is let. The grounds around the Farmhouse take a lot of keeping in order and it was this that occupied most of Sue's and my outdoor life and, strictly speaking, this should not be left too long.

"Sue also has a property near the Farm which is let and when she left I said I'd see to it while I was around, but now I'm not able to, I still feel that it's part of my duty to make sure all is right there for her, as she has very little mind for those sort of things. I understand that her tenants are planning to leave soon, so that would mean having to replace them . . . . so although there are demands on me that I should eventually try to satisfy, not one of them do I consider really urgent."

In response to this information, the Doc said that it was his intention to go to Tunbridge Wells again that August and if I so wished, I could stay on with him until then and accompany him to the Tunbridge Wells conference. Of course, to have the extra months in Florence was a big bonus for me considering I had only originally thought in terms of spending days or weeks with him, so I readily agreed to stay.

As to the question of money and being able to support myself while in Italy, he said that should present no problem as he would let me have any money that I felt was needed. As appreciated as such an offer was, I couldn't accept it without some agreement that I would repay him once home and was able to lay my hands on some cash. We settled on that arrangement because he said that he probably could do with the sterling whilst in England anyway. So, with such practicalities out of the way, I could look forward to an extended stay in Italy.

With the Doc's help I was able to explore the deeper levels of the Ageless Wisdom and we spent much time together in studying and discussing it - and the more I knew of it the more I became convinced of its truth and value.

I was also able to acquire a great knowledge of his system of Psychosynthesis, which seemed so much more comprehensive than other approaches to psychology that I had come across. It appealed to me in a similar way as did Nature Cure and Diet Reform about twenty years earlier; they both presented a revolutionary way of approach, because they both worked from principles of health rather than disease. With Nature Cure, the main emphasis was not the study of disease in its manifold forms and the treatment of its symptoms, as was common among conventional medical practitioners, but the study of health and the conditions needed to maintain it which, when once met, allowed the healing forces within the body freedom to bring about their own cure.

So it was with Psychosynthesis: it was not based on the study of mental and emotional disorders, fears and phobias, etc. from which few of us are really free, and their treatment through conventional psychoanalytical methods, but the study of the health psyche and conditions needed for its natural expression, with emphasis upon what an individual is capable of becoming. It recognises the higher potential within man and the ability he has to develop the qualities of love, understanding, selflessness, altruism, and to enhance that which is creative, beautiful, and positive in him. All a very different matter.

Briefly, Psychosynthesis postulates a multidimensional make-up of the human being, that the many facets of the personality are consistently vying for expression and are invariably in conflict one with the other. Yet, as a system, it extends beyond the limits of personal psychology by acknowledging the existence of a higher, deeper centre, within man, a highly developed and altruistic aspect which we all possess yet so far remain unaware of.

Through a series of selected techniques, one is able first to understand various facets of the personality and the level of consciousness from which they originate, either the lower unconsciousness, the middle unconsciousness, or the higher unconsciousness, then learn to control them and eventually to bring about a state of harmony between them. Once this is achieved then, as the primary aim, one would synthesise all these psychological elements and bring them under the direction of the higher centre which exists within man, thereby making that human being a totally integrated unit.

Of course, to help demonstrate these principles, the Doc worked some of his wiles on me, which I found very revealing as I was at that time undergoing an emotional crisis due to the upheaval with Sue. Apart from that, during my whole stay with him, the length of which he admitted was unusual for him, I not only confirmed much of which I had come to believe, but had the added advantage of his years of knowledge and experience in such matters.

It was all so engrossing for me that before I knew it, the middle of August had arrived and we had to prepare for our trip to England. I was deeply indebted to him for the privilege of being able to stay with him for all those months and to learn from him as I did - for which he asked nothing in return - for his time, energy, and his constant consideration and graciousness towards me, I could never adequately express my appreciation.

He ventured the opinion that, as I had had rather a long period of concentrating on strengthening the inner side of my life, with years of silence, study, meditation, and generally being withdrawn from the world, etc., it might be advisable to spend the forthcoming period utilising that which I had acquired innerly by developing various means of expressing it. Fair comment, I thought. Providing that I found it agreeable, he recommended that I carry on with my drawing work and writing (what what?), etc., yet in doing so, he stressed, not to neglect continuing to strengthen the more abstract side of my nature. Yes, I found it very agreeable.

As to my relationship with Sue, he suggested that I write and ask her if she would like to come to Florence to see me and have a word with the Doc again before we left and then maybe if she wished, we would all return to England together This, she said in her reply to my letter, she would dearly like to do and would come immediately. When she finally arrived in Florence a few days before we were due to leave, after not seeing her for over six months, and in spite of all my resolves to be more detached, I found myself attracted to her and falling in love with her again. (or more accurately, as a moth to a flame!). We both agreed to give our relationship another try in the hope that we could handle it in a more mature manner. But within a short time the same pattern started to repeat itself and I found it difficult to be with her. I became an observer of the situation and on Dr. Sag's advice delayed my decision until we reached England.

We left Italy as planned and it was my greatest pleasure, with the Doc being so frail hysically, that I could at least be of some practical assistance to him on our long journey by rail, sea, and road, to Sundial House in Tunbridge Wells. During the two weeks at Tunbridge Wells, the relationship with Sue deteriorated even more.

I managed to see the Doc a few times privately during and after the fortnight's conference, but when he returned to Florence and Sue and I to London, (I felt obliged to assist her regarding her back problem), I was not to see him again until the Tunbridge Wells conference the following year (1968). We kept in touch by letter (more writing), through which means I brought him up to date with my doings; that I had resumed my activities with various groups, and was continuing with my drawing work, and even doing some clay modelling. With regards to Sue and I, I explained that we both spent a few weeks together at the Farm after we came back from Italy, during which time she had gone down with backache and I had to look after her all the time. I didn't mind, of course, but it seems I couldn't get anything right. I put up with it being quite convinced that we couldn't be under the same roof for long. Once again we couldn't work things out amicably so, when she was back on her feet again, it was agreed that she return to her friend in Switzerland, which she had been intending to do anyway.

I suppose the most important development to write to the Doc about was my growing aspiration to create some form of spiritual centre, possibly using the Farm premises, where people interested in such subjects could come and spend a few hours or days either in study, meditation, or in some sort of spiritual group activity. In conjunction with this would be the compilation of the fundamentals of the philosophy, an idea with which I had been toying before I went to Florence.

Another item of interest during that year, which I mentioned in my letters to the Doc, was that whilst sorting out some things in the attic at the Farm, from amongst the chaotic wreckage that existed up there, I unearthed my clarinet which, I'm ashamed to admit I was remiss enough to put away eight years before without even an oiling, or coating it with any form of preservative. Being made from the root of a rare African Blackwood, it is always necessary to treat it with something to prevent it cracking, and this should be applied routinely, not only during normal use but especially so when put in store - and I, who had a first class instrument, should have known better.

After prising off all the verdigris from the body of the clarinet and thoroughly cleaning and lubricating all the woodwork, joints, and keywork, I inserted some old reeds I had dug out and endeavoured to get a semblance of noise out of the thing. Nothing really successful at first but with a few more tries over a period of about three or four weeks, clarinet-type sounds were beginning to emerge.

Encouraged by this, occasional practice periods followed which, after about five or ten minutes of effort at each sitting, left my lips feeling somewhat like raw steak. However, I persevered and, within a month or two, my lips were strengthening and my fingers were becoming supple enough for me to knock out something that could more easily have been mistaken for a musical sound - and it felt good!

I then contacted one or two of my old musician friends who suggested that I popped in to see them during their less formal sessions, and maybe sit in for a few numbers with them. This was a good way for me to ease myself back into the scene and to see if it appealed to me again. In doing so, I got to know more musicians, some who were not around during the 50s, and who invited me to various other places to play. I was soon spending two or three nights a week just doing the rounds sitting in, and all whom I met were very pleased and welcoming towards me.

On one of my forays around the London clubs, I popped in to see an old pianist chum of mine, Johnny Parker, who was playing at Ronnie Scott's old place. After I stepped up on the stand in response to Johnny's invitation to play a few numbers with his group, he enthusiastically presented me to his audience with a light-hearted yet complimentary build-up, then with a twinkle in his eye, he turned to me and asked, "Well, what is it going to be tonight, Cy, Ma Rainey or Ma harishi?"

A particular mention must be made of Max Collie, who, during this period, generously invited me to his band rehearsals which he held at his home in Bromley. He had come to England from Australia during my absence from the scene and was therefore one of the many current musicians who had not been around during the 50s period. He was now building his reputation as a band leader and trombonist, regularly rehearsing a full band which included Ron McKay on drums, an old buddy of mine who had played with me some eighteen years previously. Being able to sit in on these rehearsal sessions helped me greatly in getting my lip back in trim again.

I recall dropping in to a jazz pub, "Iron Bridge Tavern" in the East End, for a blow with a group and meeting, for the first time, guitarist Tony Shapiro, who suggested I go along to a small cellar club in West London with him where he was regularly booked. That sounded fine to me. It was arranged that I first go to his flat for a meal, meet his wife and a couple of friends, then all go on to West London to this club.

I must confess that the invitation to eat with him was a far greater attraction to me at that time than was the club session which was to follow. I had been living alone for so long now, doing my own cooking (such as it was), and the prospect of dining out with someone who appreciated my vegetarian inclinations, which he did, and was willing to cater for was an occasion to be fully savoured. There were two other guests for dinner that evening (who said they were fans of mine of the 50s), and it was a delight for me to have a family-type meal again in good company, a meal which, incidentally, was well up to expectations.

After dinner, as planned, we all went to this club, a small, dark, dingy, elongated cellar hall where, under a small, dimly lit brick archway at one end, a group of musicians were in the process of setting up. It was a tight squeeze for the five-piece to fit into such a space but that wasn't an uncommon state of affairs in small jazz clubs. I didn't recognise any of the musicians, mainly, I suppose, because they were younger than I and weren't around when I was playing previously.

Our little group of non-players seated ourselves among the audience in the shadows along the wall about halfway down the hall. By the time the band had played about half a dozen numbers, the friends I came with were getting rather persistent in their eagerness to hear me play with the band, so in order to pacify them, and satisfy myself, I unwrapped my horn and, as the band was halfway through a blues number that I was familiar with, I tentatively joined in with them from where I was sitting. After their initial bewilderment, the musicians twigged what was happening and, visually affirming their approval, were then good enough to accompany this unexpected wailing that was emerging from out of the darkened depths of the audience - and allowed me the freedom to lead through the choruses up to the end of the number.

After the impromptu applause died down and Tony had announced me over the microphone, I was beckoned over to the bandstand to be formally introduced to the rest of the band. As far as I remember, apart from Tony on guitar, it included, Chez Chesterman, trumpet, and Phil Franklin, drums. I was then positioned in the front line and invited to play the rest of the session with them, after which, in spite of being in a technically raw state, they wanted to book me to play on their future sessions.

So, by the time I saw the Doc in the Sumer of 1968, I not only had my drawings to show him, sketches of some of the structures I had modelled, a few poems that 'came through', and a paper outlining my proposed scheme for the formation of a spiritual centre, but I had started practising my clarinet again and had also on occasion been sitting in on sessions with some musical friends.

As was his way, the Doc encouraged me in all these efforts, recommending that I continue with these modes of self-expression and see which ones if any came to the fore. He particularly praised my drawing work, using words like 'beautiful', and 'magnifico', and asked me if I would be willing for him to reproduce some of them in a book he was writing, after which he would either return them to me or I could donate them to his Institute. Of course, I willingly gave him those he said he particularly liked saying that he should feel free to use them in any way he wished - and as far as I know, even though he died in 1974, if they weren't published as he intended, they are still available at his institute in Italy.

As to my musical work, I was being increasingly asked to play guest spots at various venues in and around London (for real money too!) and happily, not only meeting lots of my old friends and supporters, but acquiring many new ones.

After one particular session in town, I was approached by an enthusiastic ex-Cy Laurie Club member asking me if I was thinking of reforming my band as he was having a special anniversary party a few months hence that would be attended by lots of other ex-club friends of his, and that, for the prestige value alone, he would pay anything to feature my band there (. . . . . anything?). I explained to him that I didn't have a band any more and, so far, I was really only dipping my toe in for the time being, just testing the water. However, if it would be of any help, I could certainly get a group together for that particular occasion, and not to worry about the fee, it would only be the going rate as it would be my pleasure to play with an organised band again.

I mentioned this possible venture to Phil Franklin, the drummer I had played a few gigs with recently, and he said he would be dead keen to help get something like that going. So with this added encouragement, I contacted Colin Smith who was with my band in '58, and who not only was one of the finest trumpeters around, but also a good friend with an interest in some of the more serious-type things, that I was interested in, even if only in a mild way.

I met him for a meal one evening before we both went on to a Mayfair night spot, The Georgian Club, where he had a regular gig. After sitting in for a few numbers, I was asked by the Management if I would be available to play there regularly - some people do have good taste. Without unduly committing myself, I said I'd be delighted to give it a whirl but wasn't sure for how long as I had tentative plans to re-form my own band.

I was happy to find that this sort of response was often repeated at other venues where I ventured to display my reviving talents. It was nice to know that I hadn't been com- pletely forgotten and I felt that if the band idea didn't work out, I could always get gigs as a roving feature player - Cy Laurie, travelling troubadour.

It struck me quite forcefully how the scene had undergone a radical change since the 50s. Possibly due to the apparently overwhelming popularity and promotional acumen of the then 'Beat' group movement, such as the Beatles and the Rolling Stones (small combinations were used to fill in during the interval periods when our bands played Liverpool's Cavern in the late 1950s), much of the jazz work seemed to have gravitated to pubs, where free admission - and rather low fees for the musicians - had become the order of the day.

There were less jazz clubs, few dance hall gigs, and hardly any concert work in existence, that I was aware of, except for the few more publicly acclaimed bands, such as those of Chris Barber, Kenny Ball, Acker Bilk. Also the style of jazz that had appeared to come to the fore was more in the way of contemporary New Orleans musicians, such as the bands of Bunk Johnson, George Lewis, and those interpreted by the Ken Colyer type bands (whose style was now referred to as "New Orleans" jazz).

It seemed that this was the style the majority of second generation British jazz musicians were inclined towards. In fact, so much so that it was rare to find a band playing in the Classic New Orleans idiom which I had endeavoured to portray and promote. I felt this was an unfortunate state of affairs as, to my mind, the Classical style has so much to offer potential jazzers, not only to its performers but also to its listeners and dancers. Maybe, with this forthcoming new band of mine, once I got into the swing of things, I could help inject a little more of the 'Classic' influence into the scene?

After Colin agreed to join me in this new band venture, I contacted Terry Pitts, my previous trombone player, who had had a lay off for some time and was found, of all places, working in an electrical shop.Yes, Terry was very keen to join. Now with the three of us in the front line and Phil on drums, I had only two more musicians to find to complete the line-up. It was not long before I was introduced to Hugh Rainey, banjo man, a superb musician, the likes of which I had not before heard in a British player. He was not only happy to join me but recommended Pete Corrigan on double bass who, though young at the time and not too familiar with the style, was eager to join the band.

With the help of Terry and Phil, I set about drafting out a publicity blurb and arranging some initial smaller gigs where we could put a bit of polish on our musical arrangements 'on site', so to speak (if the reader will recall, I was always a bit of a stickler for ordered head arrangements and professional presentation). I was pleasantly surprised how easy everything was coming together, it all seemed to be working out so well . . . . that is, until Colin rang me and asked if I would please release him from his verbal agreement to join the band as he had an offer to join Acker Bilk which he would rather not pass up. . . . .Clang!

Of course, I wouldn't even consider standing in his way in joining a full-blown professional band such as Acker's, but it did throw my plans out somewhat. On reflection, it seemed that I had been down this road before and that the same old problems of running a band were once again rearing their ugly heads . . . . . and was it really worth the trouble it forebode?

However, all was not lost. I was lucky enough to rope in Dennis Field on cornet, a steaming hot player in the style, who was a cohort of mine in the early 50s, soon after I had started the Club.

So, now with a settled line up we could get down to some serious rehearsals which, once we had a few of them under our belts, revealed the potential of the group. The close musical rapport that developed between us all in such a short time was far beyond any of our expectations.

We did our first public performance at the Hatfield Jazz Club, which was run by an old jazz collector acquaintance of mine, Ken Lindsay. The band blew a storm that night and the sparks that flew off the band was an unforgettable experience, so much so, that even to this day Pete Corrigan is ever reminding me how he was so excited, that he couldn't sleep for nights after that gig - and it wasn't entirely due to the evening's lubrication. Subsequent gigs for the band only went to confirm the high quality of technical ability, jazz feeling, and musical rapport which set this particular line-up apart from all similar bands on the scene.

Around this time I was approached by an agent who, having heard of my intentions to re-form a band, was eager to promote it and make a big thing of my come-back. The plan was to send out the prepared blurb to all the national and musical press, to circulate all the promoters who could feature the band at their venues, to contact all radio and TV producers, etc. and generally to create a big build-up so that I could then"burst onto the professional jazz scene with the maximum impact". Well, I fell for it.

I also considered that it might be an appropriate time to see if I could revive the club again, even if only for one night a week, as I had no intentions of turning fully professional again, even if the opportunity offered itself, which I thought doubtful. I contacted Mac who owned the premises in Great Windmill Street, where my previous club was situated, and although he was very pleased to see me and abundantly feted me from his customer's snack table, unfortunately, he informed me, the room was not now available. It seemed that gambling had become a lawful occupation and, sure enough, he had got in on the act and was running a very profitable gaming set-up there.

So off I went a-hunting, in search of suitable premises, as I had once before, about eighteen years before. After much gum-shoeing around Soho and its outskirts, I finally managed to book the Ballroom below the Bedford Corner Hotel, just off Tottenham Court Road. It was rather a lush looking place, probably a bit too posh for a jazz club, and some way from Soho, but it was available for a series of Sunday evenings which, in spite of the cost, was one of the conditions that was in its favour. So I took a chance and booked it for a minimum of six months, with the option to extend it after that. Now, with the tireless energy (I was led to believe) which our new Agent was going to put into our launch in conjunction with the opening of the New Cy Laurie Jazz Club, success in returning to the scene was practically assured.

And so another episode in my story was about to open up.

171

EPISODE FOUR

CHAPTER 12 - MY MUSICAL COME-BACK

1968-70 - Approaching My Mid-Forties

Having decided on a date for the grand opening of the New Cy Laurie Jazz Club in the August of 1968, I set about getting posters, leaflets, membership cards, tickets, etc., printed, and arranged all the necessary advertising so that it would all coincide with the efforts that our Agent was to make. However, it turned out that the 'tireless energy' expected from our Agent was only the energy of hot air. Apparently, no effort was spared by him to leave everything to me. In short, he had done absolutely nothing to promote either me, the band, or the club - and there was no reason forthcoming for this total neglect, apart from he had intended to get around to doing something about it. Cripes, what a let down!

So what should I do now? It was panic time! There was so little time before the opening of the club to contact the media and set up interviews etc. I hastily circularised the fact of my return to the scene by sending out the blurb that Terry and Phil had helped me prepare. I was at a great disadvantage as I was not aware of the current contact people in the appropriate media departments (press, radio, and TV) nor was I sure which of the various agents and promoters I should inform.

Although I didn't actually 'burst onto the scene with the maximum impact', as I thought could have happened, I did manage to get a good dose of publicity from my hurried efforts, including substantial write-ups and photographs in the national press such as, "The Sunday Telegraph", "Daily Sketch", "London Evening News", "The Listener", etc., and in all the current musical papers, as well as radio interviews, all of which helped to promote the band and the club for this new phase. Once again, luck came to my aid as, under the circumstances, far more interest was generated than I had expected, but certainly nothing like the intended publicity exposure which was previously planned.

In fact, if it hadn't been delayed, the announcement of my return to the scene would have coincided with the sweep of publicity which surrounded the Beatles when they went to the Himalayas to practice meditation with Mahesh, as I had done eight years before. Although such a promotional advantage for me was obviously not to be, some articles written in the press about me related to the interest in meditation which this young group had. The general gist of such articles can be seen from the following collection of snippets which I have unearthed;

MR. LAURIE MEDITATING ON HIS COMEBACK"

He was then in his late 20's. I was still at school. He was a star with a capital S. I was frankly star-struck.

"We never actually met. The nearest I ever got to him was joining hundreds of other jazz fans in a Soho club where the temperature hit 120F on an average night.

"FORTUNE"

"The year was 1958. The name of the man - Cy Laurie.

"He was - in fact, still is - a clarinettist. Until eight years ago he was doing for the clarinet what the Beatles did for the guitar later. What Elvis had done for rock 'n roll.

"Cy Laurie's band had the pull to fill an all-night session at the Albert Hall, or pack a steamer on a weekend river boat shuffle.

"Jiving 'beatniks' - as they were quaintly known - followed him everywhere.

"He was bigger than Chris Barber, Kenny Ball or Acker Bilk. He earned a fortune, had three cars, a house in the country.

"Suddenly he disappeared. Just vanished. Told people he needed a rest, left his club and never came back.

"For months the jazz world bopped with rumours. But what no one knew then was Cy Laurie had met Maharishi Mahesh Yogi.

"And, just like the Beatles were to do eight years later, the jazz man followed him to India. He abandoned his music and lived on the slopes of the Himalayas meditating and "thinking it all out"

"And now, after disappearing from the top of the tree, Cy is starting the climb back up again.

"THINNER"

"I met him in London for the first time yesterday. He's a little older and a little thinner. "And I'm out of touch. I've got many things sorted out, but I feel the need to play again"

"About the Maharishi, Cy said: "I think he's a sincere man but it's difficult to assess anyone's motives. . . I didn't find his type of meditation suitable for what I was looking for, and I suppose the Beatles haven't either".

"But I wasn't surprised that they found a need for this type of thing"

"Now Cy, 39, unmarried and starting again, is hoping to revive the jazz mood of the fifties.

"SELL-OUT"

"Once his name meant an instant sell-out. On Sunday he makes his comeback at an unknown club off London's Tottenham Court Road.

"Whether the old strains of Cy's clarinet soloing on "King of the Zulus" or "Perdido Street Blues" will get a new generation stomping again remains to be seen."

"Daily Sketch" - August 15th 1968 - Anne Nightingale.

"CY LAURIE (After eight years of meditating) RETURNS TO JAZZ"

"A long time ago, when the Beatles were almost boys, the Maharishi Mahesh Yogi came to Britain. Just as he did on his 1967 visit, he took with him a leading entertainer when he returned to India. The event wasn't surrounded with the hysterical publicity given to last year's visit, though.

"The musician was Cy Laurie, in 1960 one of the country's leading jazzmen, who had a fanatical following at his Piccadilly traditional jazz club. Then suddenly he vanished. Nobody knew where he had gone.

"Now eight years later, he is back "I had always been interested in Philosophy and yoga", he recalls, "and one evening in the club a member told me there was someone from India around. So I went to see him".

"ALONE"

"The "someone from India" was the Maharishi, who soon suggested that Mr. Laurie should return to India with him. "It wasn't much of a wrench. Although my music was very important to me, it was less important than my study."

"Mr. Laurie spent three months touring and helped the Maharishi to choose the site which the Beatles visited last year.

"Then he left and wandered on his own into the Himalayas.

174

"I was given a small hut in the hills by a man I met at one of the temples. I stayed in it for more than a year."

"During this time he didn't see one other person. His food was put outside the hut by the local villagers.

"RETURN"

"There was no fear of boredom at all", he says, "I would get up at daybreak, have a short walk in the forest, and then spend the rest of the day in study and meditation. One doesn't have much sense of time in those conditions".

"After a year in the hut he decided the time had come to leave. He met somebody who offered him the fare home and returned to England, to follow the same pattern of life.

"He felt no desire to return to the world of jazz and hadn't touched his clarinet since he left for India. He settled in a small farmhouse in the country.

"But then I felt the need for some form of self-expression, "he says "and I opened the case again and took out my clarinet. I was a bit rusty after so long, but it soon came back."

"It has come back so well that with a new band, he starts playing again - at the Bedford Corner Hotel off Tottenham Court Road - on Sunday.

"He has no intention of giving up his meditation. He hasn't seen the Maharishi since 1961, but the meditation has gone on, although it is a different form to that preached by his former mentor. Now it will have to be fitted in between playing the clarinet."

"The Evening News" - 13. 8. 1968. - John London.

"CY LAURIE? WITH THE MAHARISHI, OF COURSE! ALONE"

"Ever since 1960 the Melody maker has had callers asking, "Whatever happened to Cy Laurie"? At last we can give the answer - he discovered the Maharishi Mahesh Yogi eight years before the Beatles.

"In recent months there had been reports that Cy - whose London club was the trad Mecca of the 1950s until his disappearance eight years ago - had been sitting in at various places on clarinet. On each occasion he was secretive about his movements and then did a vanishing act.

"This week he came to MM and announced that he was back in the jazz business. But

175

first he explained the mystery - and it's a story that would need an Ian Fleming to do it full justice.

"Cy met the Maharishi in 1960, "I'd been interested in that sort of thing for years and my interest got so strong I packed up and went with him", he said.

"He travelled with the Maharishi across Europe and the Middle East, finally arriving In India where he attended the first of the Maharishi's courses of training with a few other hand-picked Europeans.

"Eventually Cy left and settled down in a mud-hut 10,000 feet up in the Himalayas. How did he manage to live?

"'In India, people with my interests are reasonably respected', Cy explained, 'There were always lots of people willing to help'.

"' I was completely isolated but still had money from the jazz days and people used to help get things for me'.

"'I was quite happy and my interest in it all is still strong. I came back to Britain in 1963 but I only recently felt the urge to play again.'

"'I hadn't seen my clarinet for about eight years, but I got it out and started sitting in with the bands to try and get my lip in shape.'

"For the past three years, Cy has been living in his old farmhouse in Essex and still spends much of his time meditating and studying.

"But now he has re-formed his band and is opening a new club on August 18, at the Bedford Corner Hotel in Bayley Street, Bloomsbury.

"The line-up, most of whom were associated with him in the past, is Dennis Field (tpt) Terry Pitts (tmb) Hugh Rainey (bjo) Peter Corrigan (bass) and Phil Franklin (dms)

"' I am staying strictly semi-pro', Cy told me, 'but we hope to take out-of-town gigs at weekends and the occasional job during the week'.

"I asked how Cy thought the scene had changed in eight years.

"'I would have expected things to improve a lot, and, I think they have.' he said, 'The thing I noticed is the number of bands who now play in pubs'.

"'The few clubs I have been to all seem to be doing very well. That surprised me, really, as I'd heard stories that music was practically dead.'

"'Another thing that surprised me was to find that most of the audiences seemed to remember who I was'.

"How does Cy see his future? 'That's a hard question,' he admitted.

"'I feel I'm in a sort of transitional stage. I do get together with groups of people - discussion groups and meditation groups, and that takes up quite a bit of my time.'

"'Keen as I am to play jazz again, that must definitely take second place'.

"Had Cy missed the fame and audience appreciation of ten years ago during his retreat in India?

"'No' he said, 'After all I'd been playing a long time, I'd had a band since 1948, and I'd spent a good many years chasing up and down the country. The glamour had rather worn off'.

"LAY OFF"

"Had an eight-year lay-off changed his sound or is he still a Johnny Dodds man?

"'I can't really say,' he admitted, 'It feels the same to me but you'll have to tell me when you hear what it sounds like'.

MELODY MAKER - August 10th 1968. Interview with Bob Dawbarn.

"BACK TO JAZZ"

"In a cutting dated December 24, 1960 headed "Illness forces Cy Laurie to Retire", that best-known British traditional clarinettist of the day was quoted as saying 'I don't know how long I'll be away, it may be a few weeks, it may be months. I anticipate spending some time in a warmer climate.

"In the event he was right about the climate, wrong about the time. He went to India, but although he was back from there by 1963 it was another five years before he actually showed himself. The completeness of his disappearance was baffling: there were, it's true, occasional rumours that he'd gone to the East to meditate, but they seemed at the time too far fetched to be credited.

"Of course in 1961 meditation was not fashionable: neither was the obscure Indian mystic who was passing through London and to whom Cy Laurie was introduced. You

Dennis Field. Phil Franklin. Self. 1968

could follow the Maharishi Mahesh Yogi to India, as Cy did, and nobody need ever find out. As with Unidentified Flying Objects there was no lack of "sightings": he was seen everywhere between the South Coast and Bombay while he was, in fact, either living in the Himalayas on fresh air, contemplation and the rent from a property in Essex, or lying low in Essex itself.

"I met him on Thursday over a coffee (predictably he's a fairly heavy non-drinker). He explained that he'd given up a band, a flourishing club in Soho, and perhaps as much fame and fortune as any British revivalist jazzman had ever had, not just because of the strains of constant playing and touring, but also because he'd been interested in philosophy and meditation almost as long as he'd been interested in music. 'When the sun comes out, the stars fade from sight,' he said, adding a warning that if you live too long in India the use of aphorisms like that can become a bad habit.

"Now, he feels the need for self-expression. 'I've tried painting,' he said, 'but for me it doesn't amount to much: and I'm trying to write. But the obvious answer is the clarinet. It was hard at first to relate tunes to titles: 'lets play so-and-so' didn't mean a thing. But it's all coming back. 'So there's a new Cy Laurie band, and from tonight, a Cy Laurie club for it to play in.

"It's in the Bedford Corner Hotel, off Tottenham Court Road, and it starts modestly with a weekly Sunday session. According to London superstition, it's in the wrong place, but Cy's reputation among revivalist jazz fans, having survived nearly eight years of silence from him, might well attract a good following. Whether he'll still be playing the same kind of Johnny Dodds-influenced clarinet (always described in the handouts as "blue-hot") remains to be seen - he thinks he hasn't changed. The interesting thing is that here is a near-myth prepared to take a chance on being a hit once more."

Sunday Telegraph - 18. 8. 1968. - Peter Clayton

"BEATLE TRAIL-BLAZER"

"Cy's New Life"

"The Beatles were still a club act when jazzman Cy Laurie blazed the Himalayan trail in search of the secrets of meditation.

"He left behind a successful career, his own theatrical agency, a London house, a farm and his three cars. At the age of 35, he simply disappeared.

"That was in 1960. Then the Beatles were upon us. As record after record rocketed to the top of the charts and the fans' screams continued unabated, they seemed to tire of success.

"They decided to follow the teachings of the Maharishi Mahesh Yogi, and to study meditation. And off they went to the mystic East to get away from it all.

"Their decision created a huge stir. Yet they were simply following the path trod years before, by Cy Laurie.

"Last Summer, Laurie reappeared. And this week, he explained what prompted his decision to quit.

"Cy, who prefers to keep his address secret said: "My music meant a lot to me - but not as much as my interest in meditation."

"A chance meeting in London with the then obscure Maharishi made such a deep impression on Laurie, he beat a path across the world to a mud hut nearly ten thousand feet up in the Himalayas.

"There he studied meditation and yoga. He was also, he said, the Maharishi's sole companion on a tour of Europe, the Middle East and India to spread the "gospel" of meditation.

179

"Now he's back, with his own band, playing good old New Orleans jazz. But now he works as a semi-professional.

"When I came back, I found I needed some form of self-expression', he said, 'I tried painting and writing poetry - then started playing the clarinet again. I hadn't touched one for eight years.'

"For those fans who remember the exuberant jazzman of pre-1960 days, he still parades his musical talent every Sunday evening at Romford's King's Hall.

"SHOWCASE" - "Recorder/Review" - 23. 5. 1969. Graham Weaver.

"JAZZ - THE RETURN OF CY LAURIE"

"Back in the late Fifties, when youth wore duffle-coats and crepe soles, sipped espresso coffee at the Partisan, scanned the "Universities and Left Review", got blisters on the sub-industrial wasteland between Reading and Slough - back in those days of innocence when pot was something you put a baby on, there was a jazz king called Cy Laurie. Cy was the East End's answer to Johnny Dodds and his band held court at his own club just off Great Windmill Street. At the Cy Laurie club we thronged to hear the 'blue-hot style' of Cy's band playing classics from the Twenties like 'Weatherbird Rag' and 'Chattanooga Stomp'. This was a time when trad was a generation's pop music, when the skip-jive was a masterful social accomplishment.

"Cy Laurie's success was a legend - three cars, a theatrical agency, and three homes. What more could a successful clarinettist want? The answer is: a great deal. In 1960 Cy suddenly disappeared from London and for years jazz buffs speculated about his vanishing act. The club and the band faded away.

"Today Cy Laurie is back in England and he is playing with a new band. The mystery has been solved - partly. Cy told me what happened in 1960 at the height of his success. 'For years I had been interested in yoga and meditation. When I left London it was because I had the opportunity to pursue my studies more thoroughly. My interest in these subjects became greater than my interest in jazz.' What had provoked Cy Laurie into leaving his Soho club was a chance meeting with the Maharishi Mahesh Yogi - this at a time when the Maharishi was unknown and eight years before he became a fashionable guru with tours lined up with the Beach Boys.

"Cy exchanged Soho for the foot-hills of northern India and after studying with the Maharishi he went off on his own to live in a mud and stone hut 10,000 feet up in the Himalayas. 'This isolation gave me the chance to draw back from life and try to work out various problems. Looking back now at the Fifties, it seems a completely different phase of my existence. All the time I was in India I did not touch my clarinet. I wasn't

180

sorry about this as I had been a professional musician for 15 years.'

"After three years in India, Cy returned to England to live in an isolated farmhouse where he continued his studies, 'I had led a withdrawn life for eight years when I felt a strong need for some sort of expression. I tried painting and writing. But jazz was the natural, ready-made form for me. I tried to play the clarinet again and this was very difficult at first because my lip was soft and I could hardly make a noise. But before long the music came back and I contacted old friends in the jazz world.

"In August Cy opened a jazz club with a six-piece band at the Bedford Corner Hotel near the British Museum. Every Sunday Cy's blue-hot style can be heard once more. 'Every week people come up to me and say: "I met my wife down the Cy Laurie club in the Fifties." The jazz scene is of course very different now. There are no concerts any more: there are hardly any professional bands left. But our style is basically the same as it was. We still draw on the same roots.'

"Cy's clarinet still has the remarkable vibrato and low-register fluency of the old days. His cornet player Dennis Field had played in the band in the Fifties and his tight, controlled style relieved by imaginative breaks fits perfectly into the new band. Drummer Phil Franklin gives the band its basic 'swing' and Cy Laurie says 'This is the best band I've ever had.' The repertoire is still drawn mostly from the music of the Twenties and Thirties with emphasis on the work of King Oliver and Armstrong.

"At the new club dancers still perform the distinctive Cy Laurie style jiving. The black fish-net stockings have to hold in a little more flesh on the girls. The men are starting to get paunches and the old Cy Laurie fans sometimes have trouble getting baby sitters. But the music has lost none of its freshness."

"THE LISTENER" - 16. 1. 69.   Richard Gilbert.

. . . . . . What nice people are employed in the newspaper business.

Bookings were now coming in for the band with increasing frequency but, not being a full time professional unit, we could not travel too far afield for too long, as all the boys had daytime jobs to which they were committed. This suited me very well as it enabled me to continue with my studies, my meditation practices, and keep up with my group meetings, as well as allowing me the time to build up my jazz guest spot work which seemed to be more demanding as the months went by. This avenue of work was not always as satisfying musically as playing with my full band, which had a rehearsed and organised repertoire, because most, but certainly not all of the combinations I was obliged to front as a feature artist were either alien to me in style and choice of numbers, or of less experienced musical calibre, or they consisted merely of pick-up groups gathered together for the occasion which therefore not only limited me

181

to playing basic simple jazz standards, but such groups were often noticeably lacking in musical cohesion.

However, the plusses of this type of work amply made up for these minor inconveniences inasmuch as I was free to travel where and when I wished, I received star treatment, I was put up in the best of hotels, the financial rewards were considerably greater (promoters, in general, found it more expedient and profitable to book a special known guest artist to front a local band than to book a whole named touring band)), there were many more opportunities for this type of work - and on top of that, I didn't have the organisational hassle which a full band of musicians involved. So musically, in effect, I had the best of both worlds and, as a result, I was really never short of work.

Although I found this situation quite satisfactory, by the Summer of 1969 further changes in my activities were on the cards.

DANCE OR LISTEN TO CY'S GREAT NEW BAND

at the NEW

CY LAURIE JAZZ CLUB

BEDFORD CORNER HOTEL

Bayley Street London WC1 (off Tottenham Court Road)

Every Sunday 7.30 - 11

Licensed Bar till 11.30

Members 5/- Guests 7/6 Membership 2/6 Half Year

(Free Membership for Students)

I had by then known Sally for some months beforehand and we were seeing quite a lot of each other, even though we didn't really have that much in common. She was a young, happy-go-lucky kind of girl, very attractive, intelligent, full of energy, and with a very loving nature, even though she could be a bit of an adorable scatter-brain at times; her priorities were mostly outward and in stark contrast to mine, she enjoyed partying, dancing, clothes, travel, lots of friends, etc., of course, very understandably so. But we got on well and became quite close for a while, even if we both knew there would be no permanency in our relationship. Nevertheless, at that time she was of great help in lightening me up a bit. Even after all this time, we still keep in touch.

The club attendance at Bedford Corner Hotel, which had started off so successfully with jam-packed audiences every week, began to fall off, as did some of the band gigs. I had fulfilled my obligation in booking the club's Hotel ballroom for the first six months and had now an arrangement with the management to use the premises on a month to month basis.

In spite of there always being a substantial hard core of enthusiastic members supporting the club, as the months went by, the overall audience numbers dwindled to a point where I was paying most of the club's rent and the whole of the band's wages from the income of my solo feature work. It was therefore not possible for me to sustain this condition for too long so, eventually, and unfortunately, I had to close the club.

CHAPTER 13 - THE FARM PROJECT

1969-71 - My Mid-Forties

Apart from the closure of the Club, the amount of band work was also becoming rather spasmodic partly, I would have thought, because I seemed to have lost some of my fervour for the administration side of things. There was no doubt about it, it was an excellent band and the musicians were a great bunch of guys and we all got on well together, but the situation being as it was, it was easier and more convenient for me to concentrate on taking solo guest gigs. This way, I could more easily fit my musical work in with the weekly evening group meetings which I didn't particularly want to sacrifice.

These meetings also seemed to be entering a new phase of activity, that is, for me anyway. On one occasion the subject got around to the workings of the mind and, as I had for many years been interested in the role and significance of thoughts and the process of thinking, I was prompted to give a little impromptu discourse as to my views on the matter. I explained how our thought life has a much deeper and far reaching significance than many of us realise, how each thought that one entertains has a decided and instantaneous effect not only upon one's own emotions and physical life, but upon the surrounding thought and emotional atmosphere, which automatically conditioned others who were within one's vicinity and susceptible to its influence.

There is a direct and potent inter-connection between the mind, the emotions, and the body. For instance, a serious negative thought can poison one's whole system by setting up a negative train of emotions which results in a sense of depression, pessimism, and even aggression, and this, in turn, creates a malfunctioning of the physical body leading to blockages in the flow of vital force, functional imbalance, and often eventual disease. This can easily be demonstrated when, for some, the witnessing of an accident, or the mere sight of, say, blood from a wound, can provoke physical nausea, and even vomiting, or fainting.

Most of us are aware of the effects of fear, jealousy, resentment, anger, etc., which can play havoc with our physical health resulting in such conditions as, sleeplessness, weight loss, asthma, skin problems, digestive troubles, and breathing difficulties. Whereas a positive thought invigorates the whole personality which stimulates every cell in the body, encouraging health, happiness, a sense of well-being, and, invariably, an outgoing feeling of love and goodwill towards all life. Either way, whatever the quality of a thought, it has a pronounced effect on others, whether that effect is immediately discernible or not. So the importance of constantly guarding our thoughts is as crucial to our relationship with others as it is to our relationship with ourselves.

I stressed how important I considered an understanding of the whole subject was, and

184

that there must come a time when the science of the mind and the part it plays in creating our future wellbeing, physically, emotionally, and mentally, would be a necessary subject in every school syllabus.

Anyway, that was the gist of what I said on that occasion. They seemed particularly impressed by its implications, so much so, that for some many meetings afterwards I was encouraged to expand on the subject - and even write a thesis or something on it which, I felt, to some extent, I could do. I'm sure such a document would have been of great help to many and I did think seriously about doing it, sufficiently so to set about making some preliminary notes, but nothing ever materialised ..... maybe one day, eh? Nevertheless, a big hooray for groups!

The value of these groups also proved itself in another aspect of my thinking which was aired at these meetings. The thoughts that I had been toying with over the past few years regarding utilising the Farm for some sort of spiritual centre were becoming much more formed by this time. The possibility of accommodating a group of like-minded people who would be able to regularly come together there for spiritual support and upliftment, where group study, meditation, and discussion in these matters would be the order of the day, and together we could develop forward looking ideas that could be usefully applied in life. Also by using the land for growing organic vegetables, the food served there would be rich in vitality and taste, and any excess produce could be sold off to some of the local health stores to help support financially any associated projects.

I voiced this likely scheme to members of two or three of the groups I was involved with at the time. This certainly seemed to arouse their interest and some were even encouraging enough to offer their help in its founding.

Earlier on in the year, I became involved with a group who were running a New Age type centre in West London called "Gandolf's Garden". I visited them occasionally to attend the talks, discussions, and meditation get-togethers which they held in a room below their craft shop. I first came across them when the organiser of their activities, Muzz Murray, interviewed me for their periodical magazine in which they plied me with lots of questions about my experiences in India.

I had mentioned to him about the possibility of creating a centre at the Farm and he too was keen to involve himself in such a project. He and some of the members of his group visited the Farm on various occasions for discussion and meditation, and obviously, the subject of establishing a centre there was invariably prominent.

As is often the case, the more I spoke of it, the clearer became my ideas, and the more keen I became to get something under way, although I knew how difficult it would be with my musical commitments and the guest spot gigs that were coming in for me by that time.

One particular booking was arranged for me to feature as a guest on a series of concerts with a jazz group in Belfast, Ireland. On arrival I was met by the promoter there who escorted me to the accommodation he had arranged for me. In conversation, I mentioned that I was a vegetarian, would he know of any restaurants in the area where I could get a suitable meal. This sort of statement had become my normal opening gambit whenever I arrived in a new town as, in those days, the general chances of locating an eating house that catered for vegetarians were very rare indeed.

Fortunately, as our familiar 'luck fairy' must have ordained, on this occasion, I was told that a good friend of this promoter was also a vegetarian who often ate at a small local restaurant and, if I wished, he would arrange that I lunch with this friend there the following day. This 'small restaurant' turned out to be a guest house presided over by John Hamilton, a practising Naturopath who not only had his consulting and treatment rooms on the premises but had a public dining room where he and his staff daily served meals for his in-house patients plus guests and visitors. During lunch on my first visit when he came into the dining room to speak to one or two of the guests, I caught his eye and he gave me a very friendly smile, and I of course, in my normal reserved manner, gingerly smiled back. I thought nothing more about it and carried on conversing with my new companion, who apparently was a patient of his and, unknown to me, had an appointment for treatment with him immediately after lunch. This he duly kept before I had finished eating.

I settled myself in the waiting room until my companion came out of the treatment room, then John Hamilton approached me and said to me, "Why don't you come and stay with me for three months? I can brainwash you."

"Brainwash me?" I said, "Why, is it dirty?"

"No, it's very clean!" he replied.

I said that I'd probably be returning there for the evening meal later on and if there was time maybe he could explain what he meant by his remark.

I returned there that evening as intended and, after we had dinner, he took me into his private room for a chat. He said that when he first saw me, his intuition told him that I was a 'sensitive', and I was clairvoyant. When I told him that I wasn't, he said that it was possibly covered up by the false ways of living of modern civilisation, but he did think that I was very sensitive. He said that he had considered the matter during the afternoon and that if I came to stay with him, he would get me back to full physical health. I duly thanked him for his concern but told him that, as far as I knew, I had no problems with my health, and that physical health was not my primary aim as I was interested in things more of a philosophical nature. He then inquired as to my background, my interests, my life-style, etc. which, unusually for me, seeing he was a complete stranger, I was quite open about.

He then said that in his opinion I seemed fairly relaxed on the whole but only working at 60% of my potential, although that is much more than most people. I explained that I had followed the principles of Nature Cure for the past twenty years or so and would have thought that my health was fairly sound, but if he thought he could help improve my level of health, I'd be more than happy to come and stay with him for a while, even if it was only during the two weeks later on in the Summer which I had put aside to be free from any musical commitments. He said it would be good if I could arrange it, that he'd very much look forward to working with me as he thought that I was a very rare person with a very rare sensitivity (the old smoothie). Of course, after that ego-massaging remark, I was sold!

I set about arranging some gigs in Ireland during those two weeks to help pay for my stay with him so that I wouldn't need to pull too heavily on my finance resources. Luckily, such gigs were not too hard to come by so, come the arranged time, I took myself off to Belfast for what turned out to be a health promoting working holiday for me, as well as providing me with some very interesting pointers for my future. I went on a strict healthy diet, eating as regularly as was possible in view of the gigs I was doing, getting as much fresh air and exercise as I could, and reading a lot of spiritually uplifting books I had brought with me. John gave me a good massage twice every day and insisted that I get as much sleep as I could. His main verdict of my state of health was that under the circumstances it was very good but owing to the irregular hours that I kept, the smoky atmospheres that I was obliged to work in, and the devitalised food that I consumed by often eating out, which he appreciated came with the territory as a professional musician, I was short on nervous energy and vitality. Only when I could live a more ordered life-style with a regulated routine of healthy meals, exercise, fresh air, sleep, etc., would I be able to work at the peak of my efficiency.

I could see the logic in this and queried whether as so many others in my profession work under the same conditions, is he implying that they too could be short on nervous energy and vitality? He countered this by stressing that although everybody is different, such a devitalised condition was more than likely to be the case with the majority. He stressed that if one was constantly over-exerting oneself, living on nervous energy, and then habitually taking stimulants in the way of coffee, tea, alcohol, etc. to artificially boost their energy levels, as so many people do, then their lack of natural vitality would not be so apparent. The real trouble is when they resort to medicinal drugs and antibiotics to suppress the build up of after effects of such stimulants. He was quite adamant that no one can break nature's laws of health and get away with it. That was all certainly in line with the views I had held for so many years.

He also pointed out that with someone like myself who didn't take such stimulants or drugs, and who was particularly sensitive to start with anyway, in following such an irregular life-style, the lack of vitality would be far more obvious. He advised that, if possible, I should try not to overdo the drain on my nervous energy as it could eventually cause a breakdown in the body's vitality reserves. Excellent advice, I thought, just up my street, even if I couldn't fully heed it. He acknowledged that he was telling me little that I didn't know but wanted to stress that good health and my late night profession were not the best of bed-mates. Although he said he realised my music was my bread and butter, I should consider not doing so many late night jobs and try to get a better balance between my work and my health. A nice idea but not too practical under the circumstances.

He enquired whether I had ever considered changing my profession. I told him that being a musician, although very enjoyable and worthwhile, was not my whole life and I was not exactly sure which direction my future would take nor what other type of occupation would be suitable for me. He unhesitatingly said that if I could spend four years of my time training to become a Naturopath, he could assure me it would be four years well spent. I explained that I would find that very agreeable and had often thought of doing so, I had a lot of faith in Nature Cure as a way of healing but, as I was aware that there was far more to man than just his physical body and that, as I understood, it was really in these more subtle areas where much of man's ill health originates, my studies had been mainly concentrated on these inner aspects of man. He was sympathetic with this view but emphasised that true Nature Cure is not just a way of healing, it's a way of living! I said I'd certainly drink to that! (Maybe that wasn't such an appropriate remark).

He then elaborated on the need to get people into a more healthy state and spoke quite vehemently on the then National Health Service, that, "it came into existence in 1947 because the then Socialist Government said that people were being deprived of the necessary health facilities, yet the health of the Nation now is no better, even worse in fact, because there's not enough beds in Hospitals, not enough Hospitals to accommodate the sick and ailing, and now after 22 years we have not only NOT caught up with the health of the Nation, but more people need treatment and some have to wait years for a operation or even a consultation. This is because the principles and premises that the Health Service subscribe to and patronise are radically wrong - it doesn't create health, it creates disease, a disease-minded community.

"The vigour of a Nation", he continued, "is directly proportional to the health of the Nation and the Nation has no standards or consideration of matters of health, only for the treatment of disease. If our health is substandard, everything else that follows from it is substandard - instead of having a disease service, we should have a health service, based upon entirely different principles and that education of such should be wide spread beginning with children in schools, the creation of new seats in Universities, new Professorships, and new Faculties, teaching the principles of HEALTH.

. . . . . Well, how about all that?

But he wasn't all talk, he worked long hours almost non-stop every day with a vital atmosphere about him, obviously dedicated to his job of bringing people back to health. I felt much admiration for him and his unbounded energy, which was in such stark contrast to my normally quiet and unobtrusive manner. He was doing an excellent and needed job, and whatever I gained from my stay there, he certainly provided me with food for thought, especially regarding changing my career. I returned from Ireland with my mind buzzing with all possible career alternatives, making lists, and making lists of lists, all with the intention of planning a new direction for myself, one that I hoped would enable me to make a more constructive contribution to life.

When I attended the annual Sundial House conferences during the late Summer of 1969, I managed to get in a few chats with Dr. Sag. He had a very full schedule for that visit, not only giving talks on Psychosynthesis and the Ageless Wisdom but he was working with smaller groups so that they could set up their own Psychosynthesis workshops in various countries around the world, which is something he had told me was part of his hopes. He enquired how I had been getting on and I gave him a general picture of my life over the past year since I last saw him. I told him that I was considering a change of career, which he was good enough to discuss with me and the possible implications of such a move, and concurred with my attitude towards it, that I try to treat it as an experiment and see what use I could make of the results.

So with growing keenness to sort out a new direction for myself and with the Doc's encouragement, I applied for a four-year course at one of the leading Naturopathic establishments, thinking that the grounding that I had had in the subject for the past twenty years or so would naturally qualify me for entry. Not so, I was rejected on the grounds that I hadn't sufficient 'O' or 'A' levels, in spite of having equivalent National Certificate qualifications. I then thought of taking up some form of social work, so I then applied for a place in University to study Sociology, Philosophy, and Psychology, subjects that would be useful if I ever wanted to put my knowledge of Psychosynthesis into practice, but was turned down for similar reasons.

I even offered myself for training as a voluntary Marriage Guidance Councillor, seeing as I had a certain amount of experience in man-woman difficulties (didn't I though!) and had certain constructive views on creating harmonious human relationships. An attraction for me in this field was that they took in to account the educational side of pre-marriage which was very much in line with my interests in Psychosynthesis. But this application too turned out to be unsuccessful after a rather humiliating interview with a trio of "respectable" local wives who concluded that, as I didn't have any academic qualifications in social work and had never officially married, I wouldn't be thought suitable for such a post. (Well, slam went that door!)

My next tactic was to try to equip myself with some 'academic' qualifications, so come that Autumn I enrolled in a local college to take their part-time day 'O' level courses, these were in Sociology, Mathematics, English, Social Economics, and Human Biology, as well as an 'A' level course in Social Economics. I felt that all this could be rather ambitious for me to attempt, especially at my age, as I was approaching my middle forties, but I could at least have a try and just see what comes of it and, if successful, apply again for the Naturopathic course or a University place the following year.

When these 'O' level courses started it came as a bit of a shock for me to find that I was thrown in amongst classfullls of generally disinterested and, at times, unruly teenagers. Needless to say, being nearly three times as old as the eldest of them, as well as being around 10 years or more older than most of their tutors, I stood out like a sore thumb. Besides which, most of these pupils seemed way ahead of me in learning ability (that is, when they were not intent on larking around), as they were repeating some of their previously failed subjects. Still, they were good fun even if disturbingly distracting at times, but then, I had made my bed and just had to make the best of it, especially when certain of the teaching methods were not exactly to my liking.

The first turn-off for me was when we were all escorted to the Chemistry Laboratory for our initial lesson in Human Biology. The tutor there, a young man probably in his early thirties, had prepared a demonstration for us to show how the movement of the limbs of an animal are controlled through the nervous system. In a large upturned glass beaker he had entrapped three live frogs, he took one out, placed it on the bench for all to see, including its two other companion frogs, sliced off its legs with a knife and connected them up to an electrical circuit to make them twitch. The sheer horror of this scene was enough to make my stomach retch, as it was for those few pupils who were forced to turn their backs in revulsion. Not only that, the agitation set up in the movement of the two other frogs left in the upturned beaker at the sight of this barbaric demonstration was so visibly apparent that one felt like grabbing them and rushing out of the laboratory to release them in the grounds before they too suffered a similar fate - which apparently was the intention.

Fortunately, such a rescue operation as this was unnecessary as there were enough of us who objected to any further suffering of these innocent little creatures to bring the demonstration to a close, much to the surprise, bewilderment, and reluctance of the tutor in charge. He just couldn't understand why there was so much fuss being made - after all, they were only frogs, and he had always included these type of demonstrations in his teaching programme (and probably would continue to do so). Afterwards, being the eldest of the pupils, I felt I should try, as tactfully as I could, to put to him a more compassionate point of view, that animals were living, feeling, creatures and should be treated as such, etc., and that there must be other ways, either through mock-up demonstrations or films, rather than continually repeating these viciously cruel acts with every set of students, etc. Judging by the blank look on his face, my efforts were obviously to no avail.

How often and how rife were these savage 'demonstrations' going on in all the learning establishments over the world? I shuddered to think - man has so much to answer for with regards to the unnecessary suffering of his younger brothers in the lesser Kingdoms. Whether such brutality is still going on these days in the name of learning, I'm not sure, but with the advent of advanced computerised graphics, I would have thought such acts were no longer necessary.

There were other examples of unprogressive teaching methods which went against the grain with me but with most of these I just bit my lip and ploughed through the courses as best I could, knowing full well that my future livelihood was not as dependent upon success in such studies as were possibly some of my younger friends.

From that Autumn my life once again took on a fullness of activity which left me little time to consider putting into operation the plans I had for utilising the Farm as a spiritual centre. What with my playing which took up about four or five nights a week (and the nocturnal hours which it entailed), and being in the throes of studying six college subjects, which meant six lots of homework to do, six lots of note taking, six lots of technical book cramming, plus the occasional essay or thesis which was required, etc. I hardly had time to squeeze in my daily meditation, let alone the necessary hour-a-day clarinet practice which I have always tried to make time for to maintain my playing standards. Also, in preparation for the coming Winter, I had started installing a central heating system at the Farm which I needed to complete before the cold weather set in, which, incidentally, added to the chaotically disordered state that the house was already in (I had been living alone by then for over two years, getting away with the minimum amount of housework that I dare - which, I am forced to confess, was virtually nil!).

So with my days so fully occupied, I had no alternative but to shelve all my ideas of the Farm Centre, the market garden, an essay on the mind, and all the other projects I had previously considered dabbling with, and instead, at least for the coming months, just try to concentrate my energies on these immediate tasks.

So the period of that Winter, right through to the Summer of 1970, turned out to be a very arduous one for me. On top of my gig work, the groups which I was attending, and the need to keep up my meditation and clarinet practice, I found the added work of the college courses rather demanding on my forbearance and power of endurance (which of course entailed a fair amount of written work, even though that which I managed to turn out was far less than was required of me).

I wasn't particularly optimistic when the time came for me to face the required series of College exams in the June as I knew full well that I really hadn't put in the necessary preparatory work which they demanded . . . . how they ever came to give me a pass in four 'O; level subjects out of five will always be a puzzle to me. Still, they did, and I certainly wasn't going to question it.

However my 'A' level in Sociology, as anticipated, was a decided no-no. I needed 'A' levels for my purposes, so in spite of the demands it would make on my time, that Autumn I enrolled for four 'A' level subjects. That was really over-ambitious of me, as I found out to my cost.

About a month or two after the courses had started, I had received a letter from Sue saying her car had broken down, she was stranded in Paris without money and without means of getting any, that her life had been unconstructive and she was beside herself as to what she should do. Could I possibly help out? Could I please see my way clear to come to Paris and bring her home? . . . . What! As soon as I read that, alarm bells and flashing warning lights were set off all over me. All my better instincts said NO! NO! NO!

But then, as my sense of compassion eventually surfaced, I thought how could I refuse her plea? She appeared to be in dire straits and I felt I should help her out as best I could. So in one of my weaker do-goody moods, I chased over to Paris but only on the condition that once back in England, as she had nowhere else to stay, she could use the back flat at the Farm for a short period until she got herself fixed up somewhere else.

It so happened that the weekend after we had returned from Paris there had been a meeting arranged at the Farm with about a half dozen interested friends who wanted to know more of my plans to turn the place into some form of spiritual centre. There had been the occasional meeting there over the previous few months but I wasn't too keen on holding them too often as, not only was I otherwise very busy with too much already on my plate (I did all the cooking, such as it was, and the required hospitality chores for people when they came), but I hadn't yet got around to putting anything down on paper about the scheme which I could offer for people to consider. Besides, the house was in such a heck of a mess that it was also too embarrassing for me to have visitors that often.

This is where Sue came to the rescue. She was fairly conversant with some of my intentions for the Farm and said she was keen to be in on the ground floor in establishing such a centre and would like to work with me on it. She offered to help me clean up the place before the expected weekend meeting (that was a task and a half in itself. There was over three years of untidiness to plough through - so much so, that whenever people came to visit, they wiped their feet on the way out!). She said she'd be able to help cater for the visitors when they came, to muck in with them all, to make the drinks, do the cooking, etc. Her logic being that such an arrangement would also make things more acceptable to enable future meetings to be held there more often. It was a very persuasive offer which, although it meant Sue staying around longer than I had anticipated, or felt advisable, for the sake of getting the project off the ground, I pro visionally accepted.

192

The particular group meeting turned out to be quite a pivotal one for me as, due to certain of the questions that arose, I was jockeyed into the position where I needed to be a bit more specific in expressing some of my aims - which was a good opportunity for me. I first had to give them a bit of background information, explaining that the philosophy to which I subscribed professed to be of ancient origin, in fact the source of all subsequent world teachings which, over the aeons, had in many ways become distorted in interpretation. As a consequence, only that, so it is said, which had been passed down directly from Master to pupil retained its original purity.

Owing to the phases of ignorance which have periodically engulfed the human mind, the essence of these original teachings were obliged to go 'underground', so to speak, and eventually its sole custodians were those historic establishments known as the Mystery Schools, such as those of the Druids, the Egyptians, the Eleusinians, the Mithraic Orders, etc., - as well as the Essenes, where Jesus was said to have acquired much of his training.

It was a recognised facet of these early cultures that those drawn to the spiritual life would be accepted into these Temples and Academies of yore for specific training in the more esoteric aspects of this Universal Wisdom Religion (or Ageless Wisdom, as it is now often called). It was not a training in just book knowledge that was offered, but the enhancing of one's whole spiritual existence. This was achieved through a planned and ordered training programme that enabled one, by means of a series of graded expansions in consciousness under the guidance of experienced mentors, to penetrate deeper into the mysterious realms of esoteric sciences.

I confessed that the whole idea of such specialised training appealed to me immensely, and that there was certainly a desire within me to have a stab at such a training programme myself, if ever one was on offer. But maybe I was born into the wrong era?

However, in the coming age, so the teaching goes, the season for the open acknowledgement of these Mystery Schools and their doctrines will again come around and, over the coming centuries, they will slowly but surely resurface in various parts of the world, according to need. But apparently this can only take place when mankind is mature enough to accept their existence and have appreciation of the value of their contribution, and also that there are sufficient numbers of suitable applicants for the type of training which they will offer to warrant their appearance. It is understood that they will not sprout up over night, but will slowly re-evolve from a series of initial experimental efforts by those who can 'test the waters', so to speak, to see if and when such a system of training establishments are able to be of use and would be acceptable to the human consciousness.

Apparently, there have been, and are, many projects being started along these lines

whose function is to help lay the necessary foundations of such learning establishments. They may as yet vary widely in their aims and methods and their work is very
elementary compared to what it will be once their potential is realised, but their mere
existence indicates the beginnings of such a world-wide resurgence. They, apparently, are not necessarily aware of each other's efforts, nor will their motivation or role
be based on similar lines. As experimental projects, some are expected to have a
degree of success, and some will possibly have their failures, but whatever the outcome of their efforts, many valuable lessons will be learnt so that from the results of
each new wave of endeavour in this field mankind will be brought nearer to the time
when such schools will be fully functioning, publicly recognised and an acknowledged
feature of the coming age.

Whether any of this is true or not was not too relevant for me. As far as I was concerned,
it all had a feel of rightness, something which presented me with an appealing vision
that was sufficient to spur me on to try to get something working in my own little way.

Having presented to this group the basis and the motive for the intended project, I then
went into a little more detail of that which I had provisionally had in mind, to start with
anyway, regarding the Farm. First, to use some of the land around the Farmhouse for
producing organic foodstuffs, which in the future, with any hopes, would develop into
a market garden, possibly to be run on a commercial basis as well as supplying the
needs of those at the Farm.

Then to make certain alterations to the house so that it would be able to accommodate, say, an added half-dozen people or so. For this, I had drawn up a few possible
plans that should fit the bill in this area.

Once the schemes were under way, I would select various relevant aspects of the
philosophy, and through group study and group agreement, create an elementary
presentation of the salient points of each of them which, together as a compilation,
would serve as a suitable introduction for those wishing to know more about the
philosophy and possibly involve themselves in the centre's activities. Such an introduction would give a general view of the many topics involved and enable newcomers
to select those which held most interest for them. Once they had a clearer idea where
their interests might lie, they could then, through the study of recommended selected
source material, familiarise themselves with the deeper aspects of that which attracts
them before going on to other related topics - and if they felt they could add to any of
the information contained in this introductory compilation, which would need to be
very fluid and open to expansion, so much the better.

In addition to this type of activity, the principles of Natural Healing, Psychosynthesis
and meditation methods would be available, if it would help add to their progress, so
that they, in their turn, might eventually be more able to help others in these ways.
Although rather ambitious in its scope, it seemed a worthwhile target to aim for.

Ideally then, if things went according to plan, eventually a centre would be available where those who sought a more rational and deeper meaning to life could find a congenial atmosphere where help, guidance, support, and the encouragement of others of like mind would be at their disposal, a centre of peace where they might come for varying periods according to need, a few days, weeks, months, years even - or just pop in for a quick spiritual bath. Such was the vision.

In the meantime, it was up to me to organise and help put in place as much of the foundation work as possible in readiness for the time when all the required facilities became a working reality. Although I had some idea of what might be needed, it would certainly be too presumptuous of me, with my limited knowledge and experience in such matters, to think that I could carry out such an important and responsible task on my own.

To my mind it would need a group of suitable people working in close cooperation to take on and make ready all the facets of the project which were envisaged. If their efforts were successful, possibly an organised system of training could then be devised, one that was able to cater for many of the facets of an individual's spiritual development, from extrasensory to the intuitional.

But then, if it ever reached that stage, the obvious question would arise as to who would be spiritually experienced and capable enough to supervise such a programme of training? I suppose if something of this nature was ever on the cards for such a centre, and the need was great enough, there would at sometime be someone attracted to the project who was suitably equipped for the task. However, for the time being there was quite enough to concentrate on to get the project started without trying to predict future events.

From the time of that particular meeting, my musical engagements permitting, most subsequent weekends were devoted to group get-togethers at the Farm. These were composed of a selection of different small groups, each having its own particular focus, either helping out with the gardening work, or the building alterations, or studying a particular aspect of the philosophy, or some came just to soak in the peaceful and sympathetic spirit which was being generated there.

Early on in the year of 1971, Sue and I travelled up to the North of Scotland to visit the Findhorn Centre which, at that time, was a small spiritual organisation based in a caravan park which was becoming known for successful experiments with their special organic gardening methods. They maintained that by consciously cooperating with those non-physical nature spirits who are said to be the invisible builders and custodians of the vegetable kingdom, they were able to maintain the health and vitality of the soil and achieve a specifically high standard of quality in their produce. Our intention was not only to meet Eileen and Peter Caddy, who set up this centre and to talk with their colleagues whose developed extra-sensory faculties enabled them to see and work with these nature creatures, the existence of which we had already come across in our studies, but to glean some ideas as to how we could possibly incorporate their methods into our project.

It was a very fruitful and stimulating trip for us and we came back enthused and keen to concentrate our energies on preparing the land for the Summer's produce and to try to work more in harmony with nature's requirements (as well as with each other). The only blight on the trip was to hear from one of their members that my supportive friend and confident, Cyril Scott, had died. I was an ardent admirer of his written work which I had for years found very spiritually inspiring, being so very much on my wavelength. Although I was an occasional visitor to his Eastbourne home, due to my other activities I hadn't been to see him since the previous Summer, an omission on my part which I much regretted.

Now, with the Spring of 1971 coming on, I had high hopes for the Farm Centre; the group meetings were beginning to build up an encouraging momentum, the modifications to the house were well under way, we managed to get in a lot of the preparation work needed on the land and had also begun some of the planting, etc. However, hopes were dashed, because by this time, the same old incompatibility problems between Sue and I had once again become far too acute for either of us to tolerate. So, in spite of all our good intentions in setting up the Farm Centre, that Spring saw the final parting. She decided to move into town and help out with the work at the Gandolf's Garden organisation.

I carried on as best I could but there was far too much for me to take on alone. Because I saw so much promise in this Farm project and felt, at least for that period, it should have priority over other of my activities, I wound down a lot of my gig work and postponed my 'A' level studies (I think I might have gone in over my head with them anyway), so that I could concentrate on getting this centre up and running. However, as I was footing the bill for any tradesmen that were brought in, paying for all tools and materials needed for the building work (apart from the occasional work party, I was doing most of the menial jobs myself), plus all the gardening necessities, etc., from my band earnings, I was beginning to run out of cash.

Under these circumstances, I had little alternative but to accept more gigs which, on the one hand, would bring in the 'necessary' to continue with the work, yet, on the other hand, it would leave me less time to involve myself there, which would mean that the whole project would be delayed. I couldn't continue very well on my own and without funds, so from that Spring, the number of gigs began to increase, while the work at the centre began to decrease.

I still held the weekly group discussion meetings, whenever my musical commitments permitted, and even managed to put some of my ideas on paper for future meetings, but for the time being I just had to have more money coming in.

CHAPTER 14 - VERONICA AND THE RELUCTANT SCRIBE

1971 - 1975 Approaching My Fifties

It was lucky, and very timely, that demand for my musical work was now healthily building up. I had no ambitious intentions of entering the professional entertainment field again, nor was I looking for any type of prestigious work; all that I had in mind was a sufficient number of jobs, preferably local ones, that I could enjoy and which would enable me to meet my basic domestic running expenses. I had acquired three residential pub gigs each week, plus about two or three extra weekly bookings that normally came in, which, although it helped maintain a steady inflow of cash, unfortunately left me with hardly any evening to spare for anything else. Some weekends, I managed to arrange mini tours around the country, featuring with local bands, and, I'm happy to say, with very encouraging reviews of my performances. The following is one of that period which I dug out from my time-worn and rapidly decaying archives.

"CY LAURIE"

"Following in the footsteps of Bruce Turner and Sam Rimmington, who have in recent months appeared as star solo attractions with a local band at the Birmingham Arms Salutation Stomp Jazz Club, a bigger than ever crowd welcomed Cy Laurie's first visit to this club last Friday and his first to Birmingham for many a year.

"It is a tribute to the Artesian Hall Stompers, who provided the backing, that Cy was able to fit so admirably into their framework of traditional and contemporary New Orleans music. In fact, I think the marriage was successful. I have rarely seen the band in such good form and with his sure Dodds-style clarinet, Cy Laurie was not at all overcome by the powerful Dan Pawson horn, and the resulting front line sound of Cy, Dan, and Stan, was pure joy for a New Orleans fan.

"We revelled in the old standards - "Weary Blues", "Willie the Weeper", "St. Louis Blues", and others and Cy showed himself the same quiet, courteous, and interesting guy as he ever was when raving writers talked of a Johnny Dodds reincarnation. Cy also has that quality of all great jazzmen, that of being able to inspire a band and make it swing with him . . . . Come back soon, Cy Laurie!"

Les Page, "Melody Maker" - 18th March 1971

On top of all these gigs, I had a series of concert tours for the Continent lined up, three or four of these with the Max Collie Band In Germany and Switzerland. It was on one of these sessions with Max's band that a recording was made, being the first that I had been involved in since the late 50s. It was a concert we played in Hamburg on the 7th

May, 1971, and consisted of about eight or ten standard numbers, which Max subsequently had issued on LP. Max in his wisdom arranged for another concert to be
recorded during a further tour that I did with him the following September. Here again
it consisted of a selection of about eight to ten standard numbers issued on LP.

I was still not too backward in coming forward when it came to chatting up some of the
girls at the gigs although I seemed to be overly selective when it came to getting too
friendly with any of them or asking them out. It was early in June of that year when I met
Veronica, (Ronnie) at one of my local Essex gigs, a comely, tall, golden blonde young
thing, somewhat younger than I who had a very friendly and loving nature and we
began to arrange to see each other at a few of my other jazz gigs. It was not long
before, without going into too much detail, I got around to explaining a little about
myself, where I lived, that I was living alone at the moment as a relationship had
recently come to an end, which hit me very hard, and also that most weekends I
entertained a few friends at my home where we discussed various philosophical
subjects. She told me that she too had recently broken up with her boy friend so we
found we had each other to console.

One evening some weeks later I telephoned Ronnie to invite her over to grace the
stately Laurie pile with her presence. After some slight hesitation she in her trusting
innocence decided to accept. I therefore hastily arranged to pick her up at a local
railway station before she had time to reconsider the proposition.

I duly arrived at the station at the pre-arranged time, (but Ronnie had missed the train
and when she did arrive I remember remarking 'that it was rather a late date') and after
a warm greeting by the ticket office, being the gentleman I am, I escorted her to my
car, politely opened the door to assist her into the passenger seat, forgetting to warn
her that I hadn't cleared out the old banana skins on the floor of the car where she was
due to sit . . . . . After I had helped her back into her seat, dusted her down, profusely
apologised, and checked to make sure there were no bruises about her person (not in
an obviously groping fashion I might add), I thought what an unfortunate way to start
- and end - a relationship.

But nope, it didn't turn out that way. In spite of that incident, she was still game enough
for me to drive her to the Farm that night - whether it was due to my irresistible charm
or her love of old banana skins, she's been here ever since! (What staying power for
one so young.)

I had been living alone for a few months and although the state of the place would not
exactly have qualified for an illustrated feature article in "Homes & Gardens" magazine, I considered it fairly habitable. But somehow, I had the feeling by Ronnie's initial
response on entering the house that she wasn't in total agreement with that opinion,
especially by the way she inscribed her name in the dust on the piano and counted the

half-empty milk bottles in the kitchen. In the following weeks she took up the daunting challenge, little by little, of bringing the place up to a more agreeable standard of tidiness - a chore which, incidentally, she has been saddled with ever since.

The building work had been going on steadily since the Spring of that year, most weekends we catered for various size working parties which were supervised by Harry Laverick, a regular group member and ex-architect who, each week-end, used to leave me with a list of materials to purchase and jobs to complete during the coming week in preparation for the next weekend foray.

It was the following Summer and Autumn months of 1971 which turned out to be quite a hairy one for both Ronnie and I. We had more than our share of rain and as the unfinished building work left the house exposed to the elements in places, by the constant, and often panic-stricken, manoeuvring of tarpaulin sheeting, apart from the minor upstairs soaking, we only just managed to keep the place acceptably dry. One particular weekend the weather became exceptionally vengeful when I was away on a series of gigs and Ronnie had decided to stay behind at the Farm.

Before I left I had nailed down an area of exposed roof above our bedroom with a number of 8' x 4' sheets of plywood. It was during one torrential downpour in the middle of the night that Ronnie was awakened by a heavy leakage of rain streaming into the bedroom by way of an attention-seeking sparking light socket, which thoroughly soaked the bed into the bargain.

She hastily leapt out of bed and climbed up on to the roof (access to which was by a strategically placed ladder, that was practically a fixture during that period) only to see, following a powerful gust of wind, a formation of 8' x 4' plywood sheets flying through the air which then eventually dispersed in all directions, apparently impelled by a life of their own.

It was as much as Ronnie could do to keep the rest of the hatches battened down. She left a note for me (pinned to the gate) to the effect that I should beware of being attacked by flying plywood sheets, the evidence of the night's bombardment being scattered all over the lawn and garden.

As to the garden work, that had virtually come to a standstill and much of it was too overgrown to salvage any of the sparse produce which was well hidden among the weeds. By another stroke of luck, Ronnie had an interest in that side of the work too (having a good knowledge and love of plants and trees) and by the Winter, we had cleared enough of the ground in readiness to tackle the cultivation, planting, and maintenance needed for the coming year.

For Ronnie (and she too is a very private person) this was a learning curve as she adjusted to a new way of life, being dropped in, so to speak, at the deep-end regarding me, my one-pointedness as to the Ageless Wisdom and my plans for the Farm project. Also, I met her shortly after my previous relationship had finally ended and she would be the first to admit that she went through an emotional time, but as she said some time later ' she hung in there.'

She also brought a fresh voice to the group meetings, although more a listener at first. I suggested books that I thought might interest her from my precious collection, Alice A. Bailey, Vera Stanley Alder, the Initiate books, Leadbeater, Cyril Scott, A.E. Powell and Jinarajadasa. She became vegetarian and has over the years dished-up some wonderful grub. Ronnie also has a wide appreciation of all music and is a jazz enthusiast - especially of me - he says modestly (and Trummy Young)! she is always there to support and encourage me in all I do (as I am always there for her) and our love has deepened and grown through the years and I count myself a lucky man!

With my other commitments, it wasn't easy for me to keep on top of the work all the time, even with Ronnie's help, and this resulted in many of our regular visitors becoming understandably impatient with the Centre's rate of progress, especially the expected written work. From my angle, the involvement of the groups in the intended compilation of the philosophy, which I felt should have been the main purpose of the group meetings, proved to be a non-starter. They seemed to look to me to do all the work in that area which, on top of everything else, was just not possible. That is not to say that our group discussions were unconstructive, many important and relevant issues were considered and with Ronnie taking the minutes of the meetings, we had something to go on to help maintain the continuity of the discussions.

However, mere discussion, as interesting as they were at times, was not the primary purpose and before we became too set in this kind of pattern, I felt it necessary to clarify the function of the Centre - at least, as I saw it. So in time for the meeting of late November, 1971, when much of the structure of the building work had been completed and the remaining jobs just needed to tick over for the Winter months, I had written a paper on how I saw the future role of the project. It turned out to be an introductory statement of intent, something which had really been needed for some time.

All the regular members of the groups at that time seemed in agreement with the content of the paper, yet in spite of their expressed keenness to be involved in the work of establishing such a Centre, they still looked to me, not only to keep on top of the building work, but to do all the written work as well, to get the intended compilation under way, to organise the discussion themes, and to generally steer the project in the intended direction - tasks which I had anticipated would be shared among the group.

Their point of view was somewhat understandable. It was I who originally initiated the project, it was I who formulated and proposed its intended function, it was my home around which it all centred, and it was from my own pocket that it was all funded. I suppose it was inevitable that it be considered as my 'baby', and therefore my responsibility.

So, slowly it was dawning on me that their assistance in these crucial areas was not as forthcoming as I had hoped. For the sake of keeping the project on track, I was obliged to succumb to the situation and apply myself to formulating the philosophical purposes and functions of the centre. By early March, 1972, in my efforts in this direction, to put some 'flesh on the skeleton', I had written three papers relating to the way I thought the project should go. In addition to the initial statement of intent, which I entitled "Introductory Outline of Farm Project", there was one on "Purposeful Group Activity" (in which I was able to express some of my thoughts on attaining and maintaining constructive and congenial group interplay), and another proposing a "12 Month Plan for the project.

It was really a big challenge for me to commit to paper many of the thoughts and ideas on the subject which had been floating around in my mind for some time, but I suppose as I was forced to concede to the role of administrator-of-sorts, I should take it as philosophically as I could and try to make a special effort to get the thing off the ground - at least, until such time as others might come along who would be able to take the whole project further on towards the hoped-for ideal.

In spite of the well-intentioned response to these papers during the months of '72, the number of regular group members visiting the Farm began to dwindle. There were, of course many casual visitors who came, staying for either a day or more at a time, but often their purposes were not necessarily concerned with the work and future of the centre. Some helped out with the garden work, while others liked to talk about their lives, interests, or problems, or make use of my prized collection of books, but most came to take advantage of the peaceful atmosphere and companionship which was available. No charge was ever made for any accommodation or food, etc., as I was of the mind that such facilities should always be freely available for those with spiritually motivated intentions - and if any voluntary return was forthcoming in the way of helping with the chores around the place, so much the better and it was well appreciated.

It was decided that for those whose concern was for the Centre's future, we would hold monthly discussion meetings. So, the pattern was that each month I wrote a paper on a particular theme connected with the philosophy and sent a copy to each of them at least two weeks before the forthcoming meeting. This would allow time to study the paper and more constructively contribute their thoughts to the following month's discussion.

This arrangement, in a loose fashion, went on throughout that year and well into 1973, and it seemed to work fairly well. Nevertheless, I personaly wasn't totally satisfied, as I had more meaningful aims than this in mind.

By the Spring of '73 I felt that some form of renewed effort should be made as we seemed to be getting into a rut. But where would I find the time to make such effort? We had quite a full life at that period; I was out on gigs most every night of the week and away for many weekends, there was the internal work on the house to attend to, the second fixing and decorating, etc., which I had hoped would be completed by the Summer, the work outside in the grounds such as laying lawns and general land-scaping, tree pruning, logging, and never ending maintenance tasks, as well as many other ongoing jobs. Ronnie kindly took upon her shoulders most of the internal decorating of the house and the planting and tending of the vegetable garden, this added to her domestic chores, looking after me and employment as a part-time li-brarian. There was little time left to attend to the Centre's activities.

Nevertheless, I decided to put into operation a little recruitment drive. I wrote and distributed a small booklet laying out the intentions of the Farm project and included in it a list of possible fields of research for those wishing to help in producing a compi-lation of such subjects. The response was poor and not very encouraging but it did help get the word around to an added number of interested people.

One of these was Karl Frances who, with his wife Betty, ran the Acacia House Centre in West London. It was during a visit there that we had the enviable good fortune of meeting another of my long admired authors, Vera Stanley Alder, who was a guest of the house. Ronnie and I manaaged to have a long and interesting talk with her in which I briefed her on the work in progress at the Farm. In response to her obvious interest, I offered to send her a copy of one or two of the papers that I had written on the project.

As a result of her expressed approval of our aims for the Farm, and her eventual visits there, she became a great source of encouragement for us to intensify our efforts in that direction. Throughout the Summer and Autumn, right through to the end of the year, more people were using the place as a retreat in which they could find the peace and companionship to help them in relating to their inner being. There were routine meditations, group discussions, and a general sharing of experiences, etc., which were all very well received. Unfortunately, with no help by others in realising my in-tentions of compiling an introductory course in the philosophy. Although there were many opportunities for me to expound on certain aspects of the philosophy during the periods set aside for discussions, without a more stable background in the whole doctrine, such generalised and spasmodic efforts, appreciated as they were at the time, turned out to be mere skating on the surface of the subject - which in my view, left its more significant and spiritually stimulating depths virtually untouched.

This seemed to disturb me unduly at the time, especially regarding those who seemed seriously to want to know more, as I had little time to devote to them personally. Over those months I was becoming more resigned to the fact that if I thought such an introductory presentation of the philosophy would be as important as I envisaged, I would have to attempt such a venture on my own. By the early part of 1974 this need was making itself felt so strongly that I concluded that if I was to make the attempt to satisfy it, I would really have to jettison much of my other involvements, especially my musical work, which took up so much of my time. Apart from my own gigs, I had been doing a lot of work with the Black Bottom Stompers resulting in such an overcrowded date book that it meant some weekends I was hectically chasing from one gig to cram in two, or sometimes three, performances a day. I wouldn't have minded this so much if it was not taking me away from that which I deemed more important, the Farm Centre.

I decided that, from a predetermined date, to off-load all my musical commitments and take a short sabbatical, just to see if I could get my mind around drafting out some semblance of the contemplated compilation. The date chosen conveniently to start this musical lay-off was 1st April of that year, and I had thought (optimistically) that a few months of concentrated research and the collating of the required material would be sufficient to enable me to knock out a draft outline of the scheme. Yet once again this proved to be a case of naive wishful thinking.

So on the due date, with high hopes and much enthusiasm, I once again hung up my clarinet, lined up a selection of relevant books, and cleared the decks for intensive desk work - I was raring to go. However, as I should have anticipated, with the Summer coming on and all the work that needed to be done in and around the house, I was constantly being waylaid in my writing resolves. I knew that my sabbatical was an open-ended affair and that there was no specific deadline involved, so I yielded to the pleasure of being in the open air, soaking up the sunshine with Ronnie and tackling much of the practical work during those Summer months casually in my stride, doing only that which was really pressing and doing my best to try and wind down a bit in the process - and I enjoyed the leisurely pace of it all.

However, the writing side was not entirely neglected, as I turned out a couple of papers which proved very helpful to others and to the purposes of the centre. It was during a group meeting around May ('74) that I was asked to enlarge upon my understanding of the cyclic nature of spiritual growth, not only as it applies to individuals but also to humankind in general, as well as to the world at large. Included in my attempted explanation I pointed out that, according to my studies of the subject, the world is on the threshold of a new and more creative cycle and it's effects will be particularly evident at spiritual levels. We are about to enter a veritable New Age.

The concept of the 'New Age' in those days was completely different to the distorted, and often degraded meaning which is currently associated with the term. It was then used, and still is by those who subscribe to these doctrines, to signify a coming Planetary age in which the prevalonce of disease, suffering, and injustice will be superseded by a state of health, peace, and harmony; where ignorance and selfishness will be dissolved by understanding, love, and the recognition of the creative role mankind needs to play in the overall evolution of the Planet.

It is said that conditions in preparation for this New Age have been building up for many centuries, making increasingly available opportunities for the spiritual growth of humankind. Such opportunities become particularly more accessible during the last quarter of each century, and the following year (1975) was likely to prove the beginning of a new phase for those inclined to make the needed effort. Such a concept was not new to those conversant with that and other related philosophies, but what was particularly relevant at that time was that such effort could be gainfully prepared for in that present year (1974) and I suggested that, as a group, if it was agreeable, we could work to that end.

It was because of the seriousness of interest that was aroused by members of this group to such a proposition, and the fact that I felt there was not enough 'noise' being made by the relevant organisations in relation to such an important world event, that I subsequently wrote a little pamphlet on the topic which I thought could usefully be distributed to others who might find it of help.

The pamphlet was titled, "In Preparation for 1975, - a reminder to students of Occultism", the basic thought behind it being that, if from 1975 there was to be a period of spiritual stimulation, then 1974 could be seen as the year where one could not only attune one's mind to be open and receptive to any expected higher influences, but make special effort to devise and put into practice any schemes that may enhance the quality of life of the needy. Included in this pamphlet was a section dealing with a few suggested methods as to how such preparation could be implemented.

Copies of this pamphlet were duly distributed together with an accompanying paper related to the background of the expected spiritual stimulation. The response, to my surprise, was quite encouraging, so much so that not only did it produce some helpful contacts but some even sent money, quite a bit in fact, as a contribution to 'our work' - totally unsolicited of course. Also prominent people in the New Age movement of the time requested extra copies for distribution through their particular channels. David Tansley, the eminent Radionics practitioner, wanted a quantity to include in the mailout of his specialised periodic journal. To my surprise, and delight, the whole project was sufficiently successful for me to contemplate further pamphlets on the same theme, even if they did have to be squeezed in between other jobs that demanded attention.

A steady trickle of visitors were still coming to the Farm, mainly for their personal retreat purposes and, at that period, one or two had moved into the new living quarters on a semi-permanent basis. However, the place was nowhere near achieving its intended aims as a centre for training in esoteric studies. In fact, the people who were then using the place, apart from the periods set aside where we would come together for group discussions and meditation, were continually wanting to talk about either their problems, particular beliefs, or experiences. Although such conversations on the whole served a useful purpose, it took up much time and diverted me from many other tasks that I had set myself to do, especially the intended compilation.

So, come the beginning of that Winter, when the number of visitors slackened off, I felt I really had to get my act together, discipline myself and organise my time more efficiently, so that I could put more concentrated effort into the papers I hoped to write. First off was another pamphlet on the 1975 theme which I planned to distribute in the early part of that year. This was entitled, "In Consideration of 1975", and was basically a reminder to students of esoteric thought of the significance and imminence of the period. Then in the following Spring another pamphlet was sent out, this one was called "The Significance of 1975", all aimed, incidentally, at those who were more likely to be open to such thoughts and inclined to add their penny-worth to the overall uplifting effort.

As for the compilation attempt, which was now forming in my mind as a more comprehensive training programme on the fundamentals of the Ageless Wisdom, I had only been able to work on it in a spasmodic fashion over the months. This was due to the practical work required around the place, not least was the time spent attending to the vegetable garden, as once again the planting season had come around, and the renewed effort Ronnie and I decided to make to visit some of the groups we had neglected over the years.

Included in these group visits were those connected with ecological and environmental issues such as, Conservationists, Vegetarian Society, Soil Association, Friends of the Earth, etc., all of which we discovered had small local branches, which therefore made it easier for us to keep in touch with their work. Occasional meetings with these groups were also held at the Farm throughout the year even though there was no direct connection with the philosophical side with which I was personally engaged (yet to me they were all included in the various facets of the same forward-looking type of work).

For years, in common with many others, I have held the belief that it is man who caused the pollution which plagues our natural environment, that he has abused and dangerously contaminated the whole of the Planetary atmosphere, not only physically, the results of which are there for all to see, but emotionally, through intolerance, selfishness, and aggression, and mentally also because of the unsupportable justification of his negative and harmful thinking. If this is so, he has much to answer for, and it is therefore part of his job not only to prevent further damage to our Planet's life-sustaining systems, but to make due effort to clean up the prevailing unholy mess he has been creating for so long. We all are in a way responsible, as are we all victims of its effects, and therefore we are all required to play our part in actively sanitising our world, at every level, from helping and healing wherever we can to the intelligent giving of love, support and understanding to all, and this without discrimination.

All very idealistic, but it was in this context that I support the efforts of these environmental groups. They were all doing their own thing, all working within their own fields yet, viewed from the broader framework, they had so much in common. I had made various attempts to bring them all together, not that they should amalgamate into one group, as this would be neither practical nor desirable because they each had different lines of work, but to pool their resources, to cooperate with each other in utilising common requirements such as their promotional, fund raising, and recruitment activities.

I even tried to set up a form of coordinating unit to offer such facilities and services, not only for their labour-saving and economic advantage but for helping them spread their message more effectively in their own particular fields, yet with the aid and support of a group of groups.

The intention was to have mailing lists, research facilities, speaker contacts, halls and venues, advertising channels, printing and publicity needs, etc., and the skills that go with them, even lobbyists to help influence those leaders who could support their principles. All these to be freely available to those who were intent on proclaiming and promoting the principles of working in harmony with nature, of goodwill, sharing, and relief of suffering.

I envisaged an eventual world-wide network of contacts whereby each could link up with all others and so build up an interchange of information, methods, progress, experience, etc. It all seemed far too idealistic for those I approached about helping me set up such a scheme; most treated their particular group and line of work as being specialised and therefore independent of others. It was really a non-starter at the time yet, even though these days when so much headway has been made in this direction, especially with the facilities provided by the internet, I still feel that with more cooperation between such forward looking groups, of whatever persuasion, they will be able to spread their message to, and consequently influence, a wider public - and therefore more likely to bring about their needed aims.

By the summer of '75 I had managed to get about a third of the way through the intended outline of the training programme, which then consisted mainly of jottings on the back of envelopes, which I hoped to put in some sort of order once I had enough information to determine how the whole thing was likely to work out. This project again had to be delayed when, in response to the '75 pamphlets, I was obliged to reply to the many queries requesting further information on the philosophy.

Two relevant contacts that resulted from such correspondence I feel worth mentioning; first during July of that year, I had met Benjamin Creme, another student of the Ageless Wisdom approach who was running a small meditation group in North London. I was contacted by a member of his group, Dick Benson, who had read one of my '75 pamphlets and invited to visit them. The outcome was that Ronnie and I subsequently arranged to attend one of Ben's meetings and, to my delight, he seemed to be very much working on similar lines as myself, even if his emphasis was somewhat different.

A major concept of this school of thought (and, it might be added, not exclusively to this school of thought) was that there exists on Earth certain highly evolved spiritual beings whose work in helping mankind from the more subtle levels of life is supervised by one who, during certain world periods, appears among men to help guide them on to their next phase of spiritual development. To such civilisations, it is said, did this same being come into the world in the guise of the Hindu's Krishna, the Muslim's Imam Mahdi, the Buddhist's Maitreya Buddha, the Jew's Messiah, the Christian's Christ, etc., and that in the coming age he is due to appear again to aid the spiritual progress of the world.

It was this concept, the monumental importance and imminence of this 'second coming of the Christ', that was Ben's major focus, as those whose attention have been subsequently drawn to Ben's work, which is now internationally recognised, will know full well.

There was obviously a sympathy in motivation and aim that I felt with Ben. This resulted in Ronnie and I supporting and regularly involving ourselves in his efforts, especially his meditation work. During mid-'75 there existed only a handful of us working with Ben's meditation group. In fact, sometimes only just three or four of us, Ben, Phyllis (his wife) occasionally, and Ronnie and I, and it was not uncommon for us to continue our evening meditations until way into the early hours of the morning. Of course, since those days his meditation groups have not only substantially increased in size but their off-shoots have spread to many other countries throughout the world.

Also around this period I had a letter from a member of another group explaining that, after coming across one of my '75 pamphlets, they realised that they too were studying similar teachings and they were interested in my approach and would like to know more about it. Could I give them any more information or, better still, would I like to attend one of their group meetings?

So, Ronnie and I, over a period, went to three or four of their meetings which, although interesting, seemed rather more elementary and general than anticipated. They were certainly studying various aspects of the Ageless Wisdom, as they rightly said, but it was all very casual and not in a particularly ordered way. They inquired as to our involvement in the subject and whether we would be interested in joining their group with a view to helping them understand more of what it was all about, etc. We said that we had quite a lot going on but we'd give it some thought and let them know. Ronnie had been immersed in the subject for at least four and a half years by then by being around me.

207

They did me the honour of asking me to help them in their studies. I duly explained that I considered the philosophy to be of a very deep nature and of great significance and although I had been studying it myself for the past quarter of a century or more, I was still comparatively only scratching the surface. I pointed out that to really do the subject justice, a lot of serious preliminary work should be gone through before one could study its intricacies with any effectiveness.

I was quite surprised when they unanimously responded by asking if I would be in a position to go over these preliminaries with them. I, of course, said I'd be more than happy to take them through some of the basics, as much as I myself understood them. But to do so, because I had so much already on my plate, it would mean me shelving certain other projects that I was working on.This would not be such a sacrifice under the circumstances if we all thought it would be a worthwhile exercise.

However, I explained that as I had worked with various groups before and had an idea of some of the likely pitfalls that may be encountered, to get the most out of it, it would be preferable that any work that we did as a group, should really be tackled in a more workmanlike manner than their previous efforts. To help do this, I would suggest certain guidelines that should be considered.

First, if we all agreed it was going to be an Ageless Wisdom study group, the concepts studied should be confined to only those pertaining to the doctrines of the Ageless Wisdom. In my eyes, it is a subject of great depth and to gain the most benefit, it needs to be worked on in an organised and structured way. This would entail a regularity of meetings, convenient to all, and each meeting would have a set and predetermined objective so that we all knew where we stood and what to expect.

Secondly, on their part, they should try to take the whole affair as a serious study, it should not be seen just as a series of get-togethers to indulge in interesting philosophical conversation, however pleasing it might be, but should be tackled with a definite focus and more than a touch of discipline. It would preferably include a certain amount of note-taking, possibly a bit of voluntary home-work and, most importantly, an earnest endeavour to apply its principles in their daily lives, all this according to one's personal inclination.

Thirdly, that we all should be clear that it would only be the fundamentals of the various doctrines that would be possible at this time and any deeper probing may need to be left for a later date once much of the basics had been covered. This would minimise any unnecessary diversions or confusion and, with any luck, lay more secure foundations for any subsequent and more profound delvings into the subject.

Fourthly, they should understand that whatever I personally may say on any of the topics studied, should not be taken as gospel, that it would only be my interpretation which they would be receiving and therefore, by no stretch of the imagination, be construed as a final word. Each must come to their own conclusions as to the measure of truth within the concepts studied.

Fifthly, purely as a recommendation, a basic understanding and practice of certain methods of meditation would well complement any study work which may be undertaken. This, if it was acceptable, could conveniently be fitted in as the other work proceeds.

Lastly, that although the way I've put it may all sound a bit academic, it should be seen as an experiment and taken with more than a touch of humour and, above all, something to be enjoyed. If it works out as expected and is found of use, all to the good, if not, there's nothing lost and we can either try another approach or just be happy that we have been able to make contact and be friends.

After a few light-hearted exchanges with such comments as "it sounds as if we would be going back to school". etc., I said yes, in a way it would be, but there would be no harm in that either, as most of us could benefit by having a little more mental discipline in our lives. Anyway, I left them with the thought that if, after bearing such guidelines in mind, they then felt they would really like to go ahead, I would be more than grateful for the opportunity to be of help in that way. I suggested they chew the matter over for about a month or so and if and when they wished, to let me know their thoughts on it.

Little did I suspect that I was prising open Pandora's Box, that as a result of this meeting another phase of my activities would begin.

CHAPTER 15 - ONCE MORE ON THE ROAD

1976 - 83 - My Early and Mid-Fifties

By the latter months of 1975, the usefulness of the Farm as a centre had become increasingly disappointing to me. Although there was an intermittent stream of visitors throughout the Summer and Autumn, it seemed to be attracting some of the less serious 'hippie' element, young people who were quite happy to take advantage of the free facilities offered but not particularly interested in the spiritual purposes connected with the place. One of the conditions of the free use of the facilities was that there should be no animal food consumed on the premises, that visitors should refrain from in-house smoking, yet I had reason to believe that these conditions were being violated. What I didn't want was that the place would become a 'drop in for drop outs', and that the conducive atmosphere we had endeavoured to create would be adversely effected.

Because of this, and the fact that all my efforts to generate any regular constructive group activity there had come to naught, serious thoughts of curtailing the number of visitors to the Farm were becoming more prominent in my mind. It would certainly leave me much freer to catch up on compiling the training programme - if I could discipline myself to get down to it.

In the event, it wasn't long before I was contacted by Valerie Stockwell one of the main instigators of the previously mentioned group wanting help in studying the Ageless Wisdom. It seemed that most of them were keen to go ahead with regular meetings and they were ready to start their studies as soon as it was convenient for me. It would only be a small group of about half-dozen, I was told, and that we could use the lounge of Val's house, if that would be acceptable to me.

I didn't let on that such a number would be preferable for me. I was not experienced in speaking to groups of people, especially in large numbers, and was a bit too self-conscious to bring myself to do so - I certainly didn't have the confidence to attempt any public speaking. So, as far as I was concerned, the smaller the group the better.

In a way, this invitation to help them in their studies was another lucky turn of events for me. I came to view it as a possible temporary alternative to the study course I was hoping to start at the Farm. I thought if the time and circumstances were not yet right for people to come there for any regular and substantial sort of group undertaking, I could take some of the study work out to them, such a group as this would, in addition to introducing them to the philosophy, help provide the necessary experience for me. Also having already started making notes for such a study course, they would be of use in helping me guide the group through their first few meetings and, meanwhile, I would be able to continue with the rest of the compilation work and framing the notes required for future meetings.

It was agreed that from late November 1975 Ronnie and I meet the group every Tuesday between 7.30pm and 9.30pm, and for this, Val not only kindly offered the use of her home, but laid on a goodly offering of refreshments for us. For the first meeting, for their approval, I made out a list of subjects which I thought we could include in our studies and the order in which I proposed we should take them. It was a general introductory get-together to acquaint them with the background of the philosophy and to present an outline of what they could expect. I suggested we start and close each evening with a short meditation to help align the group and, if all went well over the first few months, because of the extreme importance of the subject, we could then delve a bit deeper into the meditation side and include a study of its meaning, methods, purposes, and its relation to the philosophy.

It so happened that all did go well. So much so, that by the March of 1976 the desirability of starting another group specifically for the study and practice of meditation, just had to come about. At that time the popularity of Hatha Yoga (the Yoga related to physical postures) was rapidly increasing and classes dealing with its practice were beginning to sprout up in all sorts of locations, even being included in many official adult education courses. A couple of our group members were also certified teachers of Hatha Yoga and, as such, were in contact with various others who were involved in its practice. It was from these contacts that we were able to build up a sizeable group of people interested in studying meditation.

One of Val's group members, Vi, with keenness and industry, managed to procure for us the weekly use of a meeting room situated within the local Ursuline Convent School. Although the Mother Superior and nuns were made well aware that our meditation meetings would not be directly related to the teachings of Catholicism, they still allowed us the use of their premises. Friday was the evening chosen and from the first meeting, the subject matter was received with obvious approval by the group, which was very encouraging for me. Of course, as often happens after the first few weeks of such an effort, there are those who will eventually drop out, but this leaves others who find the work more suitable to their needs and are therefore more likely to be consistent in their interest.

So, what with the involvement in Ben's group, which we attended in his North London home at least two or three times a week, principally on Mondays and Wednesdays then the Tuesday and Friday study groups, plus the preparation work for these latter meetings, as well as the various group get-togethers that were still being held at the Farm, the pattern of my life had more or less become stabilised in these activities for the immediate future. It continued that way right throughout that year and well into the following year of 1977, when nearing the end of the planned course of study with the Ageless Wisdom group, a further group was started. This was the result of requests from various people who, over the previous months, had heard about the work we were doing and wanted some of the same.

To accommodate this additional group, the Tuesday evening study sessions were held each fortnight and the meditation work was then shifted to each alternate Tuesday. This then left the Fridays free so that the new group could be fitted in using the same alternating fortnightly arrangement of study and meditation. As this seemed to work satisfactorily, after some months of starting the Friday group, Val, who was ever ready to get the word around, suggested we put an advert in the local paper to recruit more people so that I could start a further group. Also, by using her 'phone number, she could give those who answered the advert an idea of what it was 'we were about', from the viewpoint of one who had been working with the material. It meant more work for me but I felt that if, by starting another group, we would be able to help satisfy a need, then there was no question of refusing.

The outcome of this was that by the Autumn of that year a third group had started, this time on Thursday evening, with the use of the home of one of the previous group members. This group took off fairly rapidly, possibly because some of these new members already had some background knowledge as a result of their own efforts in the 'great search'.

It was interesting for me to find that although I was using the same set of notes and jottings, as sparse as they were, for each group as a basis upon which I could construct and put over the relevant concepts, to my surprise, each group seemed to draw out of me a different viewpoint, and therefore put a different slant on the subject matter. So really, although the substance was always the same, no two groups had been given exactly the same material.

No charge was ever made for these meetings, although invariably members contributed either tea, biscuits, or other snackable-type offerings, to help those who were kind enough to host the evenings and who took it on themselves to organise refreshments.

Ben's group had also stepped up a notch by then and that too was growing in membership as his message was spreading much further afield. He apparently was gifted with the extrasensory faculty of clairaudience and as a result of the information he received from his inner contact he announced that the Christ was now in the world, that the New Age work had commenced, and that there were many people in the world eagerly waiting to hear of that momentous occurrence. Ben himself was then getting around much more, lecturing and holding meditation groups throughout the UK, and producing the literature which was to help carry his work to many other countries. He was building an active organisation which eventually, through the medium of his talks, the books he had written, newsletters, his magazine, "Share International", and recognition by the news media, was to attract people in their thousands.

Although I was sympathetic and supportive towards Ben's approach and the philosophy upon which he based his pronouncements, as well as feeling a close affinity towards him personally, I couldn't bring myself to get unreservedly swept along with the euphoria that many of his associates appeared to do when hearing of such a significant event as he was now proclaiming, at least not without some means of substantiating it for myself. I certainly did not doubt the possibility that such an event had happened, but, as usual for me, I had to reserve judgement.

Not being an 'organisation' type of person in these matters (I had a natural preference for small and informal groups), I found myself beginning to keep a certain distance from Ben's public work. Besides I personally had so many things of my own going on at this time that, even if I had wanted to, it was just not possible for me to get too involved in his growing organisation, particularly as another aspect of my life began to enter into the equation.

Although the whole pattern of my existence, for years by then, had been geared towards spiritual-type endeavours as working with Ben's group, my own study and meditation groups, ongoing involvement in compiling a study course and establishing a Centre at the Farm, as well as my own personal study and meditation efforts, there were certain changes taking place within me that seemed inconsistent with all my past hopes and aspirations in these matters. To my astonishment, not to mention bewilderment, the sense of usefulness and satisfaction that being involved in such apparently worthy activities was fast waning. I was beginning to be overtaken by an inner restlessness which was something I could neither account for nor which I desired.

I was so fortunate I was able to work in these fields which I aspired to, that of helping others, as well as myself, who were reaching out for a greater understanding of life. Yet in spite of that, there was now a certain emptiness growing within me, an increasing feeling of discontent. I was certainly not becoming disenchanted with the way of life I had assumed nor with my service offerings, such as they were, nor with my philosophical convictions. Yet somehow by this time, although my life was full, it was not fulfilling.

I was becoming very uneasy about my life direction and purposes and had recurring feelings of "what was it all for?" Had I come to the end in my need to search for a deeper meaning to life? If so, where do I go from here? Even thoughts of a change of direction were beginning to intrude upon me which, even if I had considered them seriously, would not have necessarily alleviated this dissatisfaction and disillusionment I found myself experiencing. Besides which, where else would I find such an agreeable and constructive outlet for my aspirations? These and similar questions now plagued my mind as I unexpectedly and unaccountably entered into a prolonged phase of what can be described as a sense of spiritual aridity.

Over the Summer and Autumn months of 1977 this state really took hold, I seemed to have lost a lot of my old enthusiasm and motivation and, towards the end of the year, I felt innerly quite alone, forsaken, and purposeless. I was assailed by self doubt and self questioning. Were all my years of yearning, effort, and sacrifice, just a complete waste of energy and time? What did I have to show for it all? I was in a state of sheer negativity and there seemed no clear way forward, I saw only an abyss ahead of me. I discussed it all with Ronnie as best I could, yet as sympathetic as she was, giving me as ever her loving support, there was no way it could be accounted for. I sometimes think that it must have been a bit disconcerting for her at that time too as I wasn't the most light-hearted of companions to be with. I felt I had come to a dead end and I didn't know what to do about it. I could only resign myself to the situation and until something better turned up there was no alternative but to continue as I was and just hope that life would eventually show me a way. Which, with my old friend 'luck' again coming to my rescue, in time, it did.

Through a series of coincidences, I was presented with choices that would never otherwise have entered my head. First, after over three years of total absence from the jazz scene and contact with any of my fellow jazzers of the past, I was surprised to receive a request to feature with a band booked for a month's tour of the Middle East. Of course, I had to refuse the offer as not only was I way out of practice, not having touched my clarinet for all that time, but I had a life of spiritual involvement to which, in spite of the state of deep discontent and frustration in which I had become submerged, I was committed. However, I must confess, it certainly set me thinking.

A few weeks after I was offered a tour of Scandinavia by an agent who wanted to build a group around me for the tour. This, for the same reasons, I also had to refuse, notwithstanding his constant and financially persuasive, 'phone calls from that country. It did sound appealing but, as I explained to him, even if I considered doing such a tour, it would take me some time to get my lip back again and to bring my playing up to standard. He was not deterred. He would keep on pestering me until I was ready to work for him.

However flattered and tempted I was, it was not sufficiently attractive to seriously consider such a proposition as it would take me away from the work I was doing . . . or would it? I then asked myself, what was really preventing me from returning to the musical world, even on a part-time basis? My involvement in Ben's current work of spreading his conviction of Christ's presence in the world and supporting his organisation for this purpose was becoming less relevant to me, even though the possibility of such a momentous happening was not to be dismissed indiscriminately. I should still be able to attend his meditation meetings two or three times a week as I had been doing.

Also my continuing disappointment with the progress of the Farm project did nothing to encourage my efforts in that department, even though its function as a spiritual centre could be said to be just about ticking over and therefore be fitted in around any other arrangements I might make. As to the weekly groups I was running, well there was really no intention of relinquishing them at all as I felt, either rightly or wrongly, that they kind of relied upon me for their weekly philosophical 'fix'. Besides, we had all become friends.

But there was one very pressing factor that was in favour of me returning to the musical life, and that was my financial position which was urgently becoming in need of further injections. For far too long Ronnie and I had been living extremely economically, to say the least, skimping and scraping from one meal to the next so that there was enough cash to pay for the bare essentials of country living. There were always running expenses to allow for, our electricity was fed through a meter so that we only paid as we went along for what we really needed and could afford - when that ran out, it was a case for candles all round. Telephone use was restricted to mainly incoming calls, and as for heating, that was never really a problem as we had a log fire which supplied us with a virtually free and continual source of warmth. So apart from our food, it was really only petrol for travelling requirements which had made any significant drain on any reserves we had been able to put by, and in that department we were by then just about running on empty. So playing again would be the obvious means of getting some money into the coffers. It would also provide me with a thinking-out period, a stop-gap whereby I might find a temporary diversion from the spiritual emptiness that had engulfed me, as well as possibly enabling me to assess how to proceed in my endeavours in that direction.

However, the deciding factor came when one Sunday afternoon during nature's leafless period of November 1977, I was half-way up a tree, doing a bit of pruning and lopping I believe, near the entrance gate of the Farm drive, when our 6 foot close-boarded gates creaked open to reveal Brian Masters peering up at me. Brian was a banjo playing friend from previous years, one of the musicians who was involved in getting me back on the jazz scene some nine or ten years before.

He and his girlfriend Christine were out wandering the country lanes when, so they said, they found themselves in the vicinity of the Farm. After an open-armed welcome, I invited them in for a coffee and chat and to fill me in as to what was happening in the world of jazz these days, as I had been completely out of the scene for some time. This they duly did. From what Brian had to relate, there was one piece of information which struck me rather forcibly, rates of pay for musicians had improved quite substantially over the past years, even at pub venues.

This was the final touch that prompted me to unwrap my clarinet from its years of mummification and see if I could get some sound from it, to assess, if I could, how long it would take for me to get back into shape.

After a few brief attempts to breath some life into my horn, the idea of returning to the jazz world seemed more than a likely proposition. With a few months of steady practising behind me, by the early part of 1978 I was ready to start sitting in at various local venues, and once again meeting some of my 'old muckers' in the profession.

As I had hoped, from these casual appearances I started getting bookings to play at other places, mainly pubs and clubs at that time. Throughout that year and right into 1979 I was again building up my musical connections, some of which were quite new to me.

I was rapidly getting back to my old form, technically and creatively, except for a short period where my playing standards seemed to be suffering somewhat. I was beset by an increasing difficulty in my ability to produce the tone and fluency on my instrument which I had come to expect. Was I not practising sufficiently or correctly? Were the pads on my clarinet not seating evenly, or the key mechanism not functioning properly? I tried everything I could think of yet the solution to the problem continued to evade me for some time, that is until I took the instrument into the maker's workshop with the intention of having it undergo a total overhaul. It was a fine instrument, a Selmer, the top of the range which had been presented to me during the 50s as a promotional offer.

One of Selmer's finest craftsmen, Charlie Wicks, completely stripped my clarinet and discovered that the cause of my problem was an almost indiscernible hairline crack that had appeared in the top joint. (I suppose this should not really have surprised me as it was shelved by me without the necessary preparation for a length of time on two occasions). However after replacing the top joint twice the upshot was that, as the company knew I was back in the swim again, they generously presented me once again with one of their top of the range clarinets - plus all accessories.

Apart from work coming in from various current bands, I was asked to lead a fair amount of trio and quartet groups. These were often in social clubs of which there was an increasing number featuring jazz. It was on these latter type of gigs that I felt it appropriate to adapt my choice of material to suit the wider tastes of the family audiences which normally made up the bulk frequenting these clubs. I included more of the popular music from around the early thirties and forties such as ballads, love songs, and even some fun ditties - something which I would have considered strictly taboo (as would many of my followers) in previous times. To help adapt to these type of numbers, I called upon the keenness of my teens for that style of music.

John Petters, drummer and budding promoter of those days, was a prime mover in organising many of these social club gigs for me. With John and myself a pick-up guitar and double bass, we were playing at least two or three nights a week, having all sorts of tunes thrown at us by the audience, most of which I was obliged to attempt - a novel departure for me, yet excellent training.

I also did a fair amount of work as a duo with Nevil Skrimshire, an old jazz stalwart and first class rhythm guitarist, which enabled us to tuck ourselves away in any little corner in either a small pub bar-room, a club lounge, or a cosy restaurant alcove, and just unobtrusively swing away to our heart's content. I particularly enjoyed these little duo sessions as, although the pay was not particularly brilliant, there was a certain rapport created between the two of us which lent itself to a more intimate jazz sound, a sort of 'chamber jazz', which is how I liked to describe it, yet also leaving us free to experiment with a wider variety of material.

I had earlier teamed up with soprano saxophonist, Eggy Ley, who had extravagantly ambitious ideas of both he and I moving into more professionally acclaimed circles. Backed by a rhythm section consisting of Brian Prudence, double bass, Martin Guy, drums, and either Jim Douglas, guitar, or Hugh Rainey, banjo, going out under the name of the "Cy Laurie-Eggy Ley Hot Quintet" we were doing quite a bit of work in clubs and pubs, as well as the occasional concert. We had by then found ourselves a regular weekly session at a large pub, "The Esplanade", in Southend, Essex, which was to prove a very popular jazz venue for many years to come. It was from here that the BBC had broadcast some of our quintet sessions.

Eggy invariably booked a guest musician each week and, mainly for souvenir purposes, he often recorded the sessions, some of which he even issued on cassette under his own label which he called "Viaphone". Of those issued were sessions with Digby Fairwheather, trumpet, (recorded, 2nd October, 1980, and 11th June 1981, Benny Waters, saxophone, (recorded, 4th April 1981), myself with the rhythm section playing "Dear Old Southland", (recorded 3rd, September, 1981), and Alan Elsdon, trumpet (recorded 27th, May, 1982, with Nevil Skrimshire, guitar, Geoff Downs, drums, and Alan Morgan, bass in the rhythm section).

In the meantime, various other jobs were taking me much further afield than I had anticipated, one being the Arabian Gulf tour which was offered again. (I wanted Ronnie to go with me on this tour but she had other commitments). It was on this tour over December, 1981, and January, 1982, that I had the pleasure of meeting and playing with that fine trombonist and vocalist, Mike Pointon, who was helping to organise the itinerary for the trip. Apart from Dave Mills, drums, who was responsible for setting the whole tour up, and Mike, it was basically a pick-up group of musicians selected from various UK jazz groups which went under the ingenious name of the "British All Stars".

Esplanade Southend   **With Benny Walters (sax). Hugh Rainey (banjo). Brian Prudence (bass).**

It entailed us playing mainly for British ex-pats who had arranged a series of dances, clubs, and concerts for us, some conveniently placed in the hotels where we were staying.

It was not just a jazz band playing standard jazz numbers, it was more of an entertainment showband and, as such, we were obliged to present a wide variety of items which suited such an image. Although some of the numbers we played were unfamiliar to me, the approach was right up my street as I was always inclined towards professional presentation, be it of jazz or otherwise. It certainly kept me on my toes, being billed as the feature artist on the tour.

It was on these sessions that my recent excursions into ballads, popular melodies, and fun songs, came in handy . Not only did it revive the music of my teenage interests but it also presented a challenge for me to stretch my abilities to adapt - and it was all great fun, especially some of the vocal duets I did with Mike.

Some of the sessions were recorded by a professional sound engineer and a selection

218

With the 1982 British All Stars Gulf Tour   **Back row Jim Bray, Dave Mills, Bert Murrey.**
.   **Front row Mike Pointon, Andy Dickens, Neil Buckley, Self.**

of these tracks were issued on the Polyvision label. Also at certain venues our performances were filmed and, I believe, excerpts from these were also issued, although in my personal collection I only have a few clips of what was taken, these being merely dubbings onto a standard video cassette.

I was called on again to feature on a repeat tour of the Arabian Gulf in the April of 1982, this time in company with famous comedian and raconteur of the time, Jimmy Edwards. Once again, we extended our repertoire to include a more popular selection of numbers and with Jimmy's highly amusing presentations, it turned out to be almost like a variety show, and went down extremely well into the bargain.

In spite of the American origins of the music in which I had schooled myself for so many years and the admiration I felt for the talents of its early New Orleans innovators, I had never set foot on that promised land of jazz, as had so many of my fellow jazzers. That is, not until the Spring of 1983. I was booked to play a fortnight's tour with a selection of bands in and around the New York and Boston areas. It also presented the opportunity to see my sister Marie and my niece Roz (Roslyn) - an added bonus! It turned out to be a very hectic though enjoyable series of gigs. A particular highlight of the tour was the work I did with the Harlem Blues Band, which was a special amalgamation of early jazz luminaries, particularly the sessions I played with them at New York's Central Hotel, which I understood went out on television.

This trip happened to coincide with one Beryl Bryden made to that area as a stop-over on her way to the New Orleans Jazz Festival. She and I met up in New York, a city which she had visited many times before and therefore knew all the jazz spots and many of the artists who played them. In the company of Bob Wilber, the notable American

America Spring 1983
With Pug Horton. Adelaide Hall. Bob Wilber.

clarinetist, we did the rounds together which enabled me to meet, and often play with, many of the musicians I had only previously been able to hear on record. People such as, Adelaide Hall, Doc Cheatham, Al Casey, Count Basie (who I didn't get the chance to play with as he was unfortunately wheel-chair bound at the time), Kenny Davern, et al.

Further tours abroad were beginning to be offered; France, Germany, Holland, Scandinavia, etc., most of which I was fortunately able to accept, although some I had to turn down as my musical commitments were building up here in England. Ronnie invariably accompanied me and we made the most of what leisure time there was. In fact since the late 70s, gigs had been coming in a-plenty, far more than I had originally considered doing, and I was happy to see that my musical efforts were so appreciated by audiences wherever I went - which proved to be a needed source of encouragement for me to continue playing.

So by 1983, apart from the tours I played, which took me away for days or weeks on end, the number of jobs became generally containable to about three or four a week. These included the regular Thursday evenings at the Esplanade, Southend, with Eggy Ley, and the Wednesday gig at a large pub in Buckhurst Hill, Essex, where with a line-up of Ron Weatherburn, piano, John Sirett, double bass, Steve Nice, drums, and Dennis Field, cornet, and myself, we had been 'packing them in' for the past few years. This number of weekly jobs allowed me to continue with my other involvements, such as running the series of small weekly study groups, although these and my music commitments had to be juggled, maintaining the momentum of the Farm project, which seemed to have settled down to mainly weekend meditation and discussion get-togethers, and Ben's twice weekly meditation sessions. These latter I kept up whenever I could, even though I felt that I couldn't be wholeheartedly supportive of his public pronouncements.

On most of my trips into town before attending Ben's group, I popped in to see my dear ex-concert pianist friend Gertrude Rubinstein who by that time was living alone in her four-storied North London terraced house. She was well into her 80s then, a little ball of energy yet kindly and considerate and still very involved in the philosophy which we had in common. Much time was spent during these visits in discussing the various aspects and implications of our mutual interests. She had little money at the time and often Ronnie and I brought her some goodies on our now frequent visits to her. I generally took it upon myself to do a few jobs around the house for her whilst there and to help bring her into the modern age by buying and fitting a few up-to-date items that might make her life more pleasant. Things such as a new cooker, a television set, heating appliances, etc., while Ronnie on her part, was good enough to tidy the place up and do a few household chores for her, and even at one time redecorate her lounge.

It was a great blow for us when we heard she had unexpectedly died after a road accident in the early part of 1981. On the morning of the accident I had been ringing her constantly for some hours to arrange a visit but as there was still no reply by late afternoon, Ronnie and I chased up there to see what the reason was. Her front door had been left ajar, which was not uncommon for her when she popped across the road for supplies, so we waited around for her for a while.

Fortunately a neighbour had seen us arrive and informed us that Gertrude had been knocked down by an articulated lorry whilst on a pedestrian crossing earlier that day and taken to the local hospital. The poor dear was in a terrible state and could hardly speak when we saw her, whether she recognised us or not I don't know. Sadly, after a few days in intensive care she passed away. It was left to Ronnie and I to sort out all her belongings and tie up all the loose ends of her life. Her last act of generosity was that she remembered us in her will.

Apart from Ben's group, I was still running my own groups, which by the early 1980s, had increased beyond my availability to fit them all in. Over the previous few years, at roughly six month intervals, I had started new groups, all working on similar lines but each at a different stage of the training programme. All involved were very keen to keep up the study work which seemed to have fired their imagination and enthusiasm. So much so that, because my time was so limited and the number of groups had so multiplied, before starting a new group I had to give crash courses to mid-term groups to bring them up to the stage where they could merge into the next advanced group. On top of this, for those who had completed the first tier of study I was under pressure to produce a second tier of study material.

Although it was exceedingly gratifying for me to be involved in such worthwhile work, it turned out to be very time consuming. For some years, I had been running at least five concurrent groups and, to fit them all in, I sometimes had to take two groups per evening, one from 7pm to 9pm, and another from 9.30pm to 11.30pm, which left the mid half hour between 9pm and 9.30pm for an all-in meditation of both participating groups. Others groups were fitted in during the daytime, where convenient.

As an increasing number of new people were becoming interested in taking the course of study, some of the existing group members, with my encouragement, had started forming their own off-shoot study groups. This helped to relieve the burden somewhat from my shoulders though I agreed to be on call to assist when necessary, mainly in an advisory capacity. If the truth was really known, my interest in this form of group work had been fast waning for some time and although I conducted them as conscientiously as I could, by about mid 1982 I felt that my cycle for that type of group activity was coming to an end. I also found myself withdrawing from Ben's work as his now flourishing organisation had been enterprising enough to take full-page adverts in the National Newspapers to announce that the Christ was now in the world and that soon He would declare the fact to all. As momentous as such an event would be, if true, I somehow felt quite detached from it all.

What with my reaction towards this and my group study work, as well as the growing lack of concern in the progress of the Farm as a centre, my whole life and priorities seemed to be undergoing a radical change. As far as I could see, it was all probably connected with the inner emptiness which had assailed me over the previous few years which, in varying degrees of intensity still persisted - and with no indication of a let up in that department. Also the fact that my music-making efforts and the creative outlet it afforded me was by then becoming a more demanding factor in my life, as was the encouragement of the increasingly appreciative response to it by others. There was no question about the importance that I attached to my life's spiritual quest, and to that I was still unswervingly committed, yet the aspirational zeal which had been my main driving force for the past thirty years or more was no longer so evident.

Such were the conditions which brought to a close another episode in my life.

EPISODE SIX

CHAPTER 16 - THE TOURING SHOWS

1983-88 My Late 50s - Early 60s

In the Autumn of 1983 arrangements were made for me to celebrate my 35th anniversary as a clarinettist and bandleader. Special sessions were laid on in various venues where many of the musicians who had played with me in the past were duly invited. Ronnie, together with a few of those who had followed my musical escapades in the past were the main instigators of these arrangements, which included surprise parties.

One particular session where celebrations were taking place was in an extra large bar room of the Prince of Wales pub, one of my regular venues which, although always well attended, was packed to the gills on that night. It was non-stop jazz from 7.30pm 'til gone midnight and guests galore were featured throughout the session. The only break in the music was around ten thirty when the band I was fronting refused to play after I had announced the number we were about to play. I repeatedly stamped them in to start playing but they repeatedly refused to play. What's this, I thought , mutiny in the ranks, on this special occasion? They made all sorts of excuses, the piano keys had stuck, the drum pedal had collapsed, the bass player had broken a string, etc. This went on for a good ten minutes, to the obvious amusement of the audience, I was beginning to get unsettled and embarrassed about it. Then Ronnie, to my surprise, appeared on stage bearing a candle-decked cake which she presented to me amid the mass strains of "Happy Birthday". The whole thing was totally unexpected by me, although the rest of the band were in on it from the start, and the reason for the tantalising delay, was that there was a draught coming in backstage which kept blowing out the matches when they were trying to light the candles. Murphy's Law in full operation.

In the Spring of the following year I received a call from my old acquaintance, the trombonist and budding entrepreneur, Max Collie, who told me he was thinking of putting together a touring jazz show which would feature top jazz artists, and would I be interested and available to take part. He intended to use his band as the basis for the show and each of the guest artists could use it as their backing group, which sounded like an attractive and workable scheme.

After sorting out a few minor details with Max, like having a free rein in the material I chose, a say in how I presented my numbers, the need for me to continue with my own separate guest spot engagements, the dates of which I would notify him as they came in, and, of course, my fee, etc., all was agreed.

With only a few meagre rehearsals under our belt, the resulting format featured Max and his band with guest artists Ken Colyer and myself plus a special combination of Ken, Max and his musicians forming what was billed as "The Saints Marching Band". The whole show consisted of two separate one-hour spots, the first opened with Max's band playing a selection of his known pieces after which Ken came on to lead the ensemble for a few numbers, then I made my entrance to do my special spot with the rhythm section and then I brought on the whole band for a few numbers to close the first half with me.

To open the second half, the Saints Marching Band entered from a doorway in the stalls and paraded their music around the aisles for about ten to fifteen minutes, ending up on stage to wind up this particular feature. After a few more numbers by the band, Ken was brought on stage as a solo artist just playing guitar and singing in the folk idiom. This was followed by more of Max and his band until he brought me on again to front the rhythm section to render my little two-pennys' worth after which I again brought the band on stage for my last rousing number. The show was then brought to a close with one number by the band then another with the band and Ken and finally the grand finale with all of us - tout ensemble.

It was a format that seemed to work and we did our first series of shows in September, 1984, to packed enthusiastic audiences. I have dug out a newspaper cutting of the Telford session, one of our first performances, an extract of which I include here.

"JAZZ NIGHT FIT FOR THE RETURN OF A KING"

"A quiet and gentle jazz giant of yesteryear stepped out of the past and into the spotlight at the Oakengates Town Hall last night.

"And his lilting clarinet playing riveted sequins on a programme that befitted the £1 million revamp the hall has recently undergone.

"Cy Laurie, cult figure of the fifties who retired in the sixties to study meditation and philosophy, was one of the spangles in this exciting jazz package featuring Max Collie and his Rhythm Aces.

"Cy returned to the jazz scene on a casual basis in the late seventies and in last night's performance showed he has lost none of his virtuosity.

"..... In all a superb night that left the sound of jazz engrained in the veneers of this plush looking entertainment venue - an enviable asset for Telford".

G.T. - "Shropshire Star", Thursday, September, 27th, 1984.

Thanks to Max and his agent's hard graft, bookings were coming in for venues both in the UK and on the Continent, and the show looked set for a good run and hundreds of performances.

An indication of the success of the show and my part in it can be gleaned from the following brief selection of comments by the press over that period.

". . . . Then it was the turn of the classic clarinet style of Cy Laurie, soaring and plunging through the Fats' Waller composition "Blue Turning Grey". Laurie's sound is as crisp or mellifluous as he cares to make it, his clearly stated and interpretative performance on "King of the Zulus" forming one of the show's highlights."

". . . It must then be an even greater pleasure to hear them (Max Collie's Band) when they are joined with a man who has become a legend in his own lifetime, the great Cy Laurie. A skill beyond the ability of this mere scribe would be needed to explain the qualities of this man's genius, for that it surely is,. . . ."

". . . . . I have left to the last - the best. Another of the legends, Cy Laurie, who for years had his own jazz club in Windmill Street, was the second guest.

"Immaculate in white tux, his clarinet playing was cool, clear, classic, and a lesson to any whippersnappers who may think they have mastered the instrument.

"James Green - "The Stage", December, 18th, 1985.

". . . . But the star of the evening was Cy Laurie, whose searing tone on clarinet drew, quite rightly, the biggest applause of the evening."

"Cy Laurie, an unchallenged master of the classic jazz clarinet."

It was due to such journalistic generosity that my musical reputation was more widely re-established. An added source of income for Max was the sale of the record albums containing excerpts taken from one of these concerts which he had recorded on 20th, January, 1985, at the Clair Hall, Haywards Heath. During the interval of each show, and particularly after each show, Max, and I, and occasionally Ken, would present ourselves at a special table set up in the foyer of the venue to promote and sign copies of this record. Probably due to the limited amount of material that an album could contain and as Max was keen to push his own band, my work on this record was limited to a couple of sparse showings. This resulted in many requests from punters for recordings of some of my feature numbers, which I didn't have. Even those which I did in the 50s were no longer available. However, it was by sheer coincidence that even before I started playing in Max's show a new recording of mine was in the pipeline, the story behind which I now relate.

The broad term for the various types of hot jazz, whether they be based on either the Classic Contemporary, Ragtime, or Dixieland Style, had by the early 60s been given the generic label of "Traditional Jazz", and apart from the rare three or four popular bands, such as Chris Barber, Kenny Ball, and Acker Bilk, professional wide distribution recording contracts for this Traditional type of jazz were not easy to come by. Yet there was a flourishing scene of lesser known bands playing at pubs, clubs, dance halls, and festivals, etc., who had built up their own particular following and whose demand for recorded performances of their favourite bands was an untapped source of promotion and revenue.

This situation fostered an interesting development whereby smaller recording companies who had previously specialised in reissuing certain rare tracks, mainly for the jazz buff market, were beginning to issue the works of some of these lesser known bands. There were even companies who offered an all-in service for bands who only wanted a small quantity of their recorded performances. Often this service included all the recording, mastering, and pressing requirements, plus sleeve and label design and the necessary printing and packaging that was involved. Although their charges were generally fairly high, for the private customer they took a lot of the hassle out of having to issue a record - that is, for those that could afford it. But with a sufficient following, bands were invariably able to recoup their costs, and even make a profit, by selling their recorded offerings to the punters at their gigs. This became an expanding market which eventually led to a more personal and available supply of local recorded jazz, and often a profitable one for musicians, which otherwise would never had been.

It was in this climate that I had often been approached by a goodly number from the audiences who wanted some up-to-date recordings of my work. It had been over 25 years since I was in a recording studio and now, with this obvious show of interest, I conceded that it was about time I put something on record.

I had full intentions of doing so at some time or other, when I was able to get around to organising suitable musicians, book the studio, sort out the numbers, arrange rehearsals, etc., and generally set the whole thing up - as well as to scrape around for enough cash to invest in such a project.

However, as it happened, this last condition was virtually taken out of my hands when, around the late Summer of 1984, an ex-club member and enthusiastic supporter of my musical efforts insisted on helping out financially for the production of an LP, not only for my satisfaction, he said, but for his own and many others like him. It was a timely offer which I found difficult to refuse.

I welcomed his help and told him that I would accept his offer only on the condition that we treat it as a loan and that I repay him as soon as sufficient LPs were sold to allow me to do so. He said that would be agreeable providing I included in the recorded tracks some of the more popular type numbers that I had been slipping in on most of my sessions, and also that I put the whole thing in motion by September of that year.

The result was that on the 29th of September, 1984, Hugh Rainey, banjo, Peter Corrigan, double bass, Steve Nice, drums and myself, cut a selection of tracks which epitomised the expanded and more liberal repertoire I was playing during that period.

Each member of the rhythm section had been picked for their high standard of musical ability, being well equipped to handle the material chosen. This was essential under the circumstances as, being only a quartet performance and therefore not able to support any passengers, it was my intention to portray, as best I could, a balanced mix of moods ranging from hot jazz, as on "Cakewalking Babies", to blues, "S.O.L. Blues", to swing, as on "Swing That Music", to ballads, "Someday Sweetheart", to standards, as on "September Song". Due to this varied selection the record was appropriately titled, "SHADES OF CY" and was issued by a private company that I helped to set up called "Sunstreamer Productions".

The sleeve notes of the record descriptively conveyed this new musical departure of mine by stating;

"Although it is obvious that Cy's style is rooted in the Classic New Orleans style, the varied numbers on this album and the range of moods required to do them justice are not so inappropriate to the New Orleans approach as certain purists have maintained. In fact they serve to indicate that once the essence of the idiom is mastered, it can not only be applied effectively throughout a whole spectrum of musical vehicles but by so doing can add an extra dimension to the form, quality, and expression of those vehicles - as Cy's unique handling of them here clearly demonstrates.

"Here then after over 25 years, we have available again a Cy Laurie record with the characteristic high level of musicianship and jazz content to which is now added the expertise of Ted Taylor who, as recording engineer, has done much to capture the tones and qualities of the musicians and helped to afford the listener an up-to-date sample of the various "SHADES OF CY".

The first run of 1,000 were in my hands by late November of that year and right from the start sales were encouragingly very lively, enabling me not only to repay the loan I required to get them produced but to cover the costs for another run. It wasn't long before many further runs, on both LP and cassette were needed as they were taken up by a professional record distribution company and, I venture to add, they are still in print - and still selling and are now reissued on CD.

Throughout 1985 and the following years my playing work took me abroad quite regularly, on tour, particularly to the Scandinavian countries where I featured with their

leading jazz bands. Included in these trips were Festival bookings, broadcasts, TV appearances, and recording sessions. From these latter sessions, records were issued of me playing with Denmark's Eagle Jazz Band on 23rd, March, 1985, 14th, May, 1986, and 6th, August, 1986. I'm led to believe that a further recording was issued in that country with me and the Peruna Jazzmen, but of this I have no definite information.

There was one particular Summer Jazz Festival in Denmark which caused me some considerable embarrassment. The Festival site consisted of a series of marquees of varying sizes all set up in a large field. I was to front a band in the main marquee which housed a full size stage at one end which was built at a height that afforded the crowds of spectators full view of the performing artists.

There had been heavy rain during the day and Ronnie and I were standing beneath a large awning which was sheltering the stage from the elements. I was not due on till late so about half an hour before we were talking to a group of musicians and in the middle of our conversation a gust of wind must have lifted the awning and it seemed gallons of water emptied over us. We all scattered but the water soaked my head and drenched my jacket and the front of my trousers from waist to knees. I was mopped up with towels from the bar and given a sweater from one of the Danish musicians but nothing could be done about the trousers. Ronnie and I tucked ourselves in behind the

Denmark   Self. Theis Jensen (tmp). Fessor Lindgren (tmb).   John Neess. Copenhagen

rear of the stage, where with the help of a couple of chuckling and sniggering musicians and their girlfriends I wiped down the excess water from the front of my hitherto well-creased trousers . . . . and I for one was not laughing.

The sight of me having to perform on stage standing there in a half turned posture in my efforts to conceal much of my water-logged trousers I'm sure did not convince those of the audience who were well acquainted with the unrestrained results of many a musician's excess drinking habits. Could that account for the particularly exuberant ovation I received after that performance?!

Another Scandinavian tour I played had to be arranged around a couple of Max's Mardi Gras shows in Essex, which proved to be a hairy feat of precision timing. After finishing a performance at a Danish Festival held on Femo, an island south of Denmark, it was arranged that Ronnie and I be picked up taken to the Femo Port where we would catch the ferry to the mainland. From there a local flight was arranged to take us to Copenhagen Airport for the journey to Gatwick where I had left my car a couple of weeks beforehand. Then we would drive home and, after a few hours rest, nip over to Basildon for the show that was to be the highlight of their Summer Festival. That was the plan.

What really happened was this;

The Femo performance finished late, I had no time to change clothes before we were taken by the Festival Organiser to the place where we were to be picked up. Of course, no pick-up car. Either he had come and gone or he hadn't arrived at all. After many frantic 'phone calls, it was found that there was no other car available so, back to the Festival.

Even though most of the audience had left the main marquee (the last of the day's sessions had finished by then) there was one from among the few stragglers there who kindly offered to help us out. He was an exceptionally large Viking-type fellow, heavily bearded (as well as being, at that time, heavily beer'ed) who led us to his car which was an early Citroen 2CV. For those who are not familiar with this model, it is a particularly small and austere vehicle, constructed of corrugated metal sheeting and mounted on a cart-wheel system of suspension which gave it the appearance of permanently pointing downhill. The top covering was a roll-back cloth sheet which, on this particular specimen, seemed to have recently been attacked by a pack of ravenous Danish rats.However, ours was not to criticise but to be thankful for this show of helpfulness by someone who confessed to being a long time fan of mine.

After Ronnie and I clambered inside this simulated dustbin, our good Samaritan shoehorned his way into the driving seat, an operation which made the whole vehicle suddenly lurch over to his side. It was in this lop-sided posture that this little car made its weaving way to the island's dockside - a journey, though very much appreciated, not to be forgotten. On arrival there, our portly driver insisted on wrenching himself out of the car so that he could shake our hands and express how much he had enjoyed my playing at the session, which he dutifully did. . . . . he then promptly fell over.

We missed, wouldn't you know, the ferry to the mainland leaving us some time to hang around in the mild air, yet not delaying us sufficiently to miss the local flight from the mainland coast to Copenhagen. The craft used for this flight was run by a company who used twin-engined machines that seemed to need an extra long warming up period before they were able to get airborne, but once off the ground they did their job right enough (even if their reputed epithet of being 'boneshakers' erred on the complimentary side). We missed our connection at Copenhagen but were able to pick up a later flight which unfortunately went to Heathrow Airport instead of Gatwick. A mad panic from Heathrow by taxi to the outskirts of Gatwick, where my car was parked, left us no time at all to get home, it was a case of going straight on to Basildon as the show there was due to start within two hours.

Hareing across the country from Surrey, through Kent, to Essex was no easy matter among the evening's rush hour traffic and with just over an hour to make a two hours journey. Max liked us all there for a sound check by 6pm even though the show wasn't due to start until 7.30pm. There was no chance of me making that! Fortunately, I wasn't the first guest on and after a panic clothes change on arrival at the theatre, I was able to make my flustered entrance on stage at the appointed cue, preventing near heart failure for Max, who had to announce me on.

Meanwhile, back home on the Farm, we were having some difficulty keeping the place dry. Not only was the roof subject to serious leakages, but each time we had a heavy downpour, the pattern on the kitchen floor became practically obscured under three inches of muddy water. This required at least a couple of hours of hard labour with sponges and buckets to clean up and dry it out. There were two obvious reasons for this state of affairs. Firstly soon after I moved in around the mid 50s, due to the very low ceiling height in all the rooms (the inhabitants it was originally built for must have been little taller than Pygmies), it was practically impossible to walk around from one room to another without assuming a perpetual stooping position. I, being not far off six foot in height, was forever knocking myself silly on the doorway beams - and still do on many an inattentive occasion.

The obvious solution then, particularly with regard to the ground floor kitchen, lounge, and bathroom, where ceilings were exceptionally, and so inconveniently, low, was to excavate the floors. This was not so difficult an operation as it sounds as many of the houses of that period never had foundations as such but were constructed on a layer of sand. This being the case with the Farm, the floors of the kitchen and bathroom were then taken down a good six inches below their original level.

However, inexperienced in this work as we then were, digging out the floors this way produced a lower level inside the house to that outside, therefore making these ground floor rooms very susceptible to flooding.

Another reason for this condition was that over the years, as the main outside ditches became clogged up, much of the excess water was being directed towards the house thus increasing the chances of such flooding.

Some many years after this floor-lowering operation took place, I learned that a council grant could be obtained on old buildings in need of genuine repair. The roof of the house, which consisted of ancient and well-weathered flaking flat peg tiles laid in overlapping fashion (well, some were overlapping) placed on bare roofing battons, of which some had either rotted or come adrift leaving the house delightfully exposed to all the glories of the heavens, must surely qualify for such council beneficence. So, after filling in the necessary documents, a council representative came to inspect the place whereupon he soberly pronounced that to be eligible for one of the grants, other works would be required to be done, such as; the old wooden casement windows would have to be replaced, the ceilings in all rooms would have to be at least 7' 6" high, a deep trench dug around the perimeter of the whole building to prevent seepage, etc. etc. - and even when all this was agreed and approved, I would only get a small percentage of the costs of such works. I thanked him very much for his trouble, and said that maybe I'd take up their offer at another time - and left it at that. So we stoically continued to suffer these inconveniences.

However, this flooding situation grew steadily worse so that by about 1987 our water-logged kitchen episodes became the frequent highlights of our domestic bliss, not something to look forward to first thing in the morning after a night of heavy rain and frequent early hour homecoming. So something radical had to be done and, as Ronnie pointed out, we should have a warm, dry and comfortable home to come back to after hareing up and down the country and continent. So, I employed the services of Allen, a local one-man builder, to help put things aright once and for all. The first thing we did was to hire a mechanical digger that not only cleared out all the offending ditches but took about a foot off the surface of the area surrounding the house (leaving us to wallow in the resultant squidgy muddy residue for weeks after thereby making the inside floor level well above that of the outside.

Then we decided to re-tile the roof, with the proper underfelt, new battening, guttering, etc., - an expensive job but by then it was really a 'must'. Allen, who was not backward in coming forward when he spotted extra work he could do, said he knew someone who dealt in pre-glazed windows and could get them at a discount price for me. I conceded that this also was a necessary job so, after a bit of price haggling, we had some new windows put in. I had misguided thoughts of it ending there. But no, all the barns around the house he rightly said needed renovating and one in particular needed completely rebuilding; then there was the inside of the house which he said he could tackle, and which I knew really needed to be done, and should have taken priority, such as insulating all the external walls, renewing much of the old plumbing and the electrics, heightening the ceilings upstairs, which could only be done by re-structuring the loft, replacing the old inefficient fireplaces in the kitchen and the lounge, . . . and on and on and on.

There was no way I could question the need for all these improvements, it very much rested on the cost, time, my availability to help, and all the upheaval that would nec-essarily be involved. After due consultation with Ronnie and my Building Society manager, I decided to 'go for it', at least until I saw to what extent the money would hold out.

One of the most intriguing jobs we tackled was the fireplace in the lounge. It was an ordinary small grate with a Victorian-type surround in a central position in one of the walls. After removing the grate and prising out the surrounds, we came across a larger cavity behind it where possibly there had been an earlier fireplace. Then on further investigation, we discovered an even older fireplace framed by an arched-brick facia, which we assumed at one time housed a dog grate. Then by digging deeper, we uncovered another ancient fireplace with an oak beam horizontally above it.

It would seem that periodically over the past 400 years or more, as interior house fashions changed, so these fireplace designs were appropriately adapted.

With the intention of reconstructing this last find we gingerly extracted the bricks and, whereupon, found to our amazement a much deeper chamber stretching back a good 4 foot. After excitingly clearing away the large volume of debris that filled this area (unfortunately, no old gold Tudor coins were in evidence), we found ourselves inside an old brick-lined alcove supported by an oak head-beam (Bresmer) perched about 5 foot 6 inches from floor level, the whole existence of which we eventually had confirmed as being the Inglenook feature of the original house, some 400 or more years ago. Now this was something that we really had to have resurrected and preserved.

After opening up this alcove, we were encouraged to find that, apart from a vertical crack about an inch wide by about 4 foot long in the middle of the back wall, the old fletton brickwork was still intact, even if most of the lime mortar bonding had deteriorated. All the old projecting brick shelves and the stepped surface construction were there in their entirety, right down to the charred surface markings which were still clearly visible on the brickwork as if the last fire had been lit only yesterday. The chimney immediately above consisted of a large cavity which narrowed into a vertical tunnel-like vent, big enough for a small boy to climb up, which was the customary means of cleaning out such a construction. For us, it was like a rare archaeological find, particularly so for Ronnie who was much more of an 'old house' enthusiast than myself. To think I had been living there for over thirty years, completely unaware of having such an original feature hidden away in my very living room.

The only dubious parts of the construction were the brick pillars either side of the front of the fire place which supported the well worn and charred oak beam. These would obviously have to be replaced, whereas the rest of the structure need only be repaired, but necessarily with the utmost care to maintain the original unique contours.

During this period of house renovation, I had also to attend to all my gig work, which invariably took me away from home. On this occasion when we had laid bare the details of this amazing inglenook discovery, I was due to make a weekend trip up North. It had been arranged for Ronnie to come with me and we left the front door keys with Allen who would continue the work on his own. After erecting all the necessary scaffolding around the Inglenook so that the floor above was well supported and safe for Allen to work we left as planned, yet eagerly looking forward to returning home to finish off this labour of love.

When we arrived back on Sunday as dawn was breaking after our overnight journey, we found that although Allen had rebuilt the brick pillars either side of the front of the Inglenook as we had asked, most of the original bricks from the rest of the structure had been carelessly discarded in a heap outside on the lawn exposed to the weathers. After some sleep Ronnie decided to clean the bricks (a job and a half in itself) and set about this tedious task with much heroic stoicism, removing all traces of the offending mortar and stacking them on a duckboard.

When Allen turned up that morning he was greeted with such a verbal reproach for throwing all our original bricks out on the lawn, that the poor fellow was on the verge of cowering backwards into the empty cavernous black hole of what only a few days before was our precious Inglenook fireplace.

After regaining his equilibrium, he tried to explain that as all these old bricks were 'as rotten as a pear' (a favourite statement of his when there was a repair job which he didn't want to tackle) and were covered with hardened mortar so tightly bonded to them that it would have taken a month of Sundays to clean them up (Ronnie had disproved that statement) he decided to throw them out. Besides, he thought, that by replacing them with nice new bricks, it would all look much better and cleaner, etc. That was not our opinion at all!

Once he had made up his mind on an issue, he was not the type to concede easily to an alternative course of action. However, as soon as the disrupted atmosphere had settled, Ronnie, donning her 'paragon of diplomacy' hat , got him to agree that he would reinstall them - as they were before.

The upshot of it was that he not only painstakingly reconstructed these old and valued bricks, exactly as they were before, but managed seamlessly to blend them into the new brick pillars to the point where the embedded black soot marks on each original brick were, as near as damn it, matched up to those of its neighbouring bricks, as one would reassemble the pieces of an intricate jig-saw puzzle. We finished up with a perfect and authentic-looking job - and Allen was once again back in our good books, and looking very pleased with himself to boot.

CHAPTER 17 - THAT RHYTHM MAN

1989 - 93 - My Swinging Sixties

It seemed that the success of the Mardi Gras show had prompted Max and his agent to add a second show to their work load. The theme they devised was around the film High Society, which featured the incomparable musical talents of the great Louis Armstrong, Bing Crosby and Frank Sinatra. I was again invited to feature in the show together with Max's band, a blues pianist, and a girl singer. The format turned out to be very similar to the Mardi Gras show except that the type of numbers played were more in the style appropriate to the period of the High Society film.

Max and I seemed to have started off on the wrong foot with this show as when I turned up at the first rehearsal to go through my numbers and plan the part that I was to play in it, I found Max had already decided to use some of the numbers previously set aside for me for his band's performance. OK, I thought, a bit disappointing as I was looking forward to doing my Crosby bit, but it was Max's show and there were lots of other good numbers I could choose from, even if they weren't as appropriate to the theme as I had intended.

But this proved to be just a minor sticking point compared to the difficulty I experienced soon after the show got under way. I felt I was continually being restricted in what I did and what I had hoped to do eventually gave rise to some unnecessary differences between Max and I. We played our first High Society show in the latter part of 1986 from which time we received some encouraging press reviews yet, in spite of its comparative success, over the months there was a growing feeling of frustration on my part which was never really resolved. A recording of the show was issued - without my inclusion - and after nearly a year of working with the show under such dispiriting conditions, it reached a point where I finally had to pull out of it which, unfortunately, reflected on my involvement in the Mardi Gras show obliging me to pull out of that one as well.

I had quite a fair following around the country at the time and was often told that I was missed by not being in the shows. One of my followers even offered to back me financially in a show of my own if I could set something up. I was obviously very flattered by such a proposal but at the time felt that a project of that nature would prove a bit too involved for me to take on alone. However, I thanked him very much and said I would 'think about it', assuring him that my response was not so much a courteous put-off, but a genuine intention to consider the practical possibilities of such a project.

After some serious thought on the subject and discussion with others who might be able to help, it didn't appear to be such a daunting task as I first thought. In fact, with the support of the professional connections I had made as a solo feature artiste and the reputation I had built up in Max's shows, to get a show of my own on the road was an opportunity I was encouraged to take. But I thought that if this was really a possibility, how would I go about it? I couldn't very well seek the advice of Max and his agent after our disquieting break up. Besides, I would want to present something more organised and professional than a 'jazz band show'. It would need to be thoughtfully staged, littered with a wide range of numbers as suited to the variety of tastes of a normal theatre audience, yet still being decidedly jazz orientated.

It needed to have specific musical themes which, by combining selected tunes, could tell their own little stories. It would also need to be visually attractive including special lighting and sound effects and interesting costume changes. Above all, there should be an abundance of glamour on display, preferably with dancers etc. Although all apparently ambitious, I thought that if I was really to have such a show of my own, it would have to be a fully staged professional production. It couldn't be anything less.

However, for something of this nature, to be really effective, it would require a professional director and producer, as well as artists, staff finance, and wherewithal needed to pull off such a production, not to mention an agent to sell it.

The practicality of it all had been brewing in my mind for some months when, as if by chance (or luck), over a period of about a couple of weeks I met Helen Gould again, a glamorous vocalist who I had first met some years earlier when we were both individually booked as feature artists for a large multi-band jazz celebration; and then I was offered a gig with that fine pianist, Allan Bradley, who I hadn't seen since the early 80s.

On separate occasions, I mentioned to Helen and Allan the possibility of getting a show together with novel presentations etc., and they both said they were keen to involve themselves in anything of that nature that I could muster up. Allan is a first class musician, very professional, inventive, and with a pronounced (even sometimes a little distorted) sense of humour, whom I felt would be a great asset to have as a feature accompanist on stage. Helen apart from her excellent vocal, dancing, and acting talents, was a very attractive fun-loving girl and very easy to get along with. I thought that with the three of us, we had the nucleus of a group around which we could construct a possible stage show.

I then got down to mapping out a likely workable format which would include most of the ideas I had been toying with over the past few months. I laid this likely format out to Ronnie, Helen, and Allan, explaining how the whole show would be divided up into various musical acts, each of which not only featured one of the members of the band, (the personnel of which I had yet to decide), but which would be built around some specific musical theme. Also included would be some fun numbers. The tittle of the show would be taken from the feature song, originally composed by Fats Waller and Andy Razaf (of 'Aint Misbehavin' fame), called "That Rhythm Man". Well, the three of them seemed quite enthused with the idea and impatient to put it all into practice - and that was good enough for me.

Having now formed the basis of this new show, I then had to make the whole thing a workable, and profitable proposition, something that would appeal not only to the serious jazz enthusiast but also to those of wider tastes who look for a full evening's entertainment.

However, before any rehearsal work could be considered, I first needed to get a sympathetic group of musicians

together, who would adapt to and muck in with the fun side of the show. With my old friend Nevil Skrimshire on guitar, who was also very adept at whistling, believe it or not, (and in tune I might add), John Sirett on bass who doubled on tuba, and that renowned jazz drummer, Colin Bowden, I had the basis of a line up ready to go into preliminary rehearsals.

I arranged the general running order of the show so that it would cover two one hour sets, each divided into separate phases where we could present an abundance of different musical items depicting a variety of changing moods and tempos, including, hot jazz, ragtime, stomps, blues, gospel music, ballads, popular song, and fun numbers, all performed by a top class line-up, plus a touch of dance and lots of glamour. To give a brief idea of what an audience was to expect, I include a few selected quotes from my original 'Programme Sequence' draft notes;

"Opening"

From behind closed Tabs, tom-toms by drummer for 4 bars before opening Tabs to spotlight drummer, Colin.

237

Spotlight John, bassist who enters from wings to accompany drummers rhythmic beat in B minor,

Ditto . . . . Nevil, guitar,

Ditto . . . . Allan, piano, who then sings verse to "That Rhythm Man" to introduce Cy who, once on centre stage, then introduces all the members of the group.

Phase 1

Item 1; 'A Moi d'payer'.   -   Cy, arrangement as per.

Item 2; 'Birth Of The Blues'   -   "   "   "

Item 3; 'Forty And Tight',   -   Cy, with Colin featured on washboard. Exit Cy.

Phase 2

Train whistles and shouts of "All Aboard!". Enter Helen with suitcases.

Item 1; 'Hold That Train', Helen vocal, with train noises, etc.

Item 2; 'Skylark', Helen vocal, featuring Nevil, guitar and whistling.

Item 3; 'Nice Work If You Can Get it', Helen vocal, with rhythm chase chorus.

Phase 3

Enter Cy.

Item 1; 'A Fine Romance', Helen and Cy, - arrangement as per.

Item 2; 'I Guess I'll Get The Papers And Go Home', Allan solo, piano and vocal,

. . . . . during which time, artists off stage donning fluorescent sheets, skull masks, etc., in preparation for next scene.

Phase 4

Item 1; 'Skeleton In The Closet', Thunder and lightning effects, eerie screams, wailing, and such noises. Cy feature with players suitably attired and brandishing their ghostly props in support of Helen, who dances exaggeratingly in her luminous skeleton outfit on blacked-out front stage under ultra-violet lights.

Item 2; 'The House Is Haunted', Cy, vocal feature.

Item 3; 'Dance Around In Your Bones', Allan, piano feature, with Nevil, guitar and whistling, backing Helen's wild skeleton antics, again on blacked-out stage under ultra-violet lights.

Item 4; 'I Aint Got Nobody', Helen covers her skeleton gear and dons fluorescent face mask to show only a disembodied head floating around stage to Cy's off stage vocal.

Close. All on stage for reprise of 'Skeleton In The Closet' to accompany dancing skeleton.

Play off, then Tabs.

INTERVAL

2nd HALF

Opening

Phase 5

Item 1; 'Perdido Street Blues   -   Cy, arrangement as per.

Item 2; 'S'wonderful',   -   Cy,   "   "

Phase 6

Item 1; 'Why Don't You Do Right', - Helen in sparkling strapless dress.

Item 2; 'After You've Gone',   - Helen and Cy, swinging stomp.

Item 3; 'Blues In The Night',   -   "   " vocal duet.

Item 4: Nevil   - Guitar solo feature with whistling. All others off stage to don rain gear.

Phase 7

Item 1; 'Run Little Raindrop Run'. Thunder and lightning effects as players enter wearing souwesters, galoshes, assorted rain hats and colourful umbrellas, etc. Cy and Helen duet.

239

Item 2; 'Stormy Weather',   - Cy feature, arrangement as per.

Item 3; 'Isn't It A Lovely Day', Helen feature with Cy backing. All off stage except for Allan;

Item 4; 'Garden In The Rain',   - Allan piano and vocal feature.

Except for Allan, all on stage for reprise of 'Run Little Raindrop Run', while Allan prepares for his novelty spot.

Phase 8

Item 1; 'World Is Waiting For The Sunrise', - Allan dressed in cook's kitchen gear - pots and pan novelty solo feature.

Item 2 'Waiter And The Porter And The Upstairs Maid', - Allan, Helen, Cy, trio vocal fun number.

Item 3; 'In The Still Of The Night',   - Cy, moody clarinet feature.

Item 4; 'King Of The Zulus'   - Cy feature, plus Colin drum feature, to dramatic ending.

Finale

All on stage for reprise of 'That Rhythm Man' and acknowledgement of all artists. Rousing ensemble to the closing of Tabs.

Tabs reopen to players forming line on front stage, all hold hands for final opening and closing of Tabs.

. . . . . and there you have it, a slick and entertaining production, carefully timed and executed - or at least intended to be so.

A few rehearsals was all I needed to assess the practicality of the project. Once I saw how the whole thing was shaping up and was happy with the results, I then needed to find a producer, director, and experienced theatre staff, who could oversee and fashion the show and, with the possible addition of a small troupe of dancing girls to round it all off, and of course, someone with appropriate business acumen and connections to sell it, we could make of it a first class professional production.

I knew that all this wouldn't be easy but I was keen and game to try. After many weeks on the 'phone, letter writing, and hawking the idea around to agents, etc., the little interest that I had managed to raise eventually came to nothing. It soon became painfully obvious that I was overreaching myself and that to those in the theatre world any reputation that I had in the past was long forgotten.

However, I persevered and we continued rehearsing, in a rather half-hearted manner, until I finally had to face the fact that my high hopes were not to be realised. I put the position to Ronnie, Allan, and Helen, my main partners in the project, that as I had pulled a blank in my efforts to enlist the needed theatrical notables to 'get the show on the road', I felt that I was left with three possible alternatives; either to include a special feature artist whose popularity would help carry the show and attract the necessary professional support, or failing that, to launch the show as it was, which would mean me having to foot the bill and therefore necessarily working on a low budget without all the hoped-for trimmings (my previously prospective backer had by then been obliged to channel his resources on other projects in other countries), or to forget the whole idea altogether.

They thought that to resort to this latter alternative would be a great shame seeing how much promise the show had and the rehearsals we had put in. So we plumped for the first alternative, that of trying to book someone with a popular name.

A short list of possible celebrities was made out, and the first person approached was Norman Wisdom. I had met him in the 50s at Pinewood Studios whilst he was working on a film called "Just My Luck". John Paddy Carstairs, the well known film Director of that period who was involved with the production of Norman's films, was also a dedicated follower of my band and a regular at my club, as well as being a personal friend. As a clarinet player himself, Norman joined me to play a little duet session for the folk at the studios on one of my visits there, a photo of which subsequently appeared in the Daily Mirror.

Unfortunately, Norman couldn't do the show with us at the time so I went through the list of the few other possibilities, marking them off, disappointingly, as each one of them declined our offer. There seemed nothing else for it but for me to promote the whole thing myself until such time as when either members of the theatrical profession, or an agent, would take it over or I got fed-up with the job myself.

It was the latter which finally came about as I was defeated by the sheer amount of time and energy which such a promotional chore consumed. I am not by nature a salesman and the hassle of having to repeatedly telephone promoters - who hardly ever returned my calls for bookings for the show was against my temperament and better judgement. Especially when one has to deal with office staff, and particularly those in council run venues where the unsympathetic bureaucratic machine lumbers on at a snail's pace, often administered by those who have no interest in jazz nor were familiar with the names and reputations of jazz musicians. However, I did try, and although I wasn't

241

JAZZ JAPES

British comedian Norman Wisdom (right) plays clarinet with musician Cy Laurie on the set of 'Just My Luck' at Pinewood Studios. 1957. John Pratt. Hulton Archive. London.

able to maintain a full date book, I managed to keep the show going for at least a year and some.

I did this by first contacting some of the venues where I had played with Max's shows, and where, to my surprise, I found that the majority of those in management had fortunately remembered me and their audiences' agreeable response to my efforts. On the strength of this I managed to set up a few months' work which I thought would at least get us all in shape for the time when we could present it to professional promoters, and even possibly get it into the West End. Now that really was being ambitious!

However, my high hopes were somewhat diluted by the first show we did, which turned out to be peppered with minor disasters;

- the thunder and lightning effects which our drummer Colin was meant to operate by vigorously shaking a sheet of galvanised tin in front of a microphone whilst simultaneously stamping on a strategically placed lighting foot switch, all became hopelessly out of synchronisation when he hit the mike with the tin sheet, knocking it over on to his drum kit with a resounding amplified clatter of assorted symbols;

- the luminous mask that Helen had stuck on to the back of her head for the blacked-out 'I Aint Got Nobody' number, came unglued under the heat of the spot light and had to be fumbled for, picked up from the stage floor and held on by her hand, for her to finish the number - thus completely ruining the disembodied effect;

- the vinyl skin-hugging skeleton outfit which, when exposed to the heat of the stage together with the intense perspiration it produced by her energetic dancing routine, brought Helen almost to her knees during her act - not to mention the number of times she bumped into me whilst I was playing my bit in accompanying her. Ronnie who was helping backstage with the costume changes, etc. said Helen's skin was covered all over in red blotches when she came off stage to rid herself from this vinyl epidermis. Still, being the sport that she was, she took it all in good part and saw the fun side of it. She said when she came off stage that first night, she was perspiring so much that if I'd have squeezed her whilst on stage, she would have popped out of her outfit like a wet bar of soap from a clenched fist;

- the rain sequence where Helen, gracefully twirling her coloured umbrella above her head, danced around me while I played 'Isn't It A Lovely Day', managed to entwine her lovely long golden locks in the metal spokes of the umbrella - which I tried to untangle for her (not very surreptitiously, I might add), whilst she embarrassingly continued to sing her part of the song;

- my habit of holding her hand to bow together after our duet numbers and then me raising both our hands high in the air in acknowledgement of the applause, produced some disarray to the top of Helen's strapless attire - although it did wonders to extend the applause. As it was meant to be a family show, and to prevent further embarrassment to our leading lady, I was requested by her to refrain from this gesture, which I did . . . well, most times anyway.

Notwithstanding all that, the show was enthusiastically received and we were encouraged to go full steam ahead with it. First nights are seldom perfect and once we had ironed out all the little teething problems, our following performances went much more smoothly and with a swing. I thought it was a really smashing show and I made a special effort to round up more jobs, fortunately with some success, which enabled me to get the troupe together in a recording studio to put out a few of our numbers on record so that we had something to sell at the venues we played . The future looked promising.

But alas, the time and effort involved in me trying to get bookings direct became far too frustrating for me so I once again resorted to chasing the professional producers. Finally, I thought I had a bite when an agent came back to me enquiring if I'd be interested in putting the show on in the West End. Darned right I would ! He must have been a mind reader. For this he explained, I would need first to give a few preliminary performances at a small London theatre which would serve to test the waters and as a shop window to attract the necessary backers. With this in mind, the Donmar Warehouse, a small theatre in Earlham Street, London was contacted which specialised in short runs for try-out productions, it was the venue where such successful shows as Blues in the Night first had their West End debut. However the arrangements for us to play this theatre became so protracted that by the time the agent had everything set up due to the local restructuring schemes, along with other buildings, the Donmar Warehouse Theatre had notice to close down. So bang went that opportunity - I never did hear from that agent again.

After about 9 months of the show's life span, I lost Allan Bradley and Colin Bowden, both of whom had other more reliable work they could do, which was a big blow to a show with such an arranged routine. With much added and panic stricken effort, I was fortunate enough to get that versatile pianist and stride specialist, Neville Dickie to replace Allan, and Steve Nice to replace Colin. This required some minor amendments to the presentation of the show but the general format remained the same.

The show continued for a few months more with this line-up but it all got too much for me and it finally folded. To have thought the whole thing ambitious was a gross underestimate - outrageously formidable would have been a more appropriate term . . . or even recklessly idiotic. Ah well, I suppose it was another good idea at the time.

Does anybody anywhere want a few thousand leaflets, posters, records and cassettes, of 'That Rhythm Man'?

245

CHAPTER 18 - THE TURNING OF THE WHEEL

1990 - 2001 - Into My Seventies

Following the folding of the show, my musical life consisted mainly of feature solo work, both in this country and abroad, either at clubs, concerts, or Festivals, the number of which seemed to be mushrooming all over the place. On occasions, when specifically requested, I brought the old band together for a special performance, with Dennis Field, Terry Pitts, Hugh Rainey, Pete Corrigan, and Steve Nice, under the banner of the "Cy Laurie Reunion Band", but this didn't happen more than about three or four times a year.

In 1992, when Terry Pitts decided to emigrate to Canada, we set up a recording session with the band a short while before he left. It consisted of a selection of our Classic-style jazz numbers which, I entitled "Jazz from the Roots". I thought it was a good example of the sort of music the band was turning out at that period.

My 70th Birthday Party at the 100 Club

Hugh Rainey (bjo). Self, Dennis Field (tmp), Pete Corrigan (bass), Keith Nichols (tmb).

V Laurie

This was my last studio recording but of course there have been other more recent recordings taken from live sessions which have subsequently been issued such as the concert at Wavendon, on 22nd April 1995, with Beryl Bryden's Blue Boys, and the numbers I did with Spats Langham on 15th May, 1998, at the Keswick Jazz Festival. There has also been many re-issues of my earlier stuff, broadcasts, concerts etc. on various labels, here and abroad. There was even a video taken of a session at the Sudbury Jazz Club on 1st, November, 1992, with the four piece I used to get together for such events. This was really the nucleus of the Reunion Band, with Dennis Field, Hugh Rainey, Pete Corrigan and myself. Arranging jobs for the full Reunion Band (after Terry Pitts had left) became too much of a chore for me although, when really necessary, I would book either trombonist Mike Pointon or Keith Nichols to fit the bill, which they did admirably.

In the April of 1996, Ronnie, Roger Horton (the Proprietor of London's premier Jazz venue, the 100 Club) and others, set up a special session at Roger's club to celebrate my 70th Birthday. The members of the Reunion Band were featured, as well as Neville Dickie's Jazz Celebrities, plus many of my musician friends who delighted the audience, and their fellow jazzers, with their musical contributions.

CY LAURIE

WELCOMES YOU

TO HIS **70**TH BIRTHDAY

CELEBRATION
WED 24TH APRIL 1996
AT THE
"100 CLUB"
100, OXFORD STREET, LONDON W1
MEMBERS: £5.00 NON-MEMBERS: £6.00
NON-STOP JAZZ 8PM - MIDNIGHT
WITH
CY LAURIE REUNION BAND
FEATURING
DENNIS FIELD (CNT), KEITH NICHOLS (TBN),
CY LAURIE (CLT), HUGH RAINEY(BJO),
PETE CORRIGAN (BASS), STEVE NICE (DMS)
& "THE JAZZ CELEBRITIES"
FEATURING
NEVILLE DICKIE (PNO), ALAN ELSDON (TPT),
MICKY ASHMAN (BASS), JOHNNY RICHARDSON (DMS)
PLUS MANY GUEST MUSICIANS

It turned out to be a fully-attended and joyous occasion with all the accompanying trimmings of balloons, streamers, tinsel-decked rostrum. People were queueing up to get in long before the session was due to start and, I gather, many eventually had to be turned away - a great pity because it was really a night to remember.

During the Autumn of 1997 I had been asked to do some gigs with the Frog Island Jazz Band, a group of very amiable guys who had one of the rare bands on the scene that played the Classic jazz numbers which I had specialised in during my earlier musical career. They had lost their clarinet player and I agreed to help them out for a while. However, 'for a while' turned out to be more or less permanently as they asked me to join them on a regular basis. They were - and are - a courteous bunch of fellows and I knew that clarinet players in that style were not easy to come by (more's the pity), besides most of them lived fairly locally to me which was to prove handy in getting lifts to gigs, etc., plus the attractive fees they agreed to pay me, were all an added Inducement so how could I refuse their kind offer? They knew that I had my own solo

scene going and, provided that our various jobs didn't clash too much, I agreed to join them. It meant little respite for me regarding having the occasional evening at home, but at the time I took it as all part of a busy musicians life.

For years beforehand I had, fortunately, been working quite solidly, and giving it my all, in spite of the extensive amount of travelling, irregular hours, little sleep, inappropriate fooding, etc., that was involved. In fact, the thought often occurred to me that it might be advisable to wind down my playing work, and even take a complete break for a while, so that I could get back to more regular studying and enjoy the home life that I was so fortunate to have. But now, working with the Frogs, I had virtually doubled my musical burden, and it did not take long before I realised that this workload and life-style was taking its toll on my health.

I was returning home after my tours utterly exhausted, which on some occasions took me days to get over, especially if I had further local jobs to play soon after I got back from a tour. At first I just assumed that possibly due to my advancing years, such a lack of stamina was to be expected. However, being in such good health, as I believed I was, I thought little of it at the time. Foolish me, because in March, 1998, after a very strenuous series of concerts, particularly the last one at Butlins Holiday Camp in North Wales where we were unable to get any suitable food for Ronnie and myself which was often the case, I had actually passed out for a few seconds in the middle of a meal (that we had stopped off for on the way home) which is something that I was never prone to doing.

About a couple of weeks later whilst in the middle of a day-long gig with the Frogs at the National Boat Show at Alexandra Palace, I found myself quite depleted of energy with a lessening reserve to call on requiring me to carefully pace myself throughout the session, which was a very unusual experience for me.

Over the coming months this lack of energy reserve was becoming more acute and severely affecting my daily life. I had always been an active type of person, moving from one job to another throughout the day, but now, after even a slight exertion, I was obliged to sit back and rest for a while. This went on for months with no sign of a let up, I tried all my Nature Cure know-how to shake it off but my efforts seemed to have very little effect.

Ronnie in her concern, badgered me to see the local doctor, which is something I hadn't done since I was a kid, who sent me for a series of tests before announcing that my complaint was 'atypical', it was likely to be a virus, meaning of course that as they couldn't accurately diagnose the problem, a viral infection was the only thing that they were aware of which could account for such symptoms. Anyway I was strongly advised to call a halt to my playing work and take it easy for a while. I was rather reluctant to do this as I had quite a few gigs in the book at the time, which not only provided me with a steady income but, by giving up playing, I would be giving up a way of life to which I had by then become well adapted, so from then on I did the rounds of the Complementary and Alternative Therapists, to see what they could come up with. To my dismay, none were able to satisfactorily diagnose the problem, let alone alleviate it, in spite of me trying various recommended natural treatments, all to no avail.

All this time, much to Ronnie's frustration and better judgement, I was still fulfilling all my gigs even though often hardly having the energy to get to them. The interesting thing was that once I arrived at the gig and got up on the stand, I invariably found I could play with much of my old vitality, which then lasted right up to the end of my performance - after which, I virtually crashed out. I'm sure that my Guardian Angel was working overtime for me, not to mention Ronnie's loving care and support, without which I might never have even got to some of my jobs. Who was the misguided simpleton who coined the phrase, "The Show must go on"? As a professed professional, such a statement seemed to be engraved in my subconscious and must have been an added factor in aggravating my condition.

I foolishly pressed on, continuing to fulfil all my musical commitments until one fateful night in February 1999 when halfway through a session with the Frogs, I was stricken with severe chest pains, completely unable to blow a further note. Fortunately, a local clarinet-playing friend of the Frogs had come to listen to the band that evening and

With Keith Little - Wales   Paul Dunleavy

kindly saved my bacon by nipping home to get his horn and then helpfully finishing off the session for me.

In the following weeks my local GP arranged further tests for me, the results of which were; blood pressure good, lungs O.K., heart normal, no problems with blood conditions, gall bladder, intestines, etc. In fact, nothing specific could be found, all that emphasised was that I have a complete rest which meant no more playing for a period. I really had little choice but to comply as added symptoms were then beginning to dog me and I was forced to slow down the whole pace of my living.

I played my last gig in the July of '99, confidently thinking that after a few weeks of recuperation, I'd be back on the scene as normal. Not so. The symptoms persisted and I was not even able to put in a simple clarinet practice, which would at least have helped me keep my lip in. It took some time for me to accept such a situation but I tried to be sensible about it (about time too!) and not only proceeded to rest up for a bit, which I knew I really needed, but tried to take it all as philosophically as I could by thinking that I could possibly utilise this time to advantage.

For about a year or two before all this took place, representatives of the "Just Jazz" magazine, one of the few periodicals which could be relied upon to portray the goings on and the personalities of those in the world of jazz, had been on to me for an interview with regards to my participation in the jazz scene. I was never enthusiastic about interviews, especially live ones, in fact it was normal for me to decline such invitations, so I had been putting these people off with polite murmurings of 'very many thanks for the offer chaps, I'll be in touch with you about arranging a get together for it', etc., but I never did. What with my natural disinclination for such interviews, my characteristic dilatoriness, and then my health situation, the expected interview didn't actually take place until the Summer of 2000.

Also, a couple of months beforehand, I had a call from the Jazz Curator of the "British Library's Sound Archives, who requested that I record something on tape regarding some of my experiences, for the use of future researchers as well as for posterity. Being rather flattered by this request, I agreed, in spite of not feeling in the best of health at the time. What made such a request more acceptable though was that they had chosen my old friend Mike Pointon to interview me for the purpose. Mike, not only was one of my favourite trombone players and jazz vocalists, but he was a jazz buff who organised many a radio and TV programme on the subject, so I knew I was in good hands.

The finished article was not really to my satisfaction as I was feeling particularly under par on that occasion, my voice was croaky, I could hardly gather my thoughts, and in truth felt rather than give an interview for posterity, I should have spent the day in bed.

However, chatting with Mike after we had completed the interview I explained how I could only touch on some of the experiences I had mentioned during the tapeing and he suggested, as others had frequently done in the past, especially Ronnie, that it's about time I got around to writing my memoirs. While trotting out the same old excuses to him that 'although for some time it has been my intention to write such an autobiography, but as I had too many other things going on, etc., etc.,' it dawned on me that these reasons were really no longer valid. I no longer had any musical demands to meet, I no longer had the energy to do the various jobs around the Farm, and any studying or private work I wanted to do could be fitted in as and when I felt up to it. So it seemed that providing I was able to get my mind around it, there was absolutely no obstacle to, at least making a start on my memoirs during this period of resting up.

So with these changes in circumstances and the added encouragement of Mike and Ronnie, I henceforth began rummaging around in my old files, boxes, and cupboards, to see if I could put something acceptable together that would enable me to relate in more detail some of my experiences. Hence this present effort.

As to my philosophical interests during this period, by the late 80s, although I was still managing to keep as near as possible to my meditation routine, my study periods had slackened off quite a bit, and the groups I had been running by then had dwindled down, first to two a week, then one, then monthly, until I finally disbanded them completely. As to the Farm Centre project, that had been shelved some years beforehand with no immediate plans to try to revive it.

This partial withdrawal from involvement in these areas was primarily due to the increase in my musical work, but I was also still suffering from a deep sense of spiritual discontent, a frustration which brought a total dissatisfaction with my life, a feeling that I was capable of much more than I was actually doing in that department. All of this left me with an inner void which had been with me in varying degrees of intensity for the past dozen years or more. Logically, such a condition should have spurred me on to explore other related fields of activity, to seek other means of satisfying my deeper urges, but that was not the case. It was my musical life which became my dominant activity at the time, even though I knew I could never discard my spiritual links, which would always take precedence over all else.

I went through phases of deep brooding (it was certainly not depression, but I can't think of any other way of expressing such moods to which I became prone over that period), especially after the last group meeting I held in the June of 1990. I had for some time beforehand made all my student friends aware that, due to pressure of my musical work, I intended eventually to call a halt to our meetings. Although they expressed much regret at such a decision, I explained that they had had enough from me over the years to get on with, although that doesn't mean that we should not still keep in touch and keep alive our mutual interests.

They made clear they felt what a loss it would be, not only for them but for others nor were they backward in reminding me how there must be thousands upon thousands 'out there' who could happily benefit by the work we have covered. I was inclined to agree and told them that if, as they had often mentioned to me, they had gained from our studies together, there was nothing stopping them from starting their own groups, to give what they had gained to others that they too could gain. They kindly flattered me by saying that they couldn't do it with others as I had done with them, not having the experience, background, and knowledge, etc., which I had, and besides which, they added, even if they did try forming their own groups as I suggested, their notes would certainly not be sufficient for the job, and it would probably mean them having the use of some of my notes instead.

Well if that is the case, I conceded , as my notes were merely 'jottings', and sparse ones at that, which even I had trouble in deciphering, I suppose as a last contribution to our work, I could a least make an effort to put them in some sort of usable order. It was then put to me that if they had something like that as a framework for them to work with, they could not only use them for their own group efforts but maybe, to widen their use, they could be sent out as a basis for a correspondence course - or even be put into book form!

"Whoops, hold on a minute," I objected, "I don't mind putting my jottings into some sort of order but if you were thinking of using them for a correspondence course, it would mean me writing the whole thing out properly, organising it into a series of separate papers, and making all the various concepts fit into an easily understandable sequence, and so forth,. Do you realise the amount of work that would entail? Can you imagine how much writing I would have to do?"

"Well . . . . . .?" they said.

I fell right into the trap, didn't I? Wasn't it one of the major precepts of the teachings, I was forcibly reminded, to always be aware of opportunities where we could be of help to others, especially those who may benefit by an understanding of the Ageless Wisdom philosophy? I was then persuaded, or more accurately, importuned, to assure them that I would set about such a task. There was little I could say to wriggle out of it. They were quite right in making such a point, and after all, wasn't it what I wanted to do many years ago for the Farm project? So how could I now refuse their request.

However, in conceding, I felt I had to make clear to them that if and when I had completed it, for whatever purposes it was to be used, especially if it was to be disseminated to a wider number of people rather than just for small private groups, two things I would like to see happen: one, that they administer the whole thing themselves (of course, in liaison with me on any really sticky points where they thought I could help), and two, and most important of all, due to my wish to keep this side of my life separate from any of my other activities, especially my musical doings, I would be able to maintain my anonymity. For this latter purpose therefore, everything I write would be in the third person so that it would be the content of the concepts themselves which would be the sole reason for them being accepted, or rejected, and not the one who compiled them, who would be merely the interpreter and presenter.

So after that last meeting in June of 1990, with my assurance to them, I set about tackling this daunting undertaking. However, it worked out that in going over my old notes, coordinating and arranging all the various ideas they contained and putting them into a more formal and sequential order, etc., reawakened my interest in the spiritual realities of life, resulting in a rekindling of my previous aspirations, not only to the level of enthusiasm of my earlier years, but further beyond, driving me deeper, wider, and more fully into the search which has since sustained me through the more recent years of my life.

With hindsight, I gather such a prolonged period of outer orientation which I had experienced was the result of a needed inner consolidation, one which I have since come to understand is on occasions associated with a person's spiritual growth. The desolation and frustration which I felt, if I had been able to recognise it, was more than likely due to some type of spiritual digestive process which, until it is adequately expressed, would inevitably lead to a state of dissatisfaction.

253

Another factor I suppose was the intrusion of that age-old principle that the more one knows, the more one knows how much one doesn't know, which tends to put one's life more into perspective with regard to the greater existence - which can become quite overwhelming at times. However, although such a perspective may often invoke a feeling of discontent, in the end it can provide further incentive to attain.

Be that as it may, at the time of this last meeting, I little suspected such reasons for my lack of spiritual inspiration, nor the advantages to me of such an enterprise as organising my old notes. My intentions in that respect were merely to make the needed effort so that I could hand the whole shebang over to them. As to the possibility of it ever being put into book form, I explained to them that it would be more expedient to first try it out as a correspondence course, give it maybe a few years to assess its worth, then we could decide whether or not it would be appropriate to put it into book form.

I also told them that as it was my intention to write my autobiography sometime in the future anyway I'd first like to see how that would be received. Then, if it seemed there was a call for such a work on the Ageless Wisdom, maybe we can do it as a group effort, treat it as our own little contribution to those who seek a greater understanding of life's eternal verities, and who, as do we, ardently yearn to relate more intimately to their spiritual source.

BY WAY OF AN EPILOGUE

Thus so far is my story, the shy young lad from London's East End, who by sheer luck and to his utter amazement, became a prominent figure in the field of jazz, yet who, at the height of his popularity, gave up his fame, family, home, his friends, possessions, his enviable bank balance, his life style, and his worldly pleasures, to follow the star that leads to 'enlightenment.

As dramatic as it sounds, there is nothing unique about one endeavouring to search for a deeper meaning to life - it has been a pursuit undertaken by countless individuals throughout the ages, and increasingly more so at this present time. If I have been included in their number, then I must consider myself well favoured, I claim no special credit. In fact, if the doctrines which I have followed hold any truth, over the next century or two, as the world enters more deeply into the New Age experience, an ever increasing number of people will be coming into the world whose spiritual potential will be far in advance of those existing today. Their accumulative effect upon the collective human consciousness is expected to totally regenerate the spiritual nature of the whole of mankind.

If indeed this is so, and I sincerely pray it will be, I make no apologies for mentioning it, principally because it has been central to much of my motivation and also because of the hope such a vision of the future can give. The same can also be said of other aspects of the philosopy, some of which I touched on throughout these memoirs. In mentioning them, it has certainly not been my object to either imply that I am privy to privileged information, which is available for all who wish to seek it, or to attempt to convert others to my way of thinking, which I have always held must be left to each individual to initiate their own search in these matters. (However, if any of my comments happen to spark off a helpful line of inquiry, all to the good.)

Nor has it been my intention to try to impress because I have been endowed with this urge to find some answer to those intractable questions as to the origins, purpose, and destiny of humankind. On the contrary, I have tried to play down many of my responses and the changes which have occurred within my being as a result of my quest.

Although I haven't actually bared my soul to write about such personal matters for someone who is such a private individual as I, and to reveal certain intimate aspects of my life for all to see, has not been easy; yet, I'm bound to admit that it has proved to be a valuable exercise for me, and from that alone I have gained much. It has stirred up many long forgotten memories, and rekindled old thoughts and emotions - many much cherished. Yet on the other hand it has also opened up some old wounds which at times were not too easy to deal with, and on occasions made me question whether to continue with this memoir (or not). Nevertheless, I did, and as I feel overall that I have been privileged in having such an extremely fortunate life, it may be of help for others to know about it.

I could easily have spent my days as a nine-to-five engineering draughtsman, a very creative and expressive occupation, and possibly have brought up a family who would by now be grown up and children'd off themselves while I spend a leisurely pensioned retirement - and I probably would have been very happy about it in the bargain!

Or I could have attained an even wider measure of acclaim in the entertainment world, as have other of my peers, if I had continued to build up my musical reputation and helped lead the phase of the 'Trad Boom', which proved to be to the advantage of so many of my fellow jazz musicians while I was away in India.

But it didn't turn out that way. My destiny has taken me in a different direction, one which has opened up unexpected worlds of interests and contacts and which, incidentally, is there for all to explore if the urge to do so is strong enough. If my understanding of the reincarnation process is correct, a life of seeking, such as mine, is often a necessary leg of the journey on 'the way back'.

When I was asked recently to briefly sum up my life so far, and, if it was possible for me to have my life over, would I do the same again? I replied to the effect that on looking back over the years, I would not change the theme and purpose of my life, even if I could, but I would certainly try to make more of the many opportunities which have been presented to me. So much has passed me by due to my lack of awareness, understanding, and foresight. But that said, I think I have managed to make some progress and I have nothing but homage to pay to those who have helped me in this and made my life one of considerable joy and satisfaction.

It is evident that weaving throughout the whole story like a shimmering golden thread can be seen that indefinable element called 'luck'; it is that with which I have happily been graced and which helped bring me to this present phase of fulfillment.

I have so much to be thankful for, I am not wealthy by worldly standards but have sufficient money for life's essentials, my needs are minimal, I have a roof over my head in a wonderful country environment, I have a loving partner in Veronica, (Ronnie) I enjoy good health (although temporarily I am enjoying poor health) I have been blessed with a talent for making music, I love my fellow man - and woman (especially woman), and I love our dear but sadly abused Planet.

Above all, I have a creative and satisfying philosophy which holds me in good stead and to which I am at present committed, one which ever prompts me to look for every favourable opportunity to put something back into life, to give pleasure through my music, to inform and inspire through my writings and discussions, and to help and guide through my study and meditation work.

In all, it has been a full and happy life which, in spite of some trying times, has been strewn with so many plusses which has made it all so worthwhile and fulfilling - and I know that even better things are yet to come.

Is it any wonder why I happily exclaim "Lucky ol' me!"

Summer 2000

CY LAURIE

20th April 1926 - 18th April 2002

April 18th Thursday morn-dawn - 1974

How peaceful and still, the early morning ethers
The gentle lives, bathed in mutual love, undisturbed
Sustained in tranquillity by the soft light of dawn
Showing not a sign of the coming storm
When emotions riot in fierce display
By active man who's inner strife
Upsetting natures balanced life, and
Deprived of love, repellent, coarse
Thro' confusion of desires false
Destroys that web of gentle calm
By him who needs it most as soothing balm
When will he learn that to obey
Love's loving laws will end the fray
Which creates within his heart
And knows through Love all is a part

By Cy Laurie (Copywrite)

257

MAC'S, 41 GT. WINDMILL STREET . . . . GER. 6112
PICCADILLY CIRCUS, LONDON, W.I (Opposite Windmill Theatre)

Terrific Easter Jazz Week End

ALL NIGHT SESSION
GOOD FRIDAY, APRIL 19th

12 Midnight till 7 a.m. Saturday Morning

WITH THE . . .

CY LAURIE BAND
Graham Stewart Seven
Bill Brunskills Jazzmen   Skiffle Groups

SNACK BAR   MEMBERS—7/6 GUESTS—10/-   LOUNGE

GOOD FRIDAY   EVENING SESSION AS USUAL 7.15 - 10-45 p.m.
CY LAURIE BAND & Skiffle
Members—3/-   Guests—4/-

EASTER SATURDAY
CY LAURIE BAND & Skiffle—7.15 - 10.45 p.m.
Members—4/-   Guests—5/-

EASTER SUNDAY
AFTERNOON SESSION—3 - 6 p.m. with
BILL BRUNSKILL BAND

LATE EVENING SESSION 8 - 12 midnight with
CY LAURIE BAND & Skiffle Group
Members—5/-   Guests—6/-

W. F. Arber & Co. Ltd. 459 Roman Road, Bow, E.3